William Faulkner: Self-Presentation and Performance

Literary Modernism Series

Thomas F. Staley, Editor

William Faulkner

Self-Presentation and Performance

by James G. Watson

University of Texas Press, Austin

A portion of this work originally appeared as "'My Father's Unfailing Kindness': William Faulkner and the Idea of Home," in *American Literature* 64 (December 1992), 749–761.

LIBRARY OF CONGRESS
CATALOGING-IN-PUBLICATION DATA

Watson, James G. (James Gray), 1939–
    William Faulkner : self-presentation and performance /
by James G. Watson. — 1st ed.
        p.   cm. — (Literary modernism series)
    Includes bibliographical references (p.   ) and index.
    ISBN 0-292-79131-3 (alk. paper)
    ISBN 0-292-79151-8 (pbk.: alk. paper)
    1. Faulkner, William, 1897–1962—Criticism and
interpretation.   2. Letter writing—United States—
History—20th century.   3. Faulkner, William, 1897–1962—
Correspondence.   4. American letters—History and
criticism.   5. Modernism (Literature)—United States.
6. Self-presentation in literature.   7. Narration (Rhetoric)
8. Autobiography.   I. Title.   II. Series.
PS3511.A86Z985354   2000
813'.52—dc21   99-42423

For Natty, Ruth, and Jimmy

Contents

List of Illustrations

Abbreviations Used

AA!   *Absalom, Absalom!*

AILD   *As I Lay Dying*

Appendix   "Appendix: Compson"

CSWF   *Collected Stories of William Faulkner*

Elmer   *Elmer*

EPP   *William Faulkner: Early Prose and Poetry*, ed. Carvel
         Collins

ESPL   *Essays, Speeches and Public Letters by William
         Faulkner*, ed. James B. Meriwether

FCVA   Faulkner Collection, University of Virginia

Flags   *Flags in the Dust*

FU   *Faulkner in the University: Class Conferences at the
         University of Virginia, 1957–1958*, ed. Frederick Gwynn
         and Joseph L. Blotner

GB   *A Green Bough*

GDM   *Go Down, Moses*

HAC   *Helen: A Courtship*

Hamlet   *The Hamlet*

HRHRC	Harry Ransom Humanities Research Center, University of Texas at Austin
Jerusalem	*If I Forget Thee, Jerusalem*
KG	*Knight's Gambit*
LIA	*Light in August*
Lion	*Lion in the Garden: Interviews with William Faulkner, 1926–1962*, ed. James B. Meriwether and Michael Millgate
Mansion	*The Mansion*
Marionettes	*The Marionettes*
Mayday	*Mayday*
MOS	*Mosquitoes*
MP	*Mississippi Poems*
Pylon	*Pylon*
RN	*Requiem for a Nun*
SLWF	*Selected Letters of William Faulkner*, ed. Joseph L. Blotner
SO	*"Sanctuary." The Original Text*
SP	*Soldiers' Pay*
SR	*Sanctuary*
Today	*Today We Live*
TofH	*Thinking of Home: William Faulkner's Letters to His Mother and Father, 1918–1925*, ed. James G. Watson
Town	*The Town*
TSATF	*The Sound and the Fury*
USWF	*Uncollected Stories of William Faulkner*
VIS	*Vision in Spring*
WP	*The Wild Palms*

Preface

This book evolved from my work with Faulkner's personal letters as well as his published writing and with relationships between the two that led to speculations on the question, How did he do that? I wanted to write about how he made the things he made and why he made them as he did. My speculative answer to those questions is, essentially, that he put himself forth as the artist he felt himself to be by written performances and displays recognizably based in his life as he both lived and imagined living it. From the beginning, Faulkner's was a self-presenting art, characterized by confident creation of personal modes of expression. He created in his work a world of controlled chaos, aggressively unconventional in its forms and disruptive of pragmatic thinking in its effects, which was deeply, personally his own. Self-presentation and performance are manifested both in Faulkner's life, in the guises and disguises he assumed, and in his art, where those figures and others of his emotional biography are separate but interlocking modes of representation. Self-presentation, as I mean the term, is a narrative strategy that capitalizes upon the experience of the man and artist, including of course the performative experience; by performance I mean the heightened mode of written expression that reassembles familiar experience in the forms and language of spectacle. By means of such self-affirming performances, the self and the word became one in the writing.

That thesis is set forth in expanded form in Chapter 1, "Self-Presentation and Performance," where it is illustrated from overtly performative aspects of *The Sound and the Fury* and from several self-presentational manuscripts, including drafts of Faulkner's introduction to that book. Chapter II, "Photographs, Letters, and Fictions," extends self-presentation and performance to pictorial and privately written records of Faulkner's life, especially in early photographs, in his correspondence with his mother, and in published works where those are reflected, including short stories, the verse play *The Marionettes* and Quentin's chapter of *The Sound and the Fury*. Chapter III, "Marriage Matters," treats the recurring Faulknerian motif of weddings and marriages in *The Sound and the Fury*, the two versions of *Sanctuary*, and *Absalom, Absalom!*. Much of this derives, I believe, from his complicated relation to Estelle Oldham Franklin Faulkner. Chapter IV, "Who's Your Old Man?" examines the related motif of fatherhood in terms of Faulkner's relationship to male guides and sponsors in his life and traces its expression in the short story collection *These 13*, in *Pylon* and *Absalom, Absalom!*, and in Faulkner's cinematic writing in the mid-1930s. The novelist's sense of himself as artistic "Stage Manager" and the relation of that persona to the problematics of authorial sovereignty are rooted in his reading of Melville, Hawthorne, and Thoreau in Chapter V, which focuses upon *Absalom, Absalom!*, *Mosquitoes*, and *If I Forget Thee, Jerusalem*. Chapter VI, "Old Moster," extends Faulkner's self-presentations to the self-proclaimed artist-as-God, to his extended mastery of his fictional cosmos in *The Hamlet* and in *Go Down, Moses*, and to the complex of very personal epistolary relationships with women that lies in the correspondence behind *Requiem for a Nun*.

In a larger sense, the book is about the record of William Faulkner's life in his writing, the act of its recording there, and what that record and those acts imply about the nature and meaning of his art. It is not a biography, although one side of the argument necessarily is biographical. That being the case, the book is centrally indebted to Joseph L. Blotner's *Faulkner: A Biography* (1974, 1984) and *Selected Letters of William Faulkner* (1977). It draws upon Judith Wittenberg's *Faulkner: The Transfiguration of Biography* (1979) and David Minter's *William Faulkner: His Life and Work* (1980) and on reliable biographical-historical work done since their publication, notably Richard Gray's *The Life of William Faulkner* (1994), the five volumes of Louis Daniel Brodsky and Robert W. Hamblin's *A Comprehensive Guide to the Brodsky Collection* (1982–1988), and Joel Williamson's *William Faulkner and Southern History* (1993). It draws, too, on archival materials to which Blotner had no access or, in some cases, chose not to publish. These include Philip Cohen and Doreen Fowler's work on the Rowan Oak Papers at the University of Mississippi, the

Carvel Collins and Dean Faulkner Mallard Collections in the Harry Ransom Humanities Research Center, the University of Texas at Austin, and the Faulkner Collection in the Alderman Library at the University of Virginia.

The book also depends upon a range of critical and historical studies of Faulkner, mostly of a kind. My interest is in his work rather than theoretical configurations spun from it, as will be seen by my debt to the Faulkner scholars I cite, including especially Andre Bleikasten, Michel Gresset, John T. Matthews, Thomas L. McHaney, James B. Meriwether, Michael Millgate, Noel Polk, Judith L. Sensibar, Michael Zeitlin, and Karl Zender. Other studies include the work of Richard Poirier, from whose book *The Performing Self* (1971) my thesis evolves; the work of Roland Barthes, John Berger, Carol Shloss, and Susan Sontag on photography and of Bruce Kawin on film; Louis Ruben on writers of the modern South; Wai-chee Dimock on nineteenth-century American writing; and my own and others' work with and about personal letters and manuscript books. I owe a debt of gratitude to each of those mentioned here and to everyone cited in my text.

I am especially proud to acknowledge my debts to particular people, many of them close friends and colleagues of many years, who have directly contributed to the making of this book and the way in which it is made. Noel Polk generously made time to read the entire manuscript summer by summer, offered invaluable advice on my arguments, and pointed out inconsistencies and plain wrong-headedness as needed. Others who read drafts and chapters at various stages of the composition and provided useful insights and criticism are Susan Belasco, Thomas J. Bonner, Jr., Andrea Bradley, Diane Burton, Thadious Davis, Michael Gorman, Norman S. Grabo, Cathy Henderson, Robert Hogan, Alicia Mosier, Karen Pavelka, Stephen Sumner, Gordon O. Taylor, Richard B. Watson, and Lisa Wilson. Joseph Blotner, James and Beverly Carothers, and Thomas Staley talked with me about the book over the years in Charlottesville, Lawrence, and Austin. Professors Blotner and Staley enabled my work in the Faulkner archives at the Alderman Library and the Harry Ransom Humanities Research Center, and the staffs of those great libraries helped in too many ways to recount here. The University of Tulsa Office of Research funded some of my travel to those libraries.

A portion of this book appeared previously, in revised form, in *American Literature*. Jill Faulkner Summers generously granted permission to publish Faulkner's notes on the *Absalom, Absalom!* galleys. Ms. Summers, Dean Faulkner Wells, and the Southern Media Archive at the University of Mississippi granted permission to publish photographs, some of which were provided by the Southern Media Center and the Harry Ransom Humanities Research Center at the University of Texas at Austin.

James G. Watson, Tulsa, Oklahoma

I. Self-Presentation and Performance

So he who, from the isolation of cold
impersonal print, can engender this excitement, himself partakes of the immortality
which he has engendered.

Foreword to *The Faulkner Reader*

i. The Man and the Word

Biography is a supposititious and essentially schematizing art based in the detailed reconstruction of a life. Criticism based on biography is no less speculative, no less given to schematics, and certainly no less seductive for the critic. From the outset readers and critics of William Faulkner's fiction assumed that his work is based more or less in his own life and times as a Southerner—that his "apocrypha," as he affirmed in an interview with Jean Stein in 1955, was rooted in the "actual," his fictional "cosmos" in the "postage stamp of native soil" (Lion, 255). For Faulkner this was a matter not only of adapting to his fictional purposes the geographical and historical materials ready to his hand but also of bringing to bear on them the more immediate, and for him inextricable, imperatives of his private and individual existence. This required all of his great linguistic dexterity, but it also demanded of him a tough self-knowledge. His is not a self-seeking but a self-presenting art, characterized not by fumbling after meaning (to use an ironically deprecatory term of his own) but by confident creation of expressive forms. Breaking into his own life experience, and breaking that, in turn, into diverse, often divergent segments counterposed against one another, he created a world of controlled chaos, made in his own protean image and reflective of his own multiple sense of self. Aggressively unconventional in its forms, disruptive of pragmatic thinking in its effects, Faulkner's art, once shed of its early identifications with such models as Victorian poetry,[1] was compellingly the outcome of *his* knowing and imagining, the product of *his* mind and experience. Unlike T. S. Eliot's impersonal theory of poetry, Faulkner's mind, in addition to its catalytic effect on his work, tended to express rather than to extinguish "personality."[2]

Whether or not such methods gave meaning to his life, the matter of his life decidedly gave shape and meaning to his fictions. What Richard Poirier has said of Robert Frost is true, in its way, of Faulkner: it was not that the world was too tough for him but that he was too tough for the world. "The scene of the poem," Poirier says, "is more expanded and expansive than the scene which is the world, and the poet's relationship to the scene of the poem is necessarily dynamic, exploratory, coolly executed to a degree that no comparable 'scene' in life could very well bear."[3] In the best of Faulkner's work, like Frost's, the novelist's complex social and psychological self-presentations become literal as well as literary performances that define him as a writer. Writing, for Faulkner, as his fastidiously crafted manuscripts show, always was a deed, an event at least as much as a record of events, a compulsively individual act, at once self-disruptive and self-affirming.[4] By writing he reconstructed the World in the Word, and in the World-as-Word, anything and everything were put in the service of art. Anything there is possible, everything is real.

This included, especially, the writer himself. David Minter describes one aspect of the phenomenon in his discussion of Faulkner's revision of Falkner family history in *Flags in the Dust*, where he compares not only the actual historical materials to those in the book but also the method by which Faulkner presented them there to that employed by his fictional characters:

> what we observe is not simply distortion as a sign of repression and revenge, or elaboration as a sign of benign transformation into meaning, but the two so interrelated as to be almost indistinguishable. Faced with a writer of mo-

tives so mixed and strategies so complex, some readers have concentrated on Faulkner's fidelity to facts and details, others on his distortions of them. But in the great novels he was now prepared to write, both fidelity and distortion would be crucial. For he was prepared now to dramatize minds caught up in dismembering and reconstructing. Musing over life, these minds discard and reclaim, displace and recreate, leaving signs and traces everywhere. Even as they give life, making dead figures seem potent and alive, they pass judgments, impose sentences, and display mastery: they not only participate in their maker's great rhetorical and imaginative gifts; they also share his mixed motives and complex strategies.[5]

This is an extremely accurate statement of the case. The strictly factual basis is exemplified, for example, by a representative list of fictional names: in *Soldiers' Pay*, Cecile owes her name to Jack Falkner's first wife, Cecile Hargis; in *Mosquitoes* Faulkner named himself and used easily identifiable real people thinly disguised; in *Flags in the Dust* he used Maud Falkner's maiden name, Butler, as an alias for Byron Snopes, and in *The Sound and the Fury* her mother's name, Damuddy, whose epitaph ("Her children rise and call her blessed") he gave Eula Varner Snopes in *The Town*. Less personal examples include Suratt in *Flags*, Natalie and Shegog in *The Sound and the Fury*, and the given names of Phil Stones's great-uncles Amodeus and Theophilus in *Go Down, Moses*. For the motives and methods of self-presentation from beginning to end of Faulkner's career, the fiction itself provides a wealth of metaphors.

Perhaps the greatest participant and sharer of the kind Minter describes, and one of the most intimately connected to Faulkner, is Quentin Compson. Returning to Cambridge by train on the evening of June 2, 1910, Quentin turns from the passing scene to spring in Mississippi, twilight, rain, and the smell of honeysuckle—all of this symbolizing to him "night and unrest," and producing at the edge of consciousness a sense of his collective experience as at once deeply distorted and terrifyingly real.

I seemed to be lying neither asleep nor awake looking down a long corridor of gray halflight where all stable things had become shadowy paradoxical all I had done shadows all I had felt suffered taking visible form antic and perverse mocking without relevance inherent themselves with the denial of the significance they should have affirmed thinking I was I was not who was not was not who. (TSATF, 170)

As Quentin presents himself here for his self-contemplation at Cambridge in 1910, so the scene in the novel presented itself to Faulkner in 1928 through the dark glass of his own New Haven experience in 1918, a deeply troubled yet exciting period midway between the fictional and the compositional moment. Some of the stable things of Faulkner's experience to that point were much like Quentin's, including, especially, his love for Estelle Oldham, mocked in 1918 by her marriage to Cornell Sidney Franklin, and the social and historical mores of the South itself, from which his journey to the East Coast effectively exiled him. Imaginatively sublimated (the word is Faulkner's) into art, the stable world *he* knew, with what *he* felt and *he* suffered, is reified into the shadowy paradoxical forms of life that torment Quentin. What is figured forth here is the writer-as-word, a shadow Faulkner, the formula of whose artistic self-transformation is precisely Quentin's "I was I was not who was not was not who." In this scene as in so much of Faulkner's best work, the writer, like the transmuted experience he recreates for his character, is himself "antic and perverse," obliquely self-mocking, even self-denying. And self-affirming, his parodic yet emulative energy at the core of what Richard Poirier has called "the performing self."

Performance, Poirier contends, may erupt when "a writer is most strongly engaged by what he is doing, as if struggling for his identity within the materials at hand"; it "comes to fruition at precisely the point where the potentially destructive impulse to mastery brings forth from the material its most essential, irreducible, clarified, and therefore beautiful nature."[6] By such performances, the writer "can show us, in the mere turning of a sentence this way or that, how to keep from being smothered by the inherited structuring of things, how to keep within and yet in command of the accumulations of culture that have become a part of what he is."[7] "Inherited structuring," including especially the forms and structures of actual personal experience, become in Faulkner's fictional adaptations of them the stage for his performances, his balance beams and still rings.[8] There are many such moments in *The Sound and the Fury*. In a wonderfully poetic sentence following his revery on twilight and honeysuckle, Quentin says, "I could smell the curves of the river beyond the dusk and I saw the last light supine and tranquil upon tideflats like pieces of broken mirror" (TSATF, 170). The image is one of sensory confusion and dissociation, a literal self-fragmentation fully appropriate to his preceding sense of self-dissolution ("I was I was not who was not was not who"). Nonetheless, as with the reference to the lost "stable things" of his life, the "pieces of broken mirror" still retain the implication of an anteced-ent whole that, together with its subsequent disconnection, is perfectly descriptive of Quentin's—and Faulkner's—self-presentational mode. In this sense the book itself can be described in terms of what Quentin ex-pects to achieve by his self-destruction: contemplating suicide, according to Mr. Compson, he is, in fact, "contemplating an apotheosis in which a temporary state of mind will become symmetrical above the flesh and aware both of itself and of the flesh it will not quite discard" (TSATF, 177).

Self-presentation and performance are manifested in Faulkner's life in his regularly putting himself forward in the guises and disguises of a moment—gentleman dandy, soldier, and farmer are familiar ones—as well as in his art, where these and other personae are separate but inter-locking elements of fictional representation. *Self-presentation* in fiction is a narrative strategy that capitalizes upon the experience of the man and author, including, of course, the performative experience; *performance* is a heightened mode of written expression, a means by which the self and all other selves, situations, and events of a book can be represented. If self-presentation is a *record* of a life and time, performance is the *act* of its recording.

Again, *The Sound and the Fury* offers a constructive illustration, this in a passage of authorial, rather than first-person, narration which intro-duces the Reverend Shegog on Easter Sunday morning in the final chapter.

> When the visitor rose to speak he sounded like a white man. His voice was level and cold. It sounded too big to have come from him and they listened at first through curiosity, as they would have to a monkey talking. They be-gan to watch him as they would a man on a tight rope. They even forgot his insignificant appearance in the virtuosity with which he ran and poised and swooped upon the cold inflectionless wire of his voice, so that at last, when with a sort of swooping glide he came to rest again beside the reading desk with one arm resting upon it at shoulder height and his monkey body as reft of all motion as a mummy or an emptied vessel, the congregation sighed as if waked from a collective dream and moved a little in its seats. (TSATF, 293–294)

The passage describes the vocal power by which Shegog's vision of "de power en de glory" of God is communicated to Dilsey as a personal vision of "de first en de last" (TSATF, 297). It introduces the issue of shared racial understanding and expression that the minister, by his communion with the hearts of his congregation, confirms. It has to do, as well, with Faulkner's portrayal of the imaginative powers of the artist and their effects. According to Andre Bleikasten, Faulkner offers the preacher-figure as a "double" of the novelist, a vehicle of the mythic voice that induces shared vision;[9] and according to John T. Matthews, he "figures the role of the author in his work as he strives to deliver the word that will interpret experience truly."[10] The passage also, and quite prominently, is a scene of pure performance, as antic in its literary effects as in the transformations and their resolutions that it recounts.

Surely Bleikasten oversimplifies when he argues, on grounds that Shegog's sermon sounds like sermons actually delivered, that "it is no creation at all, but only evidence of Faulkner's extraordinary mimetic abilities."[11] Bleikasten locates the "vision" of the sermon in the vision of Christian redemption for which it argues, but it is clear from this and related passages that it is not Christ but Shegog himself who is transformed for the skeptical congregation—from a black man who looks like a monkey and sounds like a white man into a tightrope dancer—and not by the word of God but by his own vocal "virtuosity." The traveling circus, whose attraction is performance and "show," is arrayed from the beginning against the Christian structures of the novel and conjoined here with its opposite in an act of Faulknerian agility that makes each a metaphor for the other.

Clearly the circus is not the only show in town. On Easter morning, when Mrs. Compson tells Jason that Dilsey will be going to church, he demands of his mother, "Go where? . . . . Hasn't that damn show left yet?" (TSATF, 279). Against an Easter Sunday scene "as flat and without perspective as a painted cardboard set upon the ultimate edge of the flat earth" (TSATF, 292), the Negro church with "its crazy steeple like a painted church" (TSATF, 292) is a one-ring circus and the visiting preacher an illusionist, both black man and white, monkey and man, preacher and ventriloquial trapezist. When he assumes a black voice, "It was as different as day and dark from his former tone, with a sad, timbrous quality like an alto horn, sinking into their hearts and speaking there again when it had ceased in fading and cumulative echoes" (TSATF, 294). His claim to Christian authority—"I got the recollection and the blood of the Lamb!"—is made in the context of blood relationship to the "Brethren and sisteren" of the congregation, a relationship that intensifies as his voice changes, in "successive waves" whelming the rock of his suffering body, to a "succubus" feeding on him (TSATF, 294). "Breddren and sistuhn," he says, speaking now in full dialect, "I got de ricklickshun en de blood of de Lamb!" (TSATF, 295). So dominant, so manifestly and insistently *present*, is his voice that it literally displaces him and his auditors: "the congregation seemed to watch with its own eyes while the voice consumed him, until he was nothing and they were nothing and there was not even a voice but instead their hearts were speaking to one another in chanting measures beyond the need for words" (TSATF, 294).

What Shegog accomplishes by this vocal performance is nothing less than the transformation of flesh (his own and his congregation's) into words—and back again into flesh reconstituted by the experience and recognizably informed by the creative Spirit of God: "when he came to rest against the reading desk, his monkey face lifted and his whole attitude that of a serene, tortured crucifix that transcended its shabbiness and insignificance and made it of no moment, a long moaning expulsion of breath rose from them, and a woman's soprano: 'Yes, Jesus!'" (TSATF, 294–295). To paraphrase Michel Gresset's account of the eyes and mouth as *organs* by which desire is vicariously fulfilled, Shegog's voice both creates and gratifies the spiritual appetite of his auditors, who "watch with their own eyes" the eucharistic consumption of his body by his words and its transcendent reconstitution. Like the sexual function of sight and speech, the specific spiritual function of Shegog's vocal organ here is, literally, "to transform being into appearance." This function Gresset characterizes as "performance": "The organ," he says, is "fundamentally that which transforms a mute, bare world into its own image," and this transformation is a function not only of sexual (or religious) desire but also "of a kind of aesthetic desire associated with the exhibitionism of the baroque."[12] This, too, applies to the Shegog scene, which is doubly constituted, consisting both of an antecedent *account* of a vocal performance and its impact and of its subsequent *transcription*. Shegog accomplishes with his voice what the "thin, frightened, tuneless whispers" (TSATF, 293) of the children's choir that introduces him cannot, and Faulkner represents that accomplishment in his own as well as in Shegog's words. Whatever mimetic character is in the scene is in the two-page sermon spoken in dialect by the minister; the aesthetic, creative, literary performance precedes, informs, encompasses, and finally transcends mimesis, and that transcendent performance is Faulkner's.

The Shegog-like figure of the physically small, inconspicuous man transformed by the elevating imaginative power of a heroic performance is a familiar one in Faulkner and often, like Shegog, he seems to take not only his outward appearance but the essence of internal identity from his maker. Several stories Faulkner wrote in the years immediately preceding *The Sound and the Fury* turn on such a figure and the power of his imagination to transform experience. The inarticulate Wilfred Midgleston of the "Black Music" (ca. 1925–1926) is a "small, snuffy, nondescript man" (CSWF, 799) who is given a vision of Faulkner's own early literary persona, the goat-god Pan. Transformed by that experience into a "farn" (CSWF, 805), his "apotheosis soared glaring, and to him at least not brief, across the unfathomed sky above his lost earth like that of Elijah of old" (CSWF, 799). Especially in the early work aspiration alone is sufficient to this literary end, as in the story "Carcassonne," written in the same period as "Black Music" and set in the same lost corner of the world Faulkner called Rincon. A prose poem more than a story, "Carcassonne" in form and content virtually is pure performance in which an unnamed dreamer, exiled to a garret in Rincon, aspires *"to perform something bold and tragical and austere"* (CSWF, 899). In the performance that leads to this declaration, Faulkner displayed his own real and imagined experience (as a horseman, aviator, tramp abroad); his reading (especially in *The Odyssey*, the Bible, medieval romance, Shakespeare, Byron, Housman); and several of his favorite poses (dreamer, isolato, poet), literary images (death-by-water, the earth-as-mother), and figures (oxymoron) including, probably, puns (on rider-as-writer [CSWF, 797]). Typescripts of the stream-of-consciousness piece call the speaker David, a name Sherwood Anderson used for Faulkner in his 1925 story "A Meeting South" and that Faulkner adopted in his New Orleans sketches and in *Mosquitoes* (1927). Mrs. Maurier in that novel is the name given in a typescript of "Carcassonne" for Mrs. Widdrington, spelled Widrington in "Black Music." At the end of the story the aspiring poet of "Carcassonne" gallops beyond the earth, like Midgleston soaring in imagination *"right off into the high heaven of the world"* (CSWF, 899).

Faulkner continued all his life to portray such paradoxical men who, as Midgleston says, have "done and been something outside the lot and plan for mortal human man to do and be" (CSWF, 821). A passage in *The Hamlet* (1940), for example, recalls Faulkner's journey to the East Coast in 1918: little Mink Snopes leaves his father's home "seeking the sea. . . . the impregnable haven of all the drowned intact golden galleons and the unattainable deathless seamaids" (Hamlet, 261). In 1921, at about Mink's age, Faulkner had described for his mother his similar excitement at returning to the sea: "Then, suddenly, you see it, a blue hill going up and up, beyond the borders of the world, to the salt colored sky, and white whirling necklaces of gulls, and, if you look long enough, a great vague ship solemnly going some where" (TofH, 145).[13] Consistent with this vision, in *The Mansion* (1959), Mink's absolute faith in cosmic justice earns him a place among "the beautiful, the splendid, the proud and the brave, right on up to the very top itself among the shining phantoms and dreams which are the milestones of the long human recording—Helen and the bishops, the kings and the unhomed angels, the scornful and graceless seraphim" (Mansion, 435–436).

ii. The Man in Manuscript

In late summer, 1933, Faulkner composed for a projected special edition of *The Sound and the Fury* an introduction in which he describes his discovery of an artistic ideal that produced in him the same transfiguring and transcendent emotion represented in these stories. Two versions have been published, one from a five-page and one from a ten-page typescript, the latter apparently the final one. The bibliographical history of the piece, compiled from the Rowan Oak Papers at the University of Mississippi by Philip Cohen and Doreen Fowler, shows him reconstructing the circumstances of the book's composition four years earlier and analyzing the artistic breakthrough it represented.[14] Images of his personal attachment to characters and situations, heavily revised and rewritten in the introduction, suggest that Faulkner was consciously drawing upon a strategy he describes using in the novel by which personal experience was dispersed in the writing and so distanced from the writer himself. Cohen and Fowler argue that one principle of revision in the introduction evolved from his sense of revealing "more about his own psychic involvement in his art than he preferred to make known."[15] Some of that he excised, but especially in the later stages of composition, revision was largely a matter of stylistic refinement and enhanced poetic effect. Certainly several passages remain in both published versions of the introduction that, for Faulkner, are remarkably self-revealing.

Thinking again of *The Sound and the Fury* in the weeks immediately following the birth of his daughter Jill on June 24, 1933, his mind turned past his newborn child to the loss of his daughter Alabama Faulkner two years before, as if her death in 1931 had been a force in the making of the novel he wrote in 1928–1929. "I, who had three brothers and no sisters," he said in the familiar passage retained in both published versions of the introduction, "and was destined to lose my first daughter in infancy, began to write about a little girl" (Miscellany, 159; SoR, 710). In the longer of the published versions, in a passage not found in the manuscripts, he added, "I did not realise then that I was trying to manufacture the sister which I did not have and the daughter which I was to lose" (Miscellany, 159). In retrospect, as the conflation of times and circumstances from his life suggests, he had come to see his writing the book as filling a literal void in the span from his childhood with his brothers when he first loved Estelle to a period of paternal grief in the early years of his marriage to her. Impossible as it was not to think of Alabama and Caddy in connection with Jill's birth, it was perhaps equally impossible not to recall then other connections in *The Sound and the Fury* between his life and his art. He had recast Estelle's April 1918 marriage to Cornell Sidney Franklin in Caddy's to Sydney Herbert Head in April 1910, and Estelle's frequent and lengthy visits to Oxford from Honolulu and Shanghai in Caddy's exile from Jefferson and her secret returns. In Caddy's sexual initiation and Miss Quentin's profligate repetition of her life, he not only portrayed a depressive version of Estelle's past but envisioned in what he would call "the dark, harsh flowing of time" a still darker future of "dishonor and shame" (Miscellany, 159) for her daughter Cho-Cho. From this reappraisal of the motives and methods of the book, he did not exclude his own anguish and his own self-portrayal.

In some versions of what he was now writing, his sense of the personal dimension of the novel becomes nearly confessional. Having conceived of "the beautiful and tragic little girl" as the sister he never had and the daughter he was fated to lose, he said in MS E, he saw that he could *be* brother and father at once.

> I could be in it, the brother and father both. But one brother could not contain all that I could feel toward her. I gave her 3: Quentin who loved her [with incest. Jason] as a lover would, Jason who loved her with the same hatred . . . jealous and outraged pride of a father, and Benjy who loved her with the complete [and] mindlessness of a child. (AL, 277; brackets indicate cancellations in the manuscript)

This statement is modified at the end of MS E, where Faulkner distances himself somewhat by extending his imaginative identification to include other characters. Until he wrote the fourth section and "made a novel of it," he said, "I was inside the book: I was Quentin and Jason and Benjy and Dilsey and T.P., learning each day what I could do, doing each day things that I had not imagined even, with joy and"—MS F continues—"peaceful eagerness and serene surprise. When I realised that it was to be a novel and printed, I knew that I would have to get out of it, get on the outside" (AL, 278). A final echo of Faulkner's "being" the brothers appears in the first typescript, following MS F, in a revised restatement of a strategy necessitated by publication of what had now gone beyond private writing. In trying to clarify Benjy's section by writing Quentin's and Jason's, TS H reads, "I was still being each of them in turn; hence the story was not clear yet. (I was thinking now in terms of print, readers) I saw that I should have to get completely out of the book" AL, 282). This, too, was excised from subsequent typescripts.

In the end, the personal matter having to do with Faulkner's creating the Compson brothers from his own complex feelings for Estelle was subsumed into a long passage about Southern writing and Southern writers generally. The first version of that appears in TS H, late in the compositional process, and was expanded in the longer of the published pieces. "Because it is himself that the Southern writer is writing about," he says there; "the writer unconsciously writes into every line and phrase his violent despairs and rages and frustrations or his violent prophesies of still more violent hopes" (Miscellany, 158). This conforms to Faulkner's practice, in both novel and introduction, of consciously distancing himself by dispersing his experience, but it hardly represents self-erasure. Indeed, the background pattern of revision and rewriting in the manuscripts emphasizes both the personal and the performative in what was retained. He had theorized in the earliest manuscript draft that "any introduction to any book, written by a fiction writer, is likely to be about 50% fiction itself" (AL, 272), yet fictional self-presentations deriving from revisions of autobiographical and historical fact were by 1933 an established and familiar strategy of Faulkner's writing, whatever the form—including poems, letters, essays, and sketches as well as fiction—and however veiled. In the introduction, as in the novel, this refined sense of self-presentation is accomplished at no cost to the intensity of the self Faulkner presents. Autobiographical and other personal matter retained in the final version still is presented in the charged language of performance that Faulkner achieved in the novel and to which he turned early and late in the compositional process. In the longer introduction, for example, Caddy remains the archetypal "fierce, panting, paused and stooping wet figure which smelled

like trees" of TS H (Miscellany, 159; cf. AL, 280); Benjy, in a passage
slightly revised from TS H that recalls the agony of his "eyeless, tongue-
less" bellowing at the end of *The Sound and the Fury* (TSATF, 320), is
"shapeless, neuter, like something eyeless and voiceless which might
have lived, existed merely because of its ability to suffer, in the beginning
of life; half fluid, groping: a pallid and helpless mass of all mindless agony
under the sun" (Miscellany, 160; cf. AL, 281).[16] Faulkner's sense of discovery as he wrote the book became a celebration of writing as an act, expressed in a passage elevated to performance not only by its language but
also by his strategically disclaiming the ability to describe the elation
that the words following portray: "the emotion definite and physical and
yet nebulous to describe," he called it, "that ecstasy, that eager and joy-
ous faith and anticipation of surprise which the yet unmarred sheets beneath my hand held inviolate and unfailing" (AL, 275; Miscellany, 160;
SoR, 709).

Faulkner's concern with the act of writing in the introduction, so evi-
dent in the intensity of such passages, extends as well to performances
at the scene of the writing he describes there, where Southerners take
"horsewhips and pistols to editors about the treatment or maltreatment
of their manuscript" (Miscellany, 157–158), where the opening section of
the novel seemed to him "to explode on the paper before me" (Miscellany,
159), and where he discovered "in a series of repercussions like summer
thunder, the Flauberts and Conrads and Turgenievs which as much as ten
years before I had consumed whole and without assimilating at all" (Miscellany, 160). A passage new to the final typescript, in which he expanded
upon the nature of Southern writers and writing, uses literal performances
to describe the ambiguous nature and situation of art as he knew it:

> in the South art, to become visible at all, must become a ceremony, a spec-
> tacle; something between a gypsy encampment and a church bazaar given
> by a handful of alien mummers who must waste themselves in protest and
> active self-defense until there is nothing left with which to speak—a single
> week, say, of furious endeavor for a show to be held on Friday night and then
> struck and vanished, leaving only a paint-stiffened smock or a worn out
> typewriter ribbon in the corner and perhaps a small bill for cheesecloth or
> bunting in the hands of an astonished and bewildered tradesman. (Miscel-
> lany, 157)

He is present in the passage, of course, in the remnant of "worn out typewriter ribbon" on which he typed it. He drew his metaphor from the trav-

eling show in the novel, by which, in juxtaposition to the church service, he ironically had defined two poles of artistic performance in Jefferson and degrees of community fascination with them. The image of a dumb show acted by mummers in this final draft of the introduction is reimagined and expanded from a reference to mime in an early manuscript fragment. What he had learned about his own reading in the course of his writing, he said in MS B, and what he worked toward in his book as he wrote, was the expressive power of a fictional moment in which character, action, and event coalesced into a single picture, soundless, as he described it, yet inherently in motion with life, partaking of that quality of writing he previously had called "silent thunder" (CSWF, 898). He called such moments here the "one physical ideality which all the novels which I had believed good had possessed":

> This was that the action, the desires of the people all came to one single head, like [when a pot boils,] that instant when a pot boils, in an [simple] anecdote so simple as to be possible or actual {(or at least credible)} in the experience of everyone who ever breathed, and that the [ones which to me were] 2 or 3 which to me were absolutely right and absolutely beautiful postulated themselves even finer than the anecdote: in a picture [so explicable] that it could be acted by lay figures and caught without dialogue by a camera. It would probably not be the same picture to all who read it, and even those who left the book with the same picture would not be moved the same way (AL, 273; brackets indicate cancellations in the manuscript; braces indicate marginal additions.)

The concept of the physical ideality is illustrated in a note at the end of the next manuscript fragment about Caddy in the pear tree. "It's fine to think you will leave something behind you when you die," he wrote, "but its better still to have made something that you yourself can die with: Much better little doomed gir[l]'s drawers climbing tree to look in window" (AL, 274). To this image, of course, he returned not only in the shorter version of the introduction, where he called it "perhaps the only thing in literature which would ever move me very much" (SoR, 710), and in the longer version, where it concludes the piece, but also in public statements and interviews he gave for the rest of his life.[17] The first description of such moments in the heavily revised passage from MS B points backward as well as forward, to his interest in comedia dell'arte drama and his experience with the university theatre group for whom he wrote *The Marionettes* in 1920.

The one-act verse play is illustrated not with photographs but with ten black-and-white drawings in which Marietta, Pierrot, and the Shade are caught in suggestive or telling attitudes as a camera might catch them. For several years previously, Faulkner had provided the university annual with similar drawings and in the two years immediately preceding *The Marionettes* he was himself much photographed. The play, like many of those photographs, is a consciously staged self-presentation, the verse, the illustrations, and the hand-printed pages in the hand-bound book declaring the William Faulkner of the title page an artist in several mediums. The action of the play is represented as the dream of the sodden Pierrot, in which, as in *The Sound and the Fury*, an idealized woman is seduced by another, more sexually dynamic lover and falls into a version of what Faulkner called later, in the introduction to the novel, "dishonor and shame" (Miscellany, 159). At one level of the play, Marietta is courted, seduced, and corrupted by Pierrot's active self, the Shade, and his paradoxically passive dreaming is a reflexive image of the poet-playwright's act of writing. In the play as in the novel, the woman in question is modeled on Estelle. Faulkner's drawings of Marietta closely resemble photographs of her at this period, and the inscription in one of the extant copies appears to address Estelle through her then two-year-old daughter. The play is inscribed "TO 'CHO-CHO,' / A TINY FLOWER OF THE FLAME, THE / ETERNAL GESTURE CHRYSTALLIZED" (Marionettes, 89).[18] In her final speech in the play, Marietta describes her own dishonor in terms of her transformation into an aging voluptuary: no longer the troubled virgin Faulkner described and illustrated as dressed in white at the outset, she now has "painted legs," "breasts, like twin moons that have been dead for a thousand years," and "heavy hair and . . . gilded eyelids" (Marionettes, 52, 53, 54).

What Faulkner said of his reading in an early draft of the introduction to *The Sound and the Fury*—that it had crystallized during the writing of the book "like when a chemist puts a precipitant into an inextricable and indistinguishable mass of matter" (AL, 273)—seems true also, in this context of multiple connections, of his writing *The Sound and the Fury*. As always, the work he knew best was his own, and it was his lifelong habit to draw upon previous work from book to book for materials and methods of presentation. Including self-presentation. In 1928–1929, in a period of "intimate difficulties," as he described it to Maurice-Edgar Coindreau ("Preface," 49), much that he consciously and unconsciously knew came into focus as he wrote. In addition to the work of writers he named in various drafts of his introduction—James and Anderson, Dostoevsky and Flaubert and Conrad, among others—personal matter in the otherwise inextricable and indistinguishable mass of his own life experience stood clear and ready to his hand. In retrospect there is a strong sense of elated self-expression as well as artistic expression in his assertion that by being "inside the book" he was "learning each day what I could do, doing each day things that I had not imagined even" (AL, 278).

Literally, he was reading and writing himself into being. As he returned to moments of particular intensity from his reading and his life, revising, reshaping, and reusing according to the shifting imperatives of this novel, he performed, in effect, an act of self-criticism on what he had done and what he had been that is paralleled as it also is reflected in the composition of the introduction. Writing the novel, it seemed to him in 1933 as it would in later self-appraisals, had been to him intensely a *time* of "physical ideality," an experience, as he put it in "Black Music," "outside the lot and plan for normal human man to do and be." As he also said in the introduction, it was not to return (Miscellany, 160–161): the discovery itself would undergird and inform other, subsequent work, but the first ecstatic moment of discovery was gone. Yet this was 1933, and there was a great deal more work yet to write. In a letter to Joan Williams twenty years later, he would use the same language in the context of a new love affair and the role of lover to a new beloved to express not the coalescence of his life experience in his art but his sense of his separation from the writing. At that distance of time from his first masterwork, he presented himself to Joan as an old man who had, at last "some perspective on all I have done. I mean, the work apart from me, the work which I did, apart from what I am" (SLWF, 348). Whatever he thought of himself then, he knew the work was still vital. In the 1933 introduction, conversely, the sustained tension between a much younger Faulkner and his work gives mutual expression to the man in his art and the artist in the man. It is this union that he claimed to have discovered in *The Sound and the Fury* and struggled so to describe in the drafts of the introduction. To capture *that* as in a photograph, whether readers saw the same picture together or not, was to present *himself* ecstatically transformed, to share something magical—"de ricklickshun en de blood of de Lamb," as it were—with his own congregation of readers.

The 1933 introduction represented both a culmination and a beginning of ideas and images, strategies, and modes of expression in a novelist whose aesthetic had developed by that time through seven novels and a large number of stories. In that work, as especially in the introduction as it evolved from draft to draft, and in major work throughout the 1930s, the emphasis increasingly is on strategies of self-presentation, both authorial now and as a telling aspect of fictional character, and on performance. The writer was a writer no matter what he was writing; the writer-as-writing was a creation of the same methods from medium to medium, be it poetry or fiction, letters or essays. Or photographs, for which he repeatedly posed in his late teens and early twenties, transforming himself by performances before the flash and glare of the studio portrait camera and the click of the simple Kodak. The camera image is an important one, not only for what photography represents as an emblematic mode of expression in the fiction but for its source in Faulkner's experience as one early mode of self-presentation in the years before he wrote novels—or was paid to write introductions to them.

II. Photographs, Letters, and Fictions

Yet it is not (it seems to me) by Painting

that Photography touches art, but by

Theater.

— Roland Barthes

---

i. Soldier and Son

In the photograph, taken in a Toronto studio in the autumn of 1918, he stands nearly erect, small against the chest-high painted marble railing and scratchy forest setting of the photographer's backdrop [Fig. 1]. His military-issue tunic is unbelted, smock-like, and formless above vague breeches wound in leggings from knee to ankle and boots that make his splayed feet disproportionately large. Eyes slightly right of the camera, a moustache like a shadow beneath a prominent nose, the thin face is less solemn than it is expressionless. The overseas cap with the broad white cadet band is an unconscious ironic counterpoint to the hand-inscribed legend at the bottom of the picture: "Royal Flying Corps." The Royal Flying Corps, for all of its romantic associations, was defunct then, having been officially renamed the Royal Air Force in April 1918.

In every aspect save that cap, which signifies cadet status, and the

Fig. 1 Cadet Faulkner, Toronto 1918 (Courtesy of the Harry
Ransom Humanities Research Center, The University of Texas at Austin, and
copyright permission of Jill Faulkner Summers)

anachronistic inscription, apparently in his mother's hand, this first photograph of William Faulkner in uniform is a static image. The figure makes
no gesture of selfhood. The ill-fitting costume, the stick, Faulkner's physical size and posture, and even his tiny moustache recall Charlie Chaplin's Little Tramp, but the Cadet lacks Chaplin's all-important sense of
ironic self-presentation. In this case, the Chaplinesque metaphor, if it is
one, is not Faulkner's but the photographer's, or an accident of the photographer's indifference to his subject. The image conveys not a subject in-
teracting with the camera but a passive subject-as-object dominated by
the camera's power. It is a record rather than a representation.

Because it is, it provides a point of reference—a negative one—for a
group of pictorial and written images by which Faulkner presented him-

self to family and friends during and immediately after World War I. In the present case, Carol Shloss's distinction between two extremes of photographic strategy is instructive. Shloss identifies one approach to the photographic "that acknowledges the autonomy of the Other and another that submerges the Other in a solitary purpose, one that defines itself by including the self-knowledge of the subject and another that disqualifies meanings generated externally."[1] In fact if not intention, the Cadet photograph "submerges" Faulkner in the "solitary purpose" of recording his uniformed image. This is not precisely the application that Shloss makes, but it seems to me to give point to the extremity of Faulkner's explicit insistence, in other photographs, on his own "autonomy" and "self-knowledge" as a self-posed subject.

Nearly always he *was* posing. Roland Barthes reminds that "Photography . . . began, historically, as an art of the Person: of identity, of civil status," and that in its presentation of "the body's *formality*" performance is central: "it is not . . . by Painting that Photography touches art," Barthes says, "but by Theater."[2] Recalling Faulkner's wardrobe and his fondness for costume, the Oxford, Mississippi, photographer J. R. Cofield remembered him as a natural photographic subject who was "never . . . fazed by a mere camera."[3] Both performance and costume are powerfully at work in a slightly earlier snapshot that is the precise antithesis of the Cadet portrait [Fig. 2]. Posed in the backyard of his family's white frame house on North Street shortly before he left Oxford for New Haven in 1918, Faulkner is dressed to convey "civil status" in the no less uniform costume of a Young Dandy in a Mississippi college town of the period: dark, tailored suit, coat fashionably drawn back from a tattersall vest, high round-collared shirt and broad striped tie. The pose is studied, slightly pretentious, the formally dressed figure with his walking stick as out of place in the homey backyard setting as the Cadet in his stock pastoral one. Yet this figure swaggers with a conscious superiority that propagandizes the image. Partly this is a matter of costume: as John Berger has suggested of tailored clothes generally, the suit Faulkner wears does not deform the subject, as the cadet uniform does, but "*preserve*[s] the physical identity and therefore the natural authority" of the wearer.[4] Dressed and posed as he is, the art in this case is all with the self-presenting subject who performs for the camera, not with the photographer. Unlike the Cadet photograph, this is a virtual *Self*-portrait.

In a third photograph, taken in New Haven between this one and the Cadet portrait, the costume is significantly modified to portray the

Fig. 2 The Young Dandy, Oxford 1918 (Courtesy of the Harry Ransom Humanities Research Center, The University of Texas at Austin, and copyright permission of Jill Faulkner Summers)

Englishness Faulkner understood was required for enlistment in the Royal Air Force [Fig. 3]. Probably this enlistment photograph was influenced by his residence at Yale that spring. The loose-fitting jacket, loose cravat, and soft-collared shirt in the head-and-shoulders portrait conform to the urbane Eastern style of dress he described in a letter to his mother from New Haven in April, when he wrote, "I wish some of the boys at the University of Mississippi could see these men. Tight clothes and pink and yellow shirts are as rare here as negroes" (TofH, 45). Returned to New Haven three years later, he sent Maud Falkner a drawing of four Yale undergraduates dressed in much the same style as here, calling them "expensively dressed tramps" [Fig. 4]. Even in group photographs, he presented himself in ways that expressed his individuality and difference. A photograph from the University of Mississippi yearbook for 1920 [Fig. 5] shows four dozen veterans of the American Expeditionary Force dutifully looking into the camera. Faulkner alone, whose right to membership in the A.E.F. Club was a self-invention, is obviously posed: he stands in three-quarter right profile, eyes upward, a cigarette holder in the right corner of his mouth and the signature cane on his shoulder.

Such photographs document the familiar roles Faulkner played at this time: the swaggering Young Dandy who bought his suits at Healy's in Memphis and had his mother tailor them for a tighter fit; the Church of England enlistee from Finchley, Middlesex, England, as his R.A.F. enlistment papers describe him; and the university poet and dandy dubbed by the editors of *The Mississippian* Count No 'Count. They testify to his attention to his public image, of course; but they are based more deeply in his most profound sense of himself as a man and, soon, as an artist. In such pictures, he characteristically looks not into the camera but *inward* at some image of himself, as if, to paraphrase Susan Sontag, his *self* was an image that the camera might make real.[5] The photographic record during and immediately after the war, together with his drawings and written accounts of himself, document a persistent pattern of Faulkner's presenting such self-constructed images in public and private performances.

There is general agreement that Faulkner's lifelong habit of role-playing was a function of his literary imagination, in which regard David Minter has proposed that "his authentic self was the self variously and nebulously yet definitely bodied forth by his fictions."[6] In the period 1918–1920, when there was as yet only unpublished, private writing through which to present himself as an artist, self-construction was all the more necessary and challenging. Indeed, for the young man who so

Fig. 3 Enlistment Photograph, New Haven 1918 (Courtesy of the Harry Ransom Humanities Research Center, The University of Texas at Austin, and copyright permission of Jill Faulkner Summers)

Fig. 4 "A few types," New Haven 1921 (Courtesy of the Harry Ransom Humanities Research Center, The University of Texas at Austin, and copyright permission of Jill Faulkner Summers)

Fig. 5 A.E.F. University of Mississippi, 1920 (Courtesy of the Dean Faulkner Wells Collection)

acutely felt his difference, at times even his alienation, from his contemporary place and time, the written and the pictured self he presented were sometimes at odds. Compared to the heightened self-presentations in his letters from Toronto in 1918, for example, the Cadet portrait is barely even military, an anti-image that problematized the soldierly identity he had claimed. This he was quick to recognize and revise.

From the outset the cadet uniform was unsuited to his self-image. He described it briefly, and accurately, in a letter to his mother when he arrived in Toronto, but it was the oddly more military summer uniform of "trunks and a cork helmet . . . and the eternal stick" (TofH, 79) that he drew for her in mid-July [Fig. 6]. There was a good bit in that letter, as well, about his instructors' heroics in the trenches of France, and the first mention of his hopes of making a flight. Although he promised the Cadet photograph all through that month, it was not forthcoming until August 11, in a letter that suggests how uncomfortably aware he was that it compromised the military persona he had been constructing for his parents. If he was not yet a veteran, he did have experience by then of a month's training. The prints he sent, he said, "are not much, for this is my 'rookie' uniform and was literally thrown at me" (TofH, 89). In the same letter he strategically offered to replace the Cadet photograph, first with one "in my summer clothes," then with a self-mocking but still serious one "standing beside a 'plane, you know, egregious; with one hand resting carressingly and protectively upon its knee cap" (TofH, 89).[7]

"Egregious" or not, the cliche he evoked on August 11 was far closer to the self he had extracted from his military experience and presented in his letters than was the studio print of the blank-faced Cadet. He assured Murry and Maud he would have a real officer's uniform in eight weeks— "my sure enough one," he called it (TofH, 89)—and he concluded the letter with still another drawing of himself to counteract the Cadet image, this one in the classic uniform of a flying officer in garrison cap, belted tunic, breeches, putties, and stick [Fig. 7]. "My new uniform," he wrote, "will be like this" (TofH, 90). The next day, still concerned with self-image, he dismissed the drawing in his summer uniform as Boy-Scout-like, supplanting it, in turn, with the handsome enlistment portrait, copies of which he had had since mid-summer but had not sent on to Mississippi. Unlike the Cadet picture, this was an official R.A.F. document of sorts, "made to go on my papers when I enlisted," as he said (TofH, 91).

Uniforms and costumes pervade the late letters from Canada. His military self-image still was not secure and he wanted no more pictures of

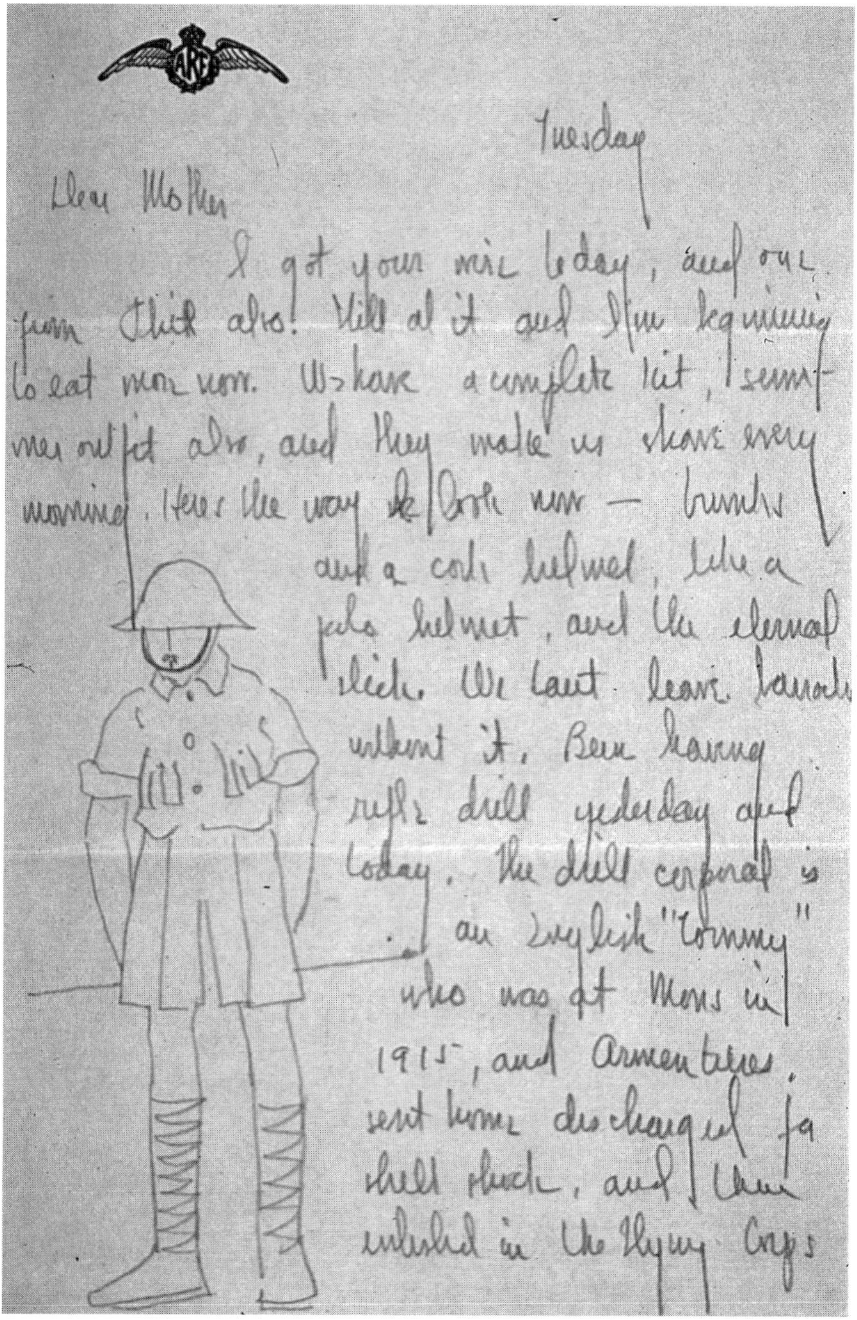

Tuesday

Dear Mother

I got your wire today, and one from Phil also! Still at it and I'm beginning to eat more now. We have a complete kit, summer outfit also, and they make us shave every morning. Here's the way we look now — breeches and a cork helmet, like a polo helmet, and the eternal stick. We can't leave barracks without it. Been having rifle drill yesterday and today. The drill corporal is an English "Tommy" who was at Mons in 1915, and Armentieres, sent home discharged for shell shock, and then enlisted in the Flying Corps

Fig. 6 RAF Summer Uniform, Toronto 1918 (Courtesy of the Harry Ransom Humanities Research Center, The University of Texas at Austin, and copyright permission of Jill Faulkner Summers)

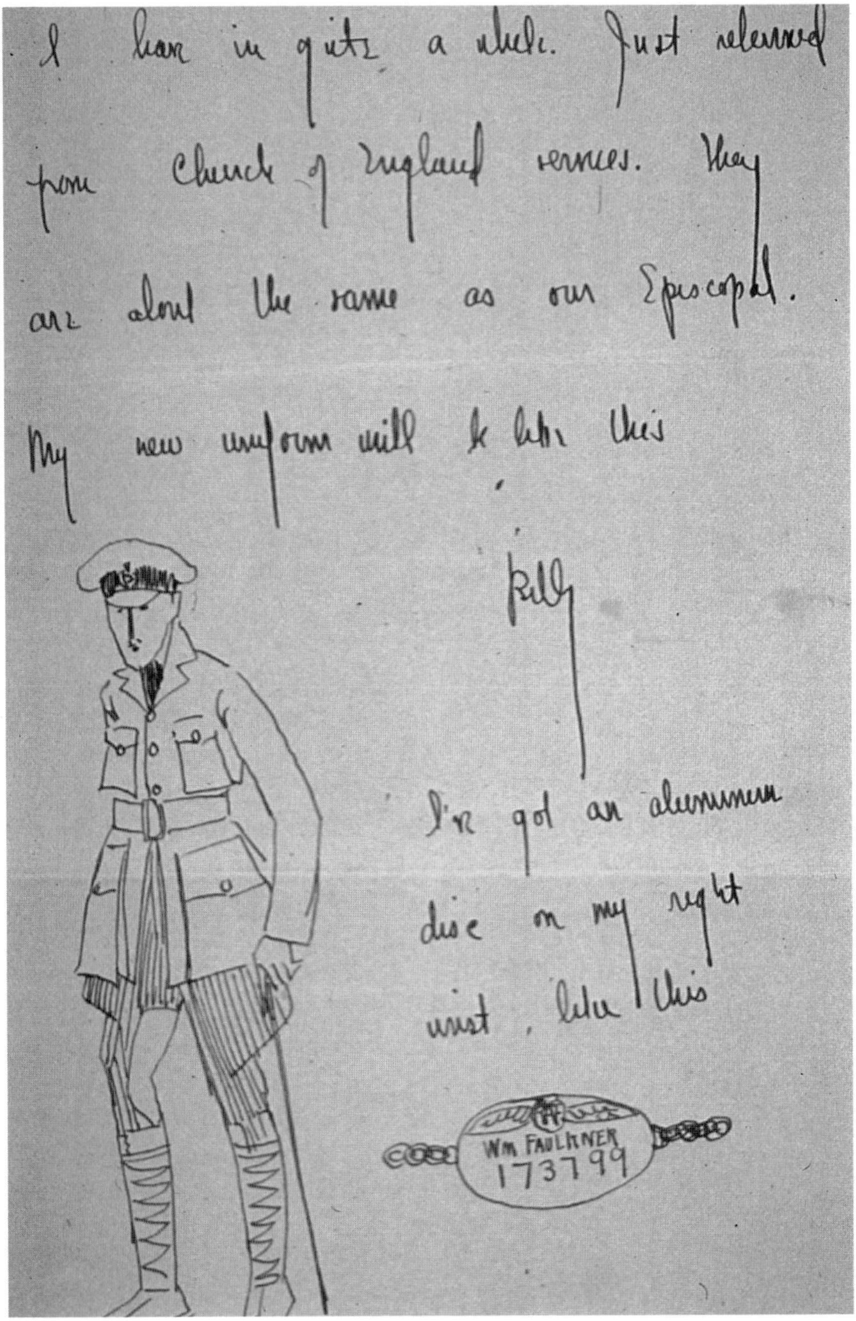

I have in quite a while. Just returned from Church of England services. They are about the same as our Episcopal.

My new uniform will be like this

Bill

I've got an aluminum disc on my right wrist, like this

Fig. 7 Flying Officer Uniform, Toronto 1918 (Courtesy of the Harry Ransom Humanities Research Center, The University of Texas at Austin, and copyright permission of Jill Faulkner Summers)

himself when he wrote his mother in October, "I cannot use the camera at all" (TofH, 113). In November he wrote that his cadet uniform was wearing out; two days before the armistice, with the war winding down, he bought new whipcord trousers and reported being mistaken for "a flying officer in mufti" (TofH, 128, 130). In December, on the day he was demobilized, he replaced his stolen cadet overcoat with one "from an officer who was hard up" (TofH, 138).

Faulkner left Toronto December 8, 1918, with no flight training and without a commission but not without the "sure enough" officer's uniform. Arrived home in Oxford, he presented himself to his family—and to the family camera—wearing the uniform he had drawn in his August letter. At the corner of the North Street house where he had stood to be photographed in a suit and vest, he posed himself for Maud Falkner's Kodak as a war-weary veteran wearing a garrison cap, tunic with pilot's brevet, and breeches [Fig. 8]. There were variations on that performance in different costumes using different props: the jaunty pilot in a garrison cap worn "hot-pilot" style, half leaning on a cane [Fig 9]; and the pensive veteran in overseas cap and Sam Browne belt [Fig. 10] from which Maud painted a still more idealized portrait embellished with color and a Canadian service flag in the background [Fig. 11]. The painting aside, there is little evidence in the snapshots of the photographer's artistry: no careful framing, no manipulation of light and shadow, no selection of detail. Rather, each is a conscious performance in which the subject presents himself for the camera to transcribe on film. Like the letters that preceded them, these snapshots give information whose value, as Susan Sontag has said of photographs, "is of the same order as fiction."[8]

Autobiographical fiction, of course—in his letters as well as photographs, and in the poetry he was writing—was a well-developed Faulknerian mode of self-making even then, and his recurrent metaphors for himself extended from one medium to another. Little of value was lost. In a letter in late August 1918, Cadet Faulkner described his tanned face and sun-faded hair as looking like "a kodak negative" (TofH, 94). By stages, the "kodak negative" of the Cadet *developed* into the Officer of the photographs he had taken in Oxford, which are not pictures of impostures so much as they are deeply autobiographical self-portraits: like the more autobiographical novels as David Minter describes them, these early photographs, though in a smaller way, also are "of his self expressive, which is to say, creative."[9]

In an essay on self-portraiture in the early prose sketches and poems

Fig. 8 War-weary Veteran, Oxford 1918–1919 (Courtesy of the Harry Ransom Humanities Research Center, The University of Texas at Austin, and copyright permission of Jill Faulkner Summers)

Fig. 9 Jaunty Pilot, Oxford 1918–1919 (Courtesy of the Dean
Faulkner Wells Collection)

Fig. 10 Pensive Veteran, Oxford 1918–1919 (Courtesy of the Dean Faulkner Wells Collection)

Fig. 11 Maud Falkner's Painting, Oxford 1918–1919 (Courtesy of the Martin Dain Collection, Southern Media Archive, Center for the Study of Southern Culture, University of Mississippi)

Faulkner wrote near this time, Michel Gresset helpfully defines a *self-portrait* as "any *signed* representation of such tendencies, actual or imaginary, as are perceived by the subject as being part and parcel of his or her psychological, mental, physical, sexual or intellectual makeup."[10] For Gresset the distinguishing aspect of the self-portrait is precisely its self-conscious awareness and presentation of otherwise invisible characteristics that the self-portraitist displays. Gresset speaks of such self-presentations as a reflexive "exchange between the subject and the subject-as-object."[11] These are terms used by theorists of photography, as well. Gresset is not concerned with photographs of Faulkner, nor with his personal letters,[12] which of course are signed, but both forms of self-presentation qualify as self-portraits according to his definition. Private photographs, especially, share several dimensions with personal letters. John Berger says of the photograph that belongs to "private experience"— the portrait in a family album and the team picture are his examples— that it "is appreciated and read in a context *which is continuous with that from which the camera removed it.* . . . such a picture remains surrounded by the meaning from which it was severed."[13] So with personal letters.

Indeed, the nature and function of the photograph as Susan Sontag describes them are inherently complementary to that of the letter.[14] Each is a subjectively crafted artifact, fragmentary and occasional, consisting of an image or images that document experience, the image in the case of the photograph being the object itself.[15] Photographs, like letters, share what Sontag calls "the presumption of veracity," and photographers, like letter writers, still are fabulists, "haunted by tacit imperatives of taste and conscience."[16] In this sense, each is a performance, the camera recording the posed subject pictorially in the way that the letter characteristically portrays both the writer in the act of writing and his or her correspondent in the act of reading. Photographer and letter writer have inherent authority over those images. However, the self-presenting subject of a photograph can subvert the authority of the camera in something of the way the receiver of a letter reverses the hierarchical power of the written by becoming an answering writer. The correspondence between subject and photographer, as between reader and writer in a circular epistolary dialogue, is responsible for the aspect of self-portraiture in each medium. The self-posed photograph of a private experience, like the personal letter, maintains as it also traverses distance: it is surrogate, Sontag says, "both a pseudo-presence and a token of absence."[17] Her description of a photograph as "a thin slice of space as well as time"[18] applies as well to a letter. Together in complement, photograph and letter accomplish what neither can completely do alone: the limitations of the photographic image—that it represents "how something looks" rather than "how it functions"—are supplied by the narrative character of the written. If it is true, as Sontag says, that "Only that which narrates can make us understand," it is equally true, as she also admits, that "Photographs, which cannot themselves explain anything, are inexhaustible invitations to deduction, speculation, and fantasy." [19]

Pictures in sequence can, and in Faulkner's case do, approximate narrative. In Cananda in 1918, Faulkner's progress from apprentice cadet to flying officer was short-circuited, first by an epidemic of the Spanish influenza that interrupted cadet training and then by the Armistice. His imaginative presentations of himself, however, developed steadily by stages that are traceable in recurrent associative patterns in his writing, drawings, and photographs. In this regard the poem "The Ace" may be read as developing, as a photographic image is developed, from his description of his deeply tanned face on August 22 as looking like a "kodak negative." Enclosed in a letter three weeks later, the poem gives imaginative expression to the written self-image Faulkner initially had explicated with a drawing, applying the same terms to the heroic figure that he wanted to be and figuratively would become in the Oxford photographs.

> The silent earth looms blackly in the dawning
> Sharp as poured ink beneath the grey
> Mists spectral, clutching fingers
>   The sun light
> Paints him as he stalks, huge through the morning
> In his fleece and leather, and gilds his bright
> Hair. The first lark hovers, singing, where
> He flashes through the shining gates of day.
>
> (TofH, 99)

The poem is not only a poetic but, embedded as it is in the first-person narrative of Faulkner's correspondence, a self-presentational performance. As it does the sun-tanned cadet in the earlier letter, "The sun light / paints" the aviator with "bright / Hair" as he "Flashes through the shining gates of day." "Huge . . . in his fleece and leather," the R.A.F. ace is significantly larger than William Faulkner, and larger than life: he transcends reality and perhaps even writing, the conjunction of which is proposed here in another of Faulkner's favorite images, that of the predawn earth as "poured ink." [20]

From the mid-1920s on, Faulkner's real and imagined experience in the R.A.F. passed into published work that regularly portrayed fictional characters by the same methods and in the same tropes as those through which he had presented himself. Such crossings, if they are not *signed* as Gresset requires of self-portraits, nonetheless point up signature concerns with identity and perception. The early story "Victory," for example, borrows the photographic metaphor from Faulkner's August 22, 1918, letter to describe the veteran Alec Gray, whose "dark face and . . . white hair looked like a kodak negative" (CSWF, 435).[21] With the pilot of "The Ace," Gray is an avatar both of Faulkner's own training in Canada and of his postwar fiction of himself as an officer: like Cadet Faulkner, Private Gray is disciplined for not shaving (TofH, 80; CSWF, 439–441), then commissioned from the ranks, as Faulkner dreamed of being commissioned, for action in the trenches akin to that Faulkner reported hearing from his Canadian ground school instructors. Seeing, and especially seeing or not seeing oneself, is very much at issue here. Another soldier in the story literally is blind. Like Donald Mahon in *Soldiers' Pay*, the blind soldier is abandoned by his fiancée as Mahon is by Cecile, and her absence is symbolized photographically in the blank card he carries in the shape of what he believes to be a photograph of her. Gray is figuratively blind, and the photographic image of him is one of several ways he is seen in the story in a complex of readings and misreadings resulting from multiple third-person perspectives. What Shloss says of the camera is true of the camera-like technique of the story, that it "sets up the world as something to be looked-at rather than as something to be experienced from-the-point-of-view-of another or as a reciprocal looking back and forth." This "obvious point"—which applies to Faulkner's Cadet photograph as well as to Gray—is not without complex implications for fictional as well as photographic perspective: as Shloss says, "it is important to recognize the discontinuities, stratifications, and crediting of a single perspective that such a configuration of visibility implies, and conversely, to recognize the interrelationships, struggles, and dialogue between differing values that are suppressed by the disposition of the community into those-who-see and those-who-are-seen."[22] As a writer of fiction Faulkner was one of those-who-see and, of course, say—one concerned, from the outset, with the formal representation in fiction of just such interrelated discontinuities as Shloss describes. As an uncommissioned non-combatant posing in Oxford as a veteran, he was also for a time his own outward image, the calculated self-presentations of the 1918–1919 photographs rendering him then one of those-who-are-seen. And, shortly, read.

The way he was seen by others did not conform always with the way he saw and presented himself. In a January 1919 letter to Herb Starr, whom he had met with Stone in New Haven, Faulkner wrote of returning home from "His Majesty's Imperial Royal Flying Corps . . . perfectly competent to be a chauffeur or to hold a job with any bunch of Wops or a Department of Streets." His parents, he said, "refuse to do the honors with the conventional fatted calf. Fact, I am a hero only to my kid brother."[23] Shortly afterward, when Faulkner entered the University of Mississippi, he added to his military costume the cape and cane of a dandy and was tagged Count No 'Count by his peers. Because some of his poses seemed to the public preposterous and phony, photographs that documented those identities were all the more important. J. R. Cofield recalled Faulkner's bringing him in 1928 "a tiny Kodak photo his mother had saved of him made back in World War I days in his RAF uniform, looking very casual. He wanted me to copy it."[24] Among other professional photographers Faulkner knew well was William Odiorne, whose portraits of him in Paris in 1925 portray a more serious, more studied Faulkner than Maud's snapshots. Posed seated in the Luxembourg Gardens, he wears a full beard rather than a moustache, a felt hat and heavy tweed suit in place of tunic and cap, and has a pipe instead of a cigarette in his mouth [Fig. 12]. By the mid-1930s, according to Cofield, Faulkner owned a sophisticated European camera and had become "a devout camera fiend." "He finally gave it up in disgust," Cofield says, "even though cameras always did fascinate him. I never took a shot that he was not at my elbow taking in the complete procedure."[25] The image of the self-posing subject as practicing photographer validates the sense of those photographs taken in uniform that Faulkner is both self-seeing and self-seen.

Not only photographs but technical facility with a camera informed some fictions. Faulkner's understanding of light and angle of perception, everywhere apparent in a lyric prose that describes landscapes as well as people with precision, is documented by detailed notes on the back of a picture he made of Jill and Mammy Callie Barr: "Camera—Leica / Lenz— 1.3, 5 F-50mm / L is at 4.5 / shutter 1/60 / Eastman Panchromatic Film / Overcast 5:00 pm / May '39."[26] The story "All the Dead Pilots" (1931), drawn from the heavily autobiographical Sartoris materials, draws as well on his factual knowledge of photography and on his own experience as a photographic subject. The narrator, who experiments during the war with a synchronized flash camera, juxtaposes contemporary photographs of the former pilots to the dog-eared snapshots taken in 1918, where they strike the same kind of poses Faulkner had affected and to the same effect.

Fig. 12 Expatriate, Paris 1926 (Courtesy of the Dean Faulkner Wells Collection)

Lean, hard, in their brass-and-leather martial harness, posed standing beside or leaning upon the esoteric shapes of wire and wood and canvas in which they flew without parachutes, they too have an esoteric look; a look not exactly human, like that of some dim and threatful apotheosis of the race seen for an instant in the glare of a thunderclap and then forever gone. (CSWF, 511)

The photograph Faulkner had Cofield copy in 1928 was just such a personal self-validation as these. The pose he once self-mockingly called an "egregious" cliche nonetheless was an "esoteric" self-image, cherished in 1931 when he published "All the Dead Pilots" as he had cherished it in 1918 when he wrote it into his letter, and traceable thirteen years later through photographic and epistolary texts to motives of personal identity.

Not incidentally, letters also are important to the story. Crippled in the leg, as Faulkner sometimes claimed to have been,[27] the narrator is a noncombat military censor whose job it is to open and read "the scrawled, brief pages of transparent and honorable lies to mothers and sweethearts" (CSWF, 512). This amounts to a rereading of Faulkner's own correspondence from Toronto, and the addition of a synchronized flash camera provides him the metaphor for that fragile moment of heroism he exhumed and reimagined from his letters and photographs then, the moment "preserved and prolonged," as the narrator says, "only on paper: a picture, a few written words that any match . . . can obliterate in an instant (CSWF, 531). This conjunction, at the conclusion of "All the Dead Pilots," is also a fictional self-presentation, one that recalls in new combination Faulkner's foreshortened military moment in Canada, his presentation of himself as an aviator on paper in various mediums, and the flash and glare of imaginative performance that informs the best of them. As with the larger context that adheres to a single photograph, as John Berger describes it— one "which is continuous with that from which the camera removed it"— individual fictions exist in their own continuous context of representation and meaning. Like the fiction of this period, the record of Faulkner's construction of self from 1918 through the 1920s is multiple, overlaid, palimpsestic—what the narrator of "All the Dead Pilots" calls a photographic "composite: a series of brief glares in which, instantaneous and without depth or perspective, there stood into sight the portent and the threat of what the race could bear and become, in an instant between dark and dark" (CSWF, 512). Years later, in a variation that itself, in this context, recalls the photographic, he said that "The aim of every artist is to arrest motion, which is life, by artificial means and hold it fixed so that 100 years later when a stranger looks at it, moves again since it is life" (Lion, 253). For this, as for the revitalization of the figuratively dead pilots in the story, the camera alone was insufficient. Only the written could restore motion to the life it arrested, only narrative can explain. In life as in art, Michel Gresset reminds us, "The actual is not the real. One is a given, a data, the other is a construct."[28]

ii. Photographs in Fiction

A photograph from a family album, taken in 1905 in front of Murry and Maud's first house in Oxford, shows eight-year-old William mounted on a spotted pony, his younger brothers Jack and John and his cousin Sally Murry Wilkins seated on the steps to his right holding the reins of two other, smaller ponies [Fig. 13]. They might be the Compson children at about the time of Damuddy's death, although no such scene and no such photograph appear in *The Sound and the Fury*. A fictional version of the same photograph, edited and elaborated in the original *Sanctuary*, does hang in an album-like arrangement of family photographs on Miss Jenny DuPre's bedroom wall: Narcissa's son Benbow Sartoris is pictured there sitting on a "pony, erect, hand on hip, a salvaged revolver-frame in his waist-band, a small negro perched like a monkey on the withers of a gaunt mule in the background" (SO, 44). In the 1930 story "Beyond," a similar brown and faded photograph of "a boy of ten, erect upon the pony" is used as a bookmark in the Allison family annals (CSWF, 790). Judge Allison takes it to heaven when he dies, where the boy on the pony is immediately recognized as the deceased Judge's deceased son Howard.[29] In "The Brooch," which dates from the same period, Howard Boyd's deceased son is represented by an empty silver frame set between silver-framed pictures of his mother and father (CSWF, 656).[30] On Armistice Day, in the early story "Ad Astra," a German pilot tells Bayard Sartoris and his companions of severing his ties to nation and family by burning the photographs of his wife and the son he has not yet seen (CSWF, 420). And in *Flags in*

Fig. 13 Children and Ponies, Oxford 1905 (Courtesy of the Dean Faulkner Wells Collection)

the Dust (1927) the same Bayard Sartoris, Benbow Sartoris's fictional father-to-be, burns the photograph of his dead twin brother with other relics of their lost life together (Flags, 204). These photographs of fictional experience are connected to one another by ties of subject and theme and by the continuity of meaning, as John Berger says, from which the fictional camera removed them. They are linked, as well, to the 1905 photograph of Faulkner and his siblings and, however obliquely, to its continuous contexts, in this case Faulkner's childhood family and home on which the fiction works variations.

In these stories and novels, whether directly or by association, the fictional photographs put forward and enhance the recurrent themes of fallen family and a discontinuous male line. In the two instances where they valorize the Faulkner figure in the original picture by focusing exclusively on him and elaborating his pose and costume, they are direct self-presentations. In the *Sanctuary* photograph, for example, the siblings of the original have been erased—Benbow, the last male Sartoris, is the only child mounted and the only one pictured. Faulkner posed him there among his male ancestors as he might have imagined himself as a child, slightly swaggering, armed, and attended by a Negro servant. The Howard Allison photograph is a less detailed but still more refined version of the original—the last son of the Allisons' ten-generation-long "name and race" (CSWF, 789), he literally is a spirit, mounted now only in the photograph and in his father's memory of him. The thematics of these "pictured" fictions are served even when the fictional photographs are not described. Or don't even exist. Together the photographs of Howard Boyd and his wife with the empty photographic frame between them, in "The Brooch," represent their married life, "that faulty whole whose third the two of them had produced yet whose lack the two of them could not fill" (CSWF, 654). The blank frame symbolizes the blank spaces in a family line broken across three generations: Boyd's surname suggests the boy he still is, and his suicide at the end of the story repeats the death of his child in a pattern of dissolution begun when Howard himself was a child and his father deserted the family. The German pilot defends his defection to the Allies in "Ad Astra" as a principled desertion: the eldest of four sons, like Faulkner, and an artist, he gives up his barony for his music, his music and family for an idea of universal brotherhood. But by burning the papers and photograph that connected him to nation and family, he breaks the continuity of meaning that defines him and leaves himself a figurative blank in a life that ironically "iss nothing" (CSWF, 426).[31] In an equally self-destructive pattern in *Flags*, Bayard burns his own literal image by burning his twin brother's photograph, and he dies on the day the son is born that he, like the German, will never see.

Whatever their uses—as historical records, for example, or family talismans—fictional photographs also bring with them the conventions and functions that govern and define actual ones. Explaining nothing themselves, as Susan Sontag has said of real photographs, they too "are inexhaustible invitations to deduction, speculation, and fantasy," and Faulkner began using them for such purposes in his stories and novels very early. In "The Leg," written sometime before 1928, a photograph serves as a kind of picture of Dorian Gray, representing not the actual Davy, an American amputee recovering in England from his wounds, but the demoniac fantasy-self of his nightmares who, he dreams, seduces and finally kills a young English woman. The proof of his crime is a photograph.

> It was dated at Abington in June of the summer just past. At that time I was lying in the hospital talking to George, and I sat quite still in the blankets, looking at the photograph, because it was my own face that looked back at me. It had a quality that was not mine: a quality vicious and outrageous and unappalled, and beneath it was written in a bold sprawling hand like that of a child: "To Everbe Corinthia" followed by an unprintable phrase, yet it was my own face, and I sat holding the picture quietly in my hand while the candle flame stood high and steady above the wick and on the wall my huddled shadow held the motionless photograph. (CSWF, 841–842)

The shadowed photograph is a shadow once removed of a photographic shadow image of Davy. By late 1925 or 1926, when this story probably was written,[32] Faulkner had presented himself in the same way as a wounded soldier in poems, letters, and photographs and declared his love for Estelle and for Helen Baird in poems and drawings that depicted him as a faun. In 1919, the year after her marriage to Cornell Franklin, he gave Estelle his copy of Swinburne's poems signed "W. Faulkner / Royal Air Force / Cadet Wing / s of A / Borden" with a drawing of RAF wings and a figuratively unprintable inscription so passionate she had to tear it from the book to take the gift with her to Honolulu. A similarly inscribed edition of Ralph Hodgson's *Poems* identified him as a member of the Royal Flying Corps.[33] In January 1926, in the manuscript book *Mayday*, he drew Helen naked before a faun that bears his own bearded face. The photograph of Davy's nightmare self and its inscription are the fictional extensions of that strategy of self-presentation and mode of performance. By describing Davy as a "huddled shadow" and, again, as a "husk of . . . shadow" (cswf, 842), Faulkner reverted to the paradox of his own posed military self-portraits: that the photographic image was reality, however outrageous, the posed subject the real man. In figure after figure, as here, such self-presentations produce self-recognitions that likewise amaze if they do not appall.

iii. *The Marionettes*

The situation of *The Marionettes*, for example, is essentially the same as that in "The Leg":[34] the seduction of Marietta is accomplished by Pierrot's sexual other self, the Shade, whom he drunkenly dreams and, in the final drawing of the play (but not in the text), confronts in a mirror across the body of the supine Marietta, the object of his love [Fig. 14]. The aesthetic basis of the dreaming artist's physical incapacity and enabling imagination may be summed up in a Shakespearean maxim about drink and lechery from a favorite play and frequent Faulkner source. In addition to drink provoking "nose-painting, sleep and urine," the drunken Porter in *Macbeth* tells Macduff, "Letchery, sir, it provokes and unprovokes: it provokes the desire but it takes away the performance" (*Macbeth*, ii, iii, 28–29). In *The Marionettes* the drink that takes away sexual performance "provokes" the dream performance that is the play. The man of words acts out his desire through his Shade in the shadow world where the words, the pictures, and the deed they depict are one. In the drawing where Pierrot confronts himself, life and art are twice doubled: the dreamer/playwright Pierrot/Faulkner looks back into the dream/play from beyond its text at the image he has created and presented as himself. His amazement (expressed here in the position of his hands) is for that creative achievement—for what, in effect, he has done and been in the night of his playmaking, verse-making, drawing, drinking, and dreaming.

Such early assertions of the power of artistic self-presentation and performance find expression in Faulkner in a number of places and ways, but especially in works phrased as dreams and having to do with love and longing. In the concluding lines of Poem X from the manuscript book *Helen: A Courtship* (1926), for example, the wakened poet familiarly insists, "So you no virgin are, my sweet unchaste: / Why, I've lain lonely nights and nights with you" (hac, 121).[35] In *The Marionettes*, however, not only Pierrot but also Marietta is a dreamer. She admits at the outset to being

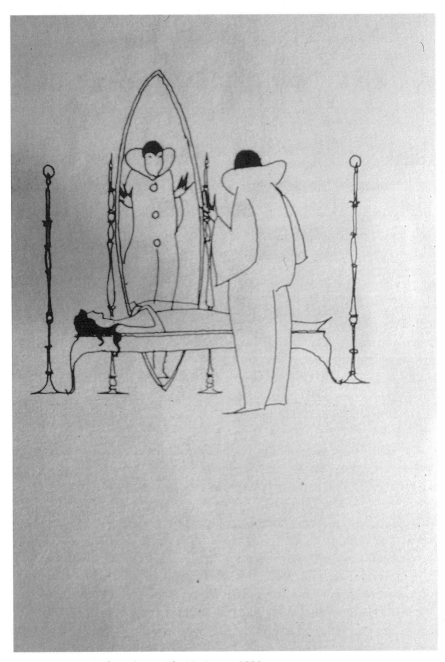

Fig. 14 Pierrot in the Mirror, *The Marionettes* 1920 (Courtesy of Jill Faulkner Summers)

"filled with desire for vague, unnamed things because a singing voice disturbed my dreams" (Marionettes, 10), the garden is a dreamscape where the moon "has cast her clothes away, / To naked dream 'till light of day" (Marionettes, 15), and a stage direction describes Marietta approaching the Shade "as though in a trance. . . . she is like a sleep walker while Pierrot continues to sing" (Marionettes, 24). This fuller context of dreaming suggests that the Shade may be Marietta's creation as well as Pierrot's, *her* ideal lover as well as *his* sexual self, and this is supported by two drawings in which she appears as aggressively offering herself to him, first stretching back toward him in the pose of a coquette [Fig. 15], then in silhouette leaning forward to kiss him [Fig. 16]. In this context, the final, aftercurtain drawing may depict Marietta as still sleeping rather than dead and the images of Pierrot within and outside the mirror manifestations of *her* dream of him, of what, to his astonishment, *she* has done and been in the night. Although she does conclude in her final speech, "The moon will play my body when I die" (Marionettes, 54), Marietta does not die in the play but insists, instead, that she is and is not changed (Marionettes, 42, 43). The choral First and Second Figures appear to agree.

From the perspective of Faulknerian self-presentation, Marietta's dreaming problematizes *The Marionettes*, not least because it raises the question of *which* William Faulkner is presented. Or how many. In his fine introduction to the play, Noel Polk raises that issue in terms of Pierrot, asking whether the play is Pierrot's "dream of himself as the would-be lover" or "a guilt-ridden dream of remorse over what he has done to Marietta" (Marionettes, xiv). Each is tenable, and Polk concludes that Faulkner seems to have intended "to synthesize both types" (Marionettes, xxix). Without proposing Marietta's agency in the creation of the Shade, Polk also proposes a third possibility, one consistent with that and with Faulkner's painful relationship with Estelle then: "that it is Marietta who has in fact deserted Pierrot, broken his heart, as it were, after having recognized in herself the power to do so, and left him to waste himself away in dissipation, rather than the other way around" (Marionettes, xxiv). This reading coincides with Estelle's behavior toward Faulkner two years previously when, informally engaged to him, she instead married the older, more urbane Cornell Franklin. Polk's sense of Marietta as both "a vulnerable, terribly wounded character" and one "associated with images of vanity and pride throughout" (Marionettes, xxiv) describes Estelle's conflicted state at that time, as well.[36] The resemblance between Faulkner's drawing of Marietta and actual photographs of Estelle, noted by

Fig. 15 Marietta the Coquette, *The Marionettes* 1920 (Courtesy of Jill Faulkner Summers)

Fig. 16 Marietta and the Shade, *The Marionettes* 1920 (Courtesy of Jill Faulkner Summers)

Sensibar, lends support to this reading, as does Polk's identification of Wilde's *Salome* and Mallarme's *Herodiade* as sources of the changed Marietta's cruelty at the end of the play (Marionettes, xxvi–xxvii).

In addition to similar language in Faulkner and Wilde, Faulkner's pen-and-ink illustrations recall Aubrey Beardsley's illustrations for *Pierrot*, especially his drawing "The Jilted Pierrot" [Fig. 17]. Beardsley, of course, also illustrated Wilde's *Salome*, and it is worth noting, in this connection, that Faulkner would associate Estelle with the infamous queen in other private writing. The drawing in the front endpapers of the manuscript book *Royal Street: New Orleans* (1926) [Fig. 18], inscribed to Estelle in 1926, constitutes a direct allusion to Beardsley's illustration "The Eyes of Herod" in *Salome* [Fig. 19]. The Herod figure was excised from that drawing, but the figures of the crowned Salome, her peacock, and one of two Beardsley cherubs were retained with a version of the Beardsleyan candle flame motif as background. Faulkner's inscription in *Royal Street*, "To Estelle, a / Lady, with / Respectful Admiration," is belied by the drawing in the front endpapers that associates her with Salome and by the sexual fear and disgust of the speaker of the concluding piece, "Hong Li." The only piece in *Royal Street* original to that collection of vignettes, "Hong Li" was added in place of the tailpiece from the collection Faulkner published as "New Orleans" in *The Double Dealer* the year before. In addition to its pointed reference to China, where Estelle was then living unhappily with her husband, "Hong Li" also incorporates language of sexual longing and reluctance that Faulkner employed in *The Marionettes*, recalling Estelle's connection to the play and Faulkner's attitude toward her there six years earlier.[37]

The Marionettes represents Faulkner's experimenting with self-presentation in early work, privately published at a time before he had learned to veil his most personal self-images and distance his intimate obsessions. The one-act verse play with its deceptively simple drawings that picture real people and situations is a multiple self-presentation as well as an artistic performance in multiple mediums. Faulkner and Estelle's relationship in 1920 was complex and troubling for them both, and if Faulkner felt they were figuratively puppets—of her parents' social ambitions, for example, or even of fate, as Polk suggests—he nonetheless must have found, as he would in his representation of himself later in relation to Caddy Compson, that one character and one perspective were not enough to express all he felt. The problem was compounded by his disjunctive sense of himself then as an artist separate from yet a part of the life of his family and community.

Fig. 17 Jilted Pierrot, Aubrey Beardsley, *Pierrot*

Fig. 18 *Royal Street: New Orleans* 1926 (Courtesy of the Harry Ransom Humanities Research Center, The University of Texas at Austin, and copyright permission of Jill Faulkner Summers)

48

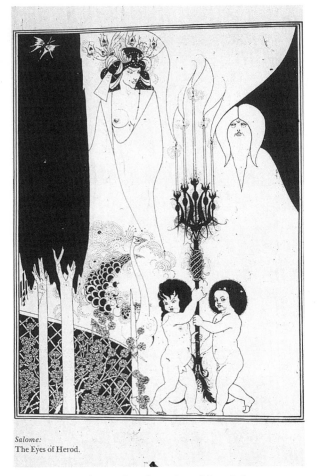

Salome:
The Eyes of Herod.

Fig. 19 Eyes of Herod, Aubrey Beardsley, *Salome*

For each of these concerns, the basically allegorical form of the play served him well. The masked characters from comedia dell'arte drama, the stock settings, and the heavy-handed action proposed parallels and meaning outside the immediate play. To represent those, Faulkner addressed and presented the interlocking issues of who he was and Estelle was but without untangling them in a text complemented, extended, and occasionally even contradicted by the drawings. The manuscript was not a mirror of their lives, although Estelle's face at one point is mirrored in Marietta's; nor yet did it overlie life like a palimpsest, one of Faulkner's favorite later figures. Yet the significance of the personal material in *The Marionettes* would have been inescapably obvious to Estelle, who was uniquely qualified to read the play personally and to recognize herself and Faulkner in it. She was the dancer, not Faulkner, and even during their informal engagement she danced and went to dances with other men while he watched; music was her realm, not his; and it was she, not he, who had entered a marriage with another lover and, returning to Oxford as a mother, was changed yet not changed, in the words of the play. Drawn from the language of the Shade's seduction song, Faulkner's inscription to Cho-Cho, the "tiny flower of the flame" of love, seems both a declaration of his own continuing love, "most respectfully tendered" (Marionettes, 82), and a reminder that Cho-Cho symbolized Estelle's infidelity to him. In his seduction song the Shade calls Marietta "a trembling pool" and himself "a flame that only you can quench" (Marionettes, 20).

Then we shall be one in the silence,
     Love!
The pool and the flame,
Till I am dead, or you have become
     a flame.

Till you are a white delicate flame,
     Love!
A little slender flame,
Drawing my hotter flame like will-o-
the-wisp in my garden.

(Marionettes, 20–21)

Judith Sensibar certainly is correct to say that *The Marionettes* is part of a recurrent pattern of self-presentation in Faulkner's work in which his relation to Estelle is deeply involved. Sensibar explains, "The author's quests for love and fame are unhappily related: pursuing one demands abandoning the other."[38] If there are implications in the play for a number of characters who were to follow the impotent Pierrot—Sensibar names George Farr and Quentin Compson, among others[39]—the Shade, in his relationship to Pierrot and Marietta, is also, and equally, suggestive of Januarius Jones and Dalton Ames. And Cornell Franklin, Estelle's actual lover-husband and Faulkner's figurative shade. In the broader contexts of fictions that were yet to be written in 1920, *The Marionettes* marks a crux in which the artist posed himself and his lover as puppets, both publicly in the four or five copies of the play that Ben Wasson sold friends and privately in the passionately inscribed copy Faulkner gave Cho-Cho for Estelle. In combination with his literary borrowings, self-presentations informed character, situation, and event, and personal matter supplied the paradoxes and ironies from which doubled perspectives on these were developed—not the least of which is the irony that the play, which is both a literary performance in itself and a record of personal performances, never was performed.

iv. "June Second, 1910"

The interest Faulkner suggested, in a draft of his introduction to *The Sound and the Fury*, in the fictional applications of photographs and photographic conventions is borne out by the fiction he wrote from the mid-1920s through the 1930s. That virtually epiphanic moment he associated with the image of Caddy in the pear tree and described as "a picture . . . caught without dialogue by a camera" was, for him, the core experience of the novel, the only thing in literature that would ever move him very much. Arguably the photographic metaphor rose to his mind in 1933 from looking back on the photographs and photographic techniques in that book and concurrent writing. Benjy's chapter, for example, might be described as a photographic montage, each section approximating that quality of a photograph that Susan Sontag describes as "a thin slice of space as well as time." It is Benjy, of course, who reports the scene of Caddy in the tree, and Faulkner subsequently spoke of "the objective picture" of Benjy's chapter as "that unbroken-surfaced confusion of an idiot" (SLWF, 44). Benjy observes without interpreting, and many of his observations have the objective quality of photographs. At mid-day on April 7, 1928, he re-enters a night scene from 1912: "The bones rounded out of the ditch, where the dark vines were in the black ditch, into the moonlight, like some of the shapes had stopped" (TSATF, 33–34). Action without dialogue is similarly framed as if caught by a camera, especially in mirrors: "Caddy and Jason were fighting in the mirror. . . . Jason was crying. He wasn't fighting anymore, but we could see Caddy fighting in the mirror and Father put me down and went into the mirror and fought too" (TSATF, 64–65). When he is at last described in the final chapter of the novel he has the features of "children in daguerrotypes" (TSATF, 274).

Quentin's pictorial imagination is as acute as his creator's, often tormentingly so. Mrs. Bland's note prompts an image of himself as a secondary figure in a photograph of Gerald into which he interposes images of Dalton Ames and Herbert Head: "What picture of Gerald I to be one of the *Dalton Ames oh asbestos Quentin has shot* background" (TSATF, 105). He adopts the photographic negative as a metaphor when he observes that Negroes are the "obverse reflection" of the white people they live among (TSATF, 86). From the outset windows are frames for external experience and mirror images are posed like slightly ominous photographs: on his return to Cambridge, the window of the lighted car frames for Quentin "my own face and a woman across the aisle with a hat sitting right on top of her head, with a broken feather in it" (TSATF, 169). He imagines Shreve at the window of a later train, at first "*seeing on the rushing darkness only his own face no broken feather unless two of them but not two like that going to Boston the same night*" and then confronting Quentin's face as it passes his on the train back to the river: "*then my face his face for an instant across the crashing when out of darkness two lighted windows in rigid fleeing crash gone his face and mine just I see saw did I see*" (TSATF, 172). These images directly partake of the dynamic stasis Faulkner ascribed to flash photographs in "All the Dead Pilots," the subjects of which are "seen for an instant in the glare of a thunderclap and then forever gone."

Each image also is a purposively posed self-presentation, a performance that Quentin acts before a camera-cum-mirror in something like the way Pierrot acts out his amazement at the end of *The Marionettes*. Like Quentin's tricking his shadow into the water, and his several visions of himself drowned in the caverns and grottoes of the sea, each is a sign of the narcissism that will destroy him. He is both without and within the pictures he makes of himself, both subject and object, himself and his shadow, alive and already drowned. Together with others which they summon, these self-presentations extend as they also complicate Quentin's sense of himself, especially, perhaps, in relation to Shreve, his roommate, confidante, correspondent, and double. And "husband," according to Spoade (TSATF, 78, 171).

Twice on June 2, 1910, Quentin's anxiety about his sexual identity finds expression in language that literally is mirrored in Shreve. As the locus of homoerotic identity in the novel, he is associated with marriage and with feminine corruption. His glasses glint "rosily" when he interrupts Quentin's reverie on Caddy's wedding, "*Roses. Roses. Mr and Mrs Jason Richmond Compson announce the marriage of.* Roses. Not virgins like dogwood, milkweed. I said I have committed incest, Father I said. Roses. Cunning and serene" (TSATF, 77); and when he and Spoade rescue Quentin from Gerald Bland, the glasses seem to Quentin "like small yellow moons" (TSATF, 167), recalling Mr. Compson's remark about women—"Delicate equilibrium of periodical filth between two moons balanced. Moons he said full and yellow as harvest moons her hips thighs" (TSATF, 128). Something of what Quentin sees reflected in Shreve's glasses is suggested, more openly, by Caddy's seeing her own desire perversely and accusingly reflected in the faces of her lovers. She tells Quentin, "*There was something terrible in me sometimes at night I could see it grinning at me I could see it through them grinning at me through their faces it's gone now and I'm sick*" (TSATF, 112). Quentin's bloodying at the hands of Gerald Bland, in this connection, may be read not only as a symbolic repetition of his confrontation with Dalton Ames, when he fainted, but also of Caddy's seduction and hymenal bloodying by Dalton, when she figuratively "died" (TSATF, 149, 151). Like the Shade whom Marietta and Pierrot dream in *The Marionettes*, Dalton is both the dynamic lover of Caddy's dreams, at whose name her blood "surged in strong accelerating beats" (TSATF, 163), and the archetypal seducer-ravager of Quentin's imagination, "*blurred within*" the womanizing Bland "*forever more*" (TSATF, 148). Like the Tommy soldiers Faulkner so envied and admired in Toronto, he "*had been in the army had killed men*" (TSATF, 148); his name, Quentin says, "just missed gentility. Theatrical fixture. Just papier-mache, then touch"; his shirts of Chinese silk resemble "Asbestos. Not quite bronze" (TSATF, 92), and Quentin associates him with Pluto, mythic lord of the underworld and abductor of Persephone: "*with one hand he could lift her to his shoulder and run with her . . . running the swine of Euboleus running coupled within how many Caddy*" (TSATF, 148). Shreve makes the repetition of Ames in Bland explicit when he joins sexuality with fighting: "If you cant be a Bland," he says, "the next best thing is to commit adul-

tery with one or get drunk and fight him, as the case may be" (TSATF, 165).
In summary, virgin Quentin (wife to Shreve's "husband") is bloodied
by Bland as his sister Caddy is seduced and bloodied by Ames (Bland's
double). From a slightly different perspective—characteristic of the multiple connections in the novel—Quentin's fight with Bland results in
blood and a black eye, like the black eye of the adulterous Uncle Maury;
Maury's eye is "sick" (TSATF, 43); and "sick" is precisely Caddy's word for
the pregnancy that forces her to marry Herbert Head (TSATF, 112), who
shares the name Sidney (spelled Sydney in the novel [TSATF, 93]) with
Cornell Sidney Franklin. To hide his own sick eye, Quentin sits on the
train to Boston by the window in which he sees his damaged face and, in
the background, a troubling reminder of low sexuality and dirty girls, the
ungentile woman with a broken feather in her hat.

In Cambridge at the end of the day, he recalls another kind of picture,
a literal one in a book that, literal or not, he describes as a Compson family photograph album. Or anti-album, since the picture he remembers and
his and Caddy's responses to it break the continuity of family that a family album conventionally is intended to establish and maintain. Alone at
the window of his Cambridge room, he thinks:

> When I was little there was a picture in one of our books, a dark place into
> which a single weak ray of light came slanting upon two faces lifted out of
> the shadow. *You know what I'd do if I were King?* she never was a queen or
> a fairy she was always a king or a giant or a general *I'd break that place open
> and drag them out and I'd whip them good* It was torn out, jagged out. I was
> glad. I'd have to turn back to it until the dungeon was Mother herself she
> and Father upward into weak light holding hands and us lost somewhere be-
> low even them without even a ray of light. (TSATF, 173)

This complex and intensely self-conscious passage incorporates several
ways of seeing from several positions and several things seen. Quentin describes not only the photograph itself but Caddy's reading of it, his reading of her and, colored by that, the transformation of the picture and
his final reading of it. What Judith Sensibar says of fictional photographs
generally applies especially to this: "Language transforms the photograph
from a record of an external reality of the other (its subjects) to an image
of the speaker/perceiver's internal reality and so seems to confirm the impossibility of an objective perception of reality. There is a shift in meaning from what the photograph denotes to what the spectator connotes." [40]

The scene is prompted by Quentin's memory of the night the previous spring when Caddy lost her virginity, and his experience of that both frames and composes the passage about the remembered picture in the album/book. Introduced by Mrs. Compson's collapse and Mr. Compson's attempt to comfort her, *"holding her hand the bellowing hammering away like no place for it in silence,"* the photograph passage is followed by Quentin's association of lost virginity with the suffocating smell of honeysuckle—*"Then the honeysuckle got into it"* (emphasis added)— and that association by a memory of himself as "little boy" again, feeling his way through the darkened Compson house (TSATF, 173). The trans-formation of the picture from "two faces lifted out of the shadow" into the image of his mother and father "upward into weak light holding hands" describes both the picture Quentin subjectively sees and the pro-cess by which he figuratively develops it, bringing it upward from the sha-dowed past. By implication and convention, photographs exclude those not pictured, and this picture is for him, as for Caddy, symbolic of paren-tal, especially maternal, abandonment, a site and sight of the Compson children's exile "below even them" that Quentin calls a "dungeon" and associates with his mother.[41] Despite the picture's being "torn out, jagged out," the image of abandonment remains in the mind's eye, a meaningful blank in a family album, as significant for the violence of its removal as for its present absence. The jagged remnant edges of the picture represent the destruction of normally clear-cut boundaries in photographs and fam-ilies. They additionally suggest Caddy's literally torn flesh, the physical consequence of her lost virginity that Quentin recalls in the framing scene and which prompts this memory.[42] Both the actual Compson fam-ily, from which a figurative camera isolated mother and father in one picture, and the collective photographic family of the album/book from which their picture is torn, foster discontinuity, disorientation, and dis-junct identity. Caddy is a King not a queen, not a child but a punishing par-ent, and home, like the picture, is a "dark place" in which Quentin must feel his way "without even a ray of light." Returning to Cambridge on the train, he describes a railway bridge "arching slow and high into space, be-tween silence and nothingness" (TSATF, 171); in his dormitory, in a pas-sage of memory prompted by that, he wanders the dark house of memory where *"hands can see touching in the mind shaping unseen door Door now nothing hands can see."* Like Eliot's Gerontion wandering blindly in the dark house of history, Quentin fumbles where neither fear nor courage can save him, his little boy's *"eyes unseeing clenched like teeth not disbelieving doubting even . . . I am not afraid only Mother Father*

Caddy Jason Maury getting so far ahead sleeping." All of this the picture he remembers and its pertinent conventions make present to him in Cambridge on the night of his drowning. Framed in his window with all they suggest, the images of the picture, the jagged-edged void, and the empty door to "*nothing*" are compressed in the thronged, transforming light of memory where they forebode his imminent dissolution: "*I will sleep fast when I door Door door*" (TSATF, 173).

v. The Idea of Home

Quentin loses himself in the attempt to locate himself on the axis of home. That his chapter of the novel, in particular, is a self-presentation based in Faulkner's personal experience has been suggested. It remains to suggest what part of his fragmented experience Faulkner drew from the circumstances of his own life and from his written representations of them in the East in 1918–1921 and in Oxford in the years following. Accounts of his apprentice years that focus solely on his poetry and fiction, including his own retrospective accounts, and some assessments of the origins and course of that work tend to represent the early career as an uninterrupted progress toward greatness.[43] In fact, it was often haphazard and accidental, however fortunate the accidents occasionally might prove to be. Letters Faulkner wrote from New Haven and New York in the decade of his twenties, for example, suggest that this, especially, was for him a time not only of adventuring and discovery but also of personal insecurity and uncertainty, of plans gone awry, goals set and forsaken. Like the military self-presentations in his letters from Toronto (1918), much of what he wrote in letters before then and after from New Haven (1918, 1921), New York (1921), New Orleans (1925), and Europe (1925) was performance. Filled with impressions of people, places, and events strange to him, unsettling, and sometimes seriously troubling, the letters reveal a range of states of mind and emotion in a young man coming of age in and sometimes through the agency of his unfamiliar milieu. They say what he felt and thought, what pleased or disappointed him, what he hoped, delighted in, and feared. Because they do these things, they offer a narrative of his life at that time—presented, it is important to remember, from his own perspective and in the limited spectrum of an epistolary relationship with his mother and father only. The twenty-year-old would-be poet from Mississippi, tutored in modernist writers by Phil Stone, reported writing only three poems in New Haven between April 5 and June 13, 1918. In that time he wrote letters to his parents at least twice each week, and significant parts of what he wrote in the sixteen of those that survive found their ways eventually into his fiction.

To Faulkner New Haven in 1918 was a double world bounded on one hand by the great university and on the other by the Winchester Repeating Arms Co. Both were new to him. At the university, though not an enrolled student, he shared a room with Phil Stone, frequented Stone's Corby Court law fraternity, and joined the ranks of students at university sporting events and outings. At the Winchester factory, where he worked in an office five-and-a-half days a week, he was one of eighteen thousand employees engaged in making explosives, half of whom, he noted in one letter, were "women and girls, in the machine shops even" (TofH, 50). This figure represented several times the population of Oxford, Mississippi, then. The plant was so large, he said, that he needed roller skates to get around. Officially, he was badge number "2A1/AGB Office/1680" (TofH, 53). In the beginning climate was a problem: he was cold all the time. It was nearly two months before his trunk of clothes arrived there, and when it did arrive, only days before his enlistment in the R.A.F., he had to repack and send it back home. What clothes he had were out of fashion in the East. He wrote that Yale University was a place where men dressed more casually than they did at the University of Mississippi; where one might go openly to a hotel or saloon for beer; and where professors drank with their students. Unlike the people in Oxford, virtually everyone in the East was in uniform, from "the convalescent French and British officers . . . with their service stripes and wings and game legs and sticks," who filled the lobbies and mezzanines of New York hotels (TofH, 45), to the Yale army and navy units he saw parade on Liberty Bond Day, when planes from a nearby base fought mock dogfights in the sky overhead and a man climbed the Woolworth Building with a bond on his back. The East had bigger trains than he had known existed, bigger hardware stores, and everything moved faster than in the South. A machine "like an enormous stock ticker" reported the war news in a New Haven newspaper window, he told Murry; streets were confusingly named George, Crown, College, Chapel, Orange; and Easterners measured distance in terms of minutes instead of miles (TofH, 47, 50, 46). New York, in particular, was a city of speed, as exciting in its complexity as it sometimes was overwhelming. In 1921 he told Maud of "Subways, surface cars, elevated trains, and taxicabs making walking a snare and a delusion. All the time, day and night, and where in the world they are all going, and so darned, darned fast, I cant imagine. I dont think they know themselves. It's grab your hat and get on, then get off and run a block and get on again" (TofH, 158).

In New Haven Faulkner felt himself surrounded by "celebrities." Among those he named: former president Taft, one of Stone's law instructors; a Canadian officer named Todd, who argued tactics with a law student named Llewellyn, who had been "in the boche army eight months, at Rheims, and was wounded in the Channel fighting at the first battle of Ypres. He had an iron cross and sent it back when we went to war" (TofH, 48); a wounded British Tommy at the Oneco Hotel; a shell-shocked British captain named Bland; and the Brick Row Book Shop poet Arthur Head, who, he said, "goes around about 40 miles an hour and passes you on the street and never sees you. His clothes look as though he had slept in them and he usually carries about six books with him" (TofH, 48). He also may have known the Yale poet Stephen Vincent Benet, who roomed that year with a Canadian intriguingly named Shreve Badger.[44] In the house where he and Stone lived was a "stupidly clever" Englishman named Bernard Reed and an Irishman named Noon, tutor and traveling companion, he reported, to a seventeen-year-old heir to two fortunes (TofH, 49, 50). Even in what was, for him, an exotic international community, with its "Poles, Russians, Italian Communists" (TofH, 54), his Southern ways and Southern speech marked him as an outsider. "These people are always saying things to me to hear me talk," he wrote his mother, "though there are lots of Southern people here" (TofH, 48). The food was different from home—pie and doughnuts for breakfast instead of hot biscuits and waffles—and if it was cheaper it was mostly "machine—or Union—made vits" (TofH, 52). He spoke later of the "desiccated grub of the one arm joints where I do my foraging" (TofH, 152). "Golly," he wrote from New Haven, "I wish I could wake up at home in the morning" (TofH, 52).

Race relations were still more different from home and more difficult to accept. He worked and ate lunch in 1918 with two "Hindoos" at the Winchester plant (TofH, 56), but he told his father in 1921, "I could live in this country a hundred years and never get used to the niggers." Analyzing East Coast mores in terms of his own experience in the South, he concluded, "You cant tell me these niggers are as happy and contented as ours are, all this freedom does is to make them miserable because they are not white, so that they hate the white people more than ever, and the whites are afraid of them" (TofH, 149).

Faulkner gradually found the collective confusion he recounted in these letters more wonderful than trying, but there were dark notes enough. He told both parents at first of being "terribly lonesome" and "home sick" in New Haven (TofH, 46, 47), and he said in mid-June, just prior to his enlistment, "At the rate I am living now, I'll never be able to make anything of myself" (TofH, 63–64). It generally has been understood that Faulkner left Oxford early in April 1918 to absent himself from home when Estelle married Cornell Franklin, and that certainly was part of his motive. Phil Stone, typically, took the longer view. In a letter about Faulkner's arrival at Yale, he wrote in part, "I don't think that he is going to be homesick; I have introduced him around to all of my friends and acquaintances, some of them rather brilliant people, and they seem to like him very much. He is a fine, intelligent little fellow, and I think that he is going to amount to a lot someday; *I certainly am glad that I got him away from Oxford for he was just going to seed there*" (emphasis added).[45]

Stone's sponsorship of his friend in 1918 marks a pattern of dependency in Faulkner's journeys away from home in the early 1920s that rarely finds direct expression in his letters, where he preferred to present himself as independent and largely self-sufficient. Yet it was Stone and Lt. Jackson Todd he conspired with to join the R.A.F. in June of that year, Stone's friends and Stark Young who arranged his affairs and looked after him in New Haven and New York in 1921, and Stone and Major Oldham who brought him home from New York to be university postmaster. Stone went with him to New Orleans in 1925, where Faulkner came under the care of Sherwood and Elizabeth Anderson, and of their friend, and soon Faulkner's, William Spratling, who accompanied him to Europe in 1925, where the New Orleans photographer William C. Odiorne also gave friendship and aid.[46] Each of these men being older or more experienced than Faulkner provided him support of a kind that balanced and in some ways made possible his otherwise solitary adventuring. And everywhere he made friends. "All these people are awfully nice to me" is a typical and recurrent remark (TofH, 51). Solitary Faulkner might have been on his trips away from Oxford, but he seldom was alone. His was a sponsored independence, and one in which his letters to and from home played a major supportive part. The postal service sustained him, and he was quick to say so. "I couldn't live here at all but for your letters," he wrote his mother from New Haven in 1918 (TofH, 53).

When he returned in 1921, the East was sufficiently familiar and he was sufficiently in control of his affairs to begin putting his travel experience to use in his art. Again, as in 1920, this involved work in several genres and mediums. A letter about the sea written October 6, 1921, concludes, with poetically expressive self-effacement, "I cant express how it makes me feel to see it again, there is a feeling of the most utter relief, as if I could close my eyes, knowing that I had found again someone who loved me years and years ago" (TofH, 145). A week later he sent Maud a crayon seascape and landscape and a sophisticated pencil sketch of four Yale undergraduates, identifying the ones without hats as seniors—a detail he would work into Quentin's "June Second, 1910" chapter of *The Sound and the Fury*. He was working steadily on unspecified short stories, and his letters then contain much more imaginative self-presentations than do those from his earlier stay.

A passage of pure performance in a letter of October 21, 1921, poses the preoccupied letter writer at the center of a manufactured mechanical chaos in a scene that evokes Charlie Chaplin's cinematic confrontations with outraged policemen.[47] The moment is as carefully paced as a scene in a silent film, a self-aware picture without dialogue (until the end), understated, comic, and ironically self-mocking. It says, in effect, Look what I can do!

> Oh, yes. I have already have stopped traffic in the streets; fame, in fact, has lighted early upon my furrowed brow. The other day I was crossing the busy corner in town, at my usual gait and failed to see the traffic cop turn his stop sign. I was thinking of something, at lest [sic] I guess I was thinking, of something, anyhow; nevertheless I didn't hear his whistle at all. So I came to as a car fender brushed the skirts of my coat and another car appeared so close to me that I couldnt see my own feet, beside a trolley that stopped resting against my hat brim. Well, I was the center of excitement, however, I did manage to climb on the fender of one of the cars while both chauffeurs and the motor man reviewed my past, present and future, liabilities, assets and aspirations in the most fluent Americanese. Well, by that time the cop got there, he bawled out all four of us, while the chauffeurs loudly called heaven to witness my thorough imbecility. They finally out-talked the cop and he turned on me, as though I had snatched a penny from the hand of his yellow haired baby daughter. "Yes," he shouted, "It was you, all right that balled the whole thing up, I seen you drooping along. What in the hell do you think you are, anyway—a parade?"
>
> No very cutting reply occuring to me until much later, I made no rejoinder. How ever, I am more careful. (TofH, 152–153)

Unlike the letter writer who had confessed to terrible lonesomeness three years earlier, the Chaplinesque figure in this passage is comic, the comedy deriving from a combination of Faulkner's self-confidence in a place that still was strange but no longer frightening and his accordant capacity to distance himself in his writing by self-deprecation.[48]

This is characteristic of the 1921 letters, in which he describes himself reading and writing and presents himself consistently in the role of the artist as a young man. Another long letter about the theft of twenty dollars and his working his way from New Haven to New York lightly fictionalizes experience and presents it in the form of a two-part story, complete with title: "Poor but Plucky, or / The Wabblings of Will" (TofH, 155). In the first part, labeled "I (New Haven)," he recounts washing dishes in a Greek restaurant where "The other dishwashers, Greeks and one Irish, thought I was a wop, and looked down on me" (TofH, 156), then working as a handyman at a Catholic orphanage, where "I thought at first that I was to wash and feed the orphans, but it evolved otherwise" (TofH, 156). "Chapter II (New York)" opens with the wry observation, "New York is a large town on the west coast of the Atlantic ocean, and is connected to America by the Brooklyn Bridge and the 14th street ferry so that as many people as possible from New Jersey and Des Moines Iowa can get here at the same time. Southern exposure and pleasant hours" (TofH, 165). In the letters that followed, the perspective on the city was "Southern," as well, and the opinions all his own. Pictures at the Metropolitan Museum were hung "without any regard for proximity, or lighting or any thing"; subway travel proved "that we are not descended from monkeys, as some say, but from lice" (TofH, 159, 157). He planned to take a portfolio of his stories from publisher to publisher in New York, he said then, and he spoke of enrolling in art school "to augment my income drawing, ads and so forth, while I get on my feet writing" (TofH, 159). These plans never were realized. In spite of his confident front and a job he was good at in the Lord & Taylor Doubleday bookstore, he gave in with only token protest to Phil Stone's and Major Oldham's plan that he return to Mississippi as university postmaster. "I hate to think of leaving the east after taking three years to get here," he wrote Maud from New Haven, "but 1800 a year is too good to let Van Hiler have" (TofH, 155). Assured by Stone that his brother Jack was no longer a candidate for the job, he agreed that "we'd better keep it in the family, I guess" (TofH, 160). He was back at home before Christmas.

Darl Bundren strikes a resonant and troubled chord from Faulkner's East Coast letters and fictions when he says on the night of his mother's death, "How often have I lain beneath rain on a strange roof, thinking of home" (AILD, 81). Faulkner always felt himself a stranger in the East in these years, however familiar it became to him, and always depended on the kindness of others when he was there. Quentin Compson, in *The Sound and the Fury* and again in *Absalom Absalom!*, is notably a stranger at Harvard, dependent there upon a single friend and likewise thinking of home in a fictional dormitory room like those Faulkner occupied at colleges in New Haven and Toronto in 1918 and later at his parents' campus home in Oxford. Clearly, as the lack of concrete geographical detail about Cambridge suggests, Quentin's Harvard is Faulkner's Yale. In *Absalom, Absalom!*, indeed, Quentin's room *is* Harvard, or all of Harvard that we know, as it also *is* for Quentin and Shreve the college room they invent in Mississippi fifty years earlier where Henry Sutpen lives with Charles Bon. In Faulkner's life as in his fiction such rooms are the sites of dreaming, the dreams the more intense for the physical confinement of the dreamer, and both Faulkner and Quentin treat them so.[49] Quentin's room in *Absalom, Absalom!* is called "this snug monastioc coign, this dreamy and heatless alcove of what we call the best of thought" (AA!, 208).

Such fictional settings echo actual ones: the Yale and the Harvard dormitories, in this instance, are mutually symbolic and therefore virtually interchangeable in terms of function and meaning. In Oxford in 1918 Stone had advised Faulkner not to marry Estelle: in spite of her near absence of mention in Faulkner's letters to his parents—or, better, *because* of it and because they were his *parents*—what he could not reveal to Maud and Murry of the trauma Estelle's marriage caused him he must surely have discussed with his friend and confidant Stone that spring in the rooms at 120 York Street in New Haven. In Toronto in 1918 he must likewise have told about the South for his Pennsylvanian roommate and friend Edward Delaney and for actual Canadians in the university dormitory where his R.A.F. cadet unit was housed from September 20 until December 6. His Southern accent might sound French Canadian to some ears, as he said in a letter from Toronto in October (TofH, 115–116), but he was as clearly a Southerner as is Quentin: his attempt at French in the letter is so garbled and written over that it is hard to think the scene he described was anything except another performance for his parents—a performance, not incidentally, that recalls Quentin's being taken for a Canadian in *The Sound and the Fury*. Faulkner was briefly an enrolled student at the University of Mississippi in 1919–1920, and later lived in the tower room in his parents' home at the former Delta Psi fraternity. Literally at home there, in a setting like those other college rooms at Yale and

Toronto, he wrote *The Sound and the Fury*, and it was there, Phil Stone recalled, that Faulkner read to him from the manuscript of the novel.[50] For Stone as for Faulkner, then, the fictional place and time of the novel must have recalled their actual past together, Quentin's dormitory at Harvard and his torment over Caddy evoking for them both, in that Mississippi setting, the rooms they shared at Yale in another spring and Faulkner's disappointed love of Estelle then. This was a situation upon which Faulkner would considerably expand in *Absalom, Absalom!*, where, as here, the fictional evocation of past places and experience extended especially to family relationships.

Longing for home in 1918 on his first extended journey away from Oxford, Faulkner had reimagined the actual New Haven and its people in his letters, reconstituting them *in* and *as* writing in ways that met his immediate emotional needs. By this means, he returned "home" figuratively in the surrogate letters he regularly sent there in his place. Home, however, remained for him an *idea*, and there are marked differences between his writing *to* home and *from* home. Disappointed by his reception in Oxford as something less than a hero when he returned from Canada, Faulkner wrote in his letter to Herb Starr, "I am coming up as soon [as I can], for I have had enough of this God forsaken place—I doubt if it sincerely inspired enough emotion in the heart of this bourgeois God of ours for him to damn it—to last me the rest of my life. I don't doubt but what they'll send me back to Oxford from Hell, so I am going to leave it as soon as I can."[51] His problem then was his parents, who wanted him in Oxford. A revealing passage in the Starr letter about choosing one's parents for their wealth strikes a particularly ironic note for so self-inventing a letter writer. "The first requirement," he told Starr, "would be at least fifty thousand a year. Then I would never have to lie about why I wanted to go anywhere, and what I intended doing when I got there. I hate people who force me to tell lies."[52]

The altered angle of this self-presentation makes all the more emphatic the essentially fictional nature of the New Haven letters with which this one contrasts. Ten years later, however, people and situations of the New Haven letters were reconstituted once again into fiction, the forms they took then modeling people and situations in the novel. This included, especially, Faulkner's father. In the 1918 letters, Murry Falkner is a conventional father and Faulkner a dutiful son who both needs and receives the support supplied him by their correspondence. Quentin, conversely, neither welcomes nor answers letters from home. The wedding invitation from "*Mr and Mrs Jason Richmond Compson*" (TSATF, 77) is a source of torment to him, and he pointedly does not *write* to his family: two of the three letters he mails on June 2, 1910, are for Shreve and the one to his father is a blank sheet wrapped around the key to his trunk.[53] Yet Quentin's father is with him all day, an absent presence whom he honors in his life and thought as Faulkner did Murry in his letters. Both fathers are inventions—as Quentin realizes and confesses when he contemplates confessing to incest: *"Say it to Father will you I will am my fathers Progenitive I invented him created I him."* In the next moment he extends his role as progenitor to Caddy, who likewise becomes the suffering offspring of his abundant imagination of his family: *"Say it to him it will not be for he will say I was not and then you and I since philoprogenitive"* (TSATF, 122).[54] As distinctly different as the actual and fictional fathers appear to be, the motives and methods of Faulkner's invention of Murry, as the letters reveal them, directly reflect upon those of Quentin's creation of Mr. Compson.

Although the majority of Faulkner's 1918 letters are addressed to his mother, his father is a surprisingly pervasive presence, both a primary and a secondary correspondent to and about whom Faulkner regularly wrote. Faulkner's biographers and memoirists, including his brothers Murry Jr. (Jack) and John, characteristically portray Murry as an ineffectual husband and father, the very figure of a family in decline.[55] His open conflicts with his wife over the years were exacerbated by his increasing disapproval of their firstborn son William, to whom Maud Falkner was most closely attached. Had Murry read his son's fiction, which he probably did not, he would have found there a parade of ineffectual or undependable fathers and some absent and unnamed, some of them in families clearly based on the Falkner family genealogy, Sartoris and Compson prominently among them. Murry's supposed absence from his son's life is another issue, and one that the letters directly address. Faulkner's brother Jack remembered that, while the boys regularly kept in touch with their mother, "Ours was not a letter-writing family as far as the menfolks were concerned. I doubt if our father ever wrote to Bill or ever received a letter from him."[56] The fact is, as his correspondence shows, Faulkner did write to and for his father in the years when he was first away from home for significant stretches of time. And as Faulkner's letters show, Murry wrote to him.

A helpful way to understand the apparent contradiction is Andre Bleikasten's sense that fatherhood in Faulkner's fiction is "a symbolic agency" rather than primarily a matter of "blood kinship." The same may be said of the letters. In fact, Bleikasten's distinction between the absence of a father-son relationship and a "relationship to absence"[57] is a particularly useful way of understanding Faulkner's relationship with Murry and one, moreover, fully accordant with epistolary conventions. Personal letters are generated by absence, and their function is to overcome separation by bridging it. If Faulkner's father was not available to him at home, he clearly was accessible in and through the letters his son wrote him from New Haven and Toronto and Paris. The Murry of those letters, essentially, is the dependable, *written* father Faulkner needed if he were to be the dutiful and appreciative son he wished to imagine himself. Establishing such a relationship required a performance of a sort to which personal letters are uniquely suited, in which the writer portrays both himself and his correspondent in ways that will prompt an answering, self-confirming letter of his own. By denying Quentin such a correspondence, Faulkner denied him his own solution to the problems they shared. This not only intensifies his isolation, it essentially denies him access to home. Nowhere is Faulkner's performance for his father clearer than in the first of the letters, written at New Haven in April, May, and early June of 1918.

On April 5, 1918, the morning after his arrival in New Haven, Faulkner wrote a long letter to Maud describing his trip, and he followed it the next day with one to Murry that specifically addresses his father's love of trains. His solicitude for his mother in the same letter—"be sure and tell Lady that I shan't starve" (TofH, 47)—typifies his assumption that his parents would share the matter of his letters and probably the letters themselves. In a note to Maud on the same day, he wrote, "Get Dad to show you his letter" (TofH, 47). What he also told Maud in his first letter, and surprisingly confessed to Murry, was his wretchedness at being away from home. Squeezed between his description of trains in his first letter to his father and an account of the cost of meals in New Haven is the admission, "I am terribly home sick and hope to hear from home by Sunday—tomorrow—anyway" (TofH, 46–47). The extent to which he depended on Murry then is indicated by a postscript to a letter in late April acknowledging his father's second letter in two weeks: "Dad, I got your letter today. Thank you, sir, and I love you" (TofH, 53).

Faulkner's admission of homesickness implies a measure of confidence in his father's support that Faulkner nurtured and Murry rewarded. Between April 9 and May 9, he received at least three letters from his father, and his expressions of gratitude extend to messages for Murry in letters to Maud. "Love to Dad & the boys" is typical (TofH, 49). In joint letters he was careful to address Murry's interests as fully as Maud's. If descriptions of the sea, teacups in a Chinese restaurant, and local poets were primarily for Maud in a letter written April 7, the passages about battles and veterans of the war would have been more to Murry's taste. Other letters to Maud address Murry secondarily through the father and son's common interests in hunting, horses, football, the outdoors, and, in one notable case, pride of family. A letter to Maud describing the 1918 Decoration Day parade in New Haven includes this reference to the Civil War and the Falkner family patriarch Col. William C. Falkner.

> And if Mammy [Callie Barr] could have seen that Decoration Day parade. The colored troops were there, veterans of the civil war, dolled up in blue suits and cigars and medals until they all looked like brigadiers.
>
> When the veterans passed, a [man] fellow named DeLacey who was watching the parade said to me—"Well, Bill, you ought to salute the old [boys] boys. It was your grandfather and his friends that put him that way." I told him that I thought they should salute me, for had it not been for my grandfather and his friends they would [b] not have had any war to go to. (TofH, 61–62; brackets indicate cancellations)

Here Faulkner evoked for his father not the defeat of the South but the heroism and daring of Murry's paternal grandfather, his own great-grandfather and namesake who, the letter affirms, still was venerated by the Falkner family men. Sharing in that nostalgia, Murry might also have shared in the underlying frustration of his son, who, like himself but unlike either the Union veterans or the Old Colonel, still had no war to go to.

The depth of Faulkner's emotion then is suggested by the literary importance he later gave materials first written into such deeply personal self-portrayals in letters that spring. Again, as the letters show, Quentin Compson's Harvard was beyond a doubt William Faulkner's Yale. The Decoration Day letter is postmarked June 2, 1918. Ten years later, together with another sentence from the letter about an Italian parade with "one nigger with an Italian flag and a cigar" (TofH, 62), the passage about his great-grandfather and the Union veterans was incorporated nearly word-for-word into the "June Second, 1910" chapter of *The Sound and the Fury*. The context, it is worth noting, is a letterly one of postoffices, envelopes, and mailings.

> Deacon wasn't at the postoffice either. I stamped the two envelopes and mailed the one to father and put Shreve's in my inside pocket, and then I remembered where I had last seen the Deacon. It was on Decoration Day, in

a G.A.R. uniform, in the middle of a parade. If you waited long enough on
any corner you would see him in whatever parade came along. The one before was on Columbus' or Garibaldi's or somebody's birthday. He was in the
Street Sweepers' section, in a stovepipe hat, carrying a two inch Italian flag,
smoking a cigar among the brooms and scoops. But that last time was the
G.A.R. one, because Shreve said:

>   "There now. Just look at what your grandpa did to that poor old nigger."
>   "Yes," I said. "Now he can spend day after day marching in parades. If
> it hadn't been for my grandfather, he'd have to work like whitefolks."
>   (TSATF, 82)

The same letter contains such significant details as a description of his
uncomfortable train trip back from the Harvard-Yale boat race on the
Housatonic River at Derby, a probable source of Quentin's back-and-forth
train and trolley trips in the novel, and a comment that addresses Quentin's need to weight himself down with flatirons: "I don't see how any one
ever drowns in the sea. You can float like a cigar box" (TofH, 62).

Murry Falkner responded to his eldest son's letters by financing a good
bit of his travel to and from Oxford from 1918 through 1925, contributing
to his support while he was away, and housing and feeding him between
times. Quentin's thoughts of Mr. Compson in the novel are the equivalent of Faulkner's correspondence with Murry, and his direct quotation of
conversations with Father approximate Murry's expressions of ideas and
opinions to which Faulkner alludes in his letters. But there is this difference: Quentin's father is not *written* but subjectively, selectively *remembered*, and that not at intervals of several days or weeks, as in Faulkner's
correspondence with Murry, but moment-by-moment. The uncertainties
of self that Faulkner in part overcame by writing Murry into a conventional fatherly role are exaggerated in Quentin, then intensified by his
recall of a "Father" whom memory portrays as a uniquely self-involved
individual, manifestly un-conventionalized and un-generalizable by his
desperately self-involved son. Quentin's recall of Father's cynicism and
several specific cruelties is a function of his need for self-torment, not
comfort. Whereas Faulkner needed familial support and generated it by
his letters, Quentin seeks signs of parental disapproval—of Caddy's sexuality, Benjy's affliction, above all his own cowardice—and he makes the
main instrument of his punishment his father, whose cynicism in the face
of his own several failures is a sign, in turn, of his own moral cowardice.

Mr. Compson is not Murry Falkner. Rather, both men are creations of their sons. Alike as the sons are in their need for paternal confirmation and the methods of gaining it, both are likewise *"Progenitive,"* to use Quentin's charged word. Like so many inversions of Faulkner's life in his art, Quentin's performance as creator of his father both reveals and conceals William Faulkner. Literally, in this respect, as well as symbolically in his chapter of the novel, he is the marionette proposed by the Shakespearean allusion in the book's title, the "poor player" of Macbeth's imagining, "That struts and frets his hour upon the stage / And then is heard no more." Like Pierrot, paradoxically, he is and is not his own "walking shadow" (Macbeth, v, v, 24–26). Faulkner put the matter in just that context when he suggested that Quentin is the creature-cum-victim of his own creation, literally the puppet of the kind of father he invents. "Father," he muses at the end of the day, "was teaching us that all men are just accumulations dolls stuffed with sawdust swept up from the trash heaps where all previous dolls had been thrown away the sawdust flowing from what wound in what side that not for me died not" (TSATF, 175–176). Read through Faulkner's epistolary creation of "Dad," Quentin's day-long evocation of "Father" is a subjectively motivated performance scripted by Faulkner obliquely from his own experience and resonant with his own deepest concerns about home.

In his last letter to his father from Europe in October 1925, Faulkner quietly acknowledged Murry's paternal authority by acceding to his father's wish that he come home. Here, as in several of the New Haven and Toronto letters, Oxford is powerfully evoked in descriptions of the landscapes he and Murry both loved. Moreover, and for the first time, home is imagined as a place where he can write. In that sense, the letter to his father satisfies vicariously both Faulkner's longing for Mississippi scenes and a new and deep-felt desire to write of home at home.

Dear Dad:—

I returned to Paris today and found your letter. I have just been thinking myself that I have been away from our blue hills and sage fields and things long enough. So I am making arrangements to come home. I will wait here a short time because I am expecting to hear from the publisher, Mr Liveright. But I'll be on the way soon. I have plenty of notes and data to last me a long time: all I need now is to settle down at home comfortable again and bang my typewriter.

I've seen strange people and different things, I've walked a lot in some fine country in France and England, but after all its not like mounting that northeast hill and seeing Woodson's ridge, or the pine hills on the Pontotoc road, or slogging along through those bare fields back of the campus in a drizzling rain. I am reasonably certain that I'll be on my way home by Nov. 1.[58]

> Much love,
> Billy
> (TofH, 218–219)

The letter culminates a relationship Faulkner established with his father over the years that he wrote to him that never deepened or matured very much—in his letters or, apparently, in his life. Nor does Quentin's with Mr. Compson show stages of development or change. Maud Faulkner kept her son's letters, and the close similarities between those from New Haven in 1918 and parts of the *The Sound and the Fury* seem to indicate that Faulkner reread them ten years later when he wrote the book. Crossings of this kind between letters and fictions are consistent with his use of letters from the start, and these confirm his sense of all writing of all kinds as an imaginative, often self-imagining, performance.[59] In his letters Faulkner remained "Billy" to both parents, and Billy never addressed his father "Dear Pardner" as Jack Faulkner did,[60] but always as Dad or Pop. Quentin, by extension, thinks of Mr. Compson more formally as Father, and his influence on his son is such that Faulkner returned to him for a more extended portrait in *Absalom, Absalom!*, where his world-weariness is cast in the somewhat different context of regional history.

In the only public tribute Faulkner made to his father in Murry's lifetime, he returned to the *written* father of his previous letters—and to Quentin's word *progenitive*—with the ironic difference that it is the father, in this case, who invented the son. He said in the introduction to the 1932 edition of *Sanctuary*:

> This book was written three years ago. To me it is a cheap idea, because it was deliberately conceived to make money. I had been writing books for about five years, which got published and not bought. But that was all right. I was young then and hard-bellied. I had never lived among nor known people who wrote novels and stories and I suppose I did not know that people got money for them. I was not very much annoyed when publishers refused the mss. now and then. Because I was hard-gutted then. I could do a lot of things that could earn what little money I needed, thanks to my fa-

ther's unfailing kindness which supplied me with bread at need despite the outrage of his principles at having been of a bum progenitive. (ESPL, 176)

Beneath the self-effacement of the "cheap idea" statement and the ironic self-portrayal as a "bum" lies the fact that Faulkner had written his first masterworks during the years between his return from Europe in December 1925 and the composition of the introduction in November 1931. Written a year after Murry's retirement from the university and eight months before his death, the tribute to his father's "unfailing kindness" recognizes Murry's practical contribution to the composition of *Flags in the Dust, The Sound and the Fury,* and the outrageous *Sanctuary* itself. It likewise recognizes the unresolved conflict between father and son at home—whatever the father may have contributed to the figures of John Sartoris ii, Jason Compson iv, and Anse Bundren. If Faulkner felt himself at odds with cultural expectations as a male artist in the South, as has been suggested, Murry must have felt his son's oddity all the more.[61] Faulkner had invented the man of "unfailing kindness" that Murry in some respects became, but Murry had invented the unemployed "bum" his wandering son seemed to him to be.

III. Marriage Matters

When you marry your own wife, you start

off from scratch. . . . . . . maybe scratching.

When you marry somebody else's wife,

you start off maybe ten years behind, from

somebody else's scratch and scratching.

Sanctuary (1931)

---

i. Matters at Hand

When Faulkner wrote the original *Sanctuary* in the winter and spring of
1929, he was preoccupied more intensely than ever before by marriage
matters. Two years earlier Estelle had filed for divorce and returned permanently to Oxford from Shanghai, bringing with her her daughter Cho-
Cho, then almost eight, and son Malcolm, three. She and Faulkner saw
each other regularly and she, at least, nourished the expectation that they
would marry when the divorce decree was granted. As that time approached, her real and imagined circumstances found their ways, with his
circumstances then, into the characters, settings, situations, events, and
language of Faulkner's fiction, most immediately and dramatically in *The
Sound and the Fury* and *Sanctuary* but recurrently, too, in the books and
stories that followed through the 1930s. Noel Polk makes the important
point that the composition of the original, or Ur-*Sanctuary*, in early 1929

probably coincided with Faulkner's final revisions of *The Sound and the Fury* manuscript.[1] Quentin Compson's preoccupation there with Caddy's seduction and marriage is indebted to the same motive force as the bitterly extended treatment of marriage matters in the subsequent book. Indeed, in significant respects the original *Sanctuary* (1929) and the revised, published in 1931, constitute a compound book-length extension of Quentin's narrative.

Faulkner's writing in 1927–1929 is deeply rooted in immediate personal circumstances, and a number of commentators have identified autobiographical details in and among *The Sound and the Fury* and the two versions of *Sanctuary*.[2] Everything we know about the period of their writing supports Faulkner's own cryptic statement to Maurice Edgar Coindreau that it was a time for him of "intimate difficulties."[3] Evidence of this is the really extraordinary fact that from January through May of 1929 Faulkner was working simultaneously, and apparently at a whitehot pace, on two separate books, in one of which he presented himself, in Quentin, as the jilted lover who fled Oxford and Estelle's wedding for New Haven in 1918 and in the other, in Horace, as the husband and stepfather he would become if he were to marry Estelle. If Horace Benbow is in some respects Quentin grown into middle age, as Polk thoughtfully suggests, Quentin's Caddy may be read as the Estelle-who-once-was and Horace's Belle Mitchell as the Estelle-who-might-be.[4] The relationships between Faulkner's life and art, in fact, are much more complex than this equation would suggest, and the parallels and intersections of the two call for a more detailed rehearsal of Estelle's and Faulkner's lives and situations to that point.

They met, of course, in Oxford as children. Estelle was seven months Faulkner's senior[5] and in the years before her marriage they were often apart, socially as well as geographically. In 1913, when Estelle was sixteen, the Oldhams enrolled her at Mary Baldwin College in Staunton, Virginia, and she was in school there for two years. She entered the University of Mississippi as a special student in 1915 and briefly that fall wore Cornell Franklin's fraternity pin.[6] Faulkner dropped out of high school at the end of that year and in 1916 began clerking in his grandfather's bank.[7] He and Estelle began to think of themselves as engaged, although she continued to see other men. In 1917–1918 she accepted a proposal of marriage from a university student, but Judge and Mrs. Oldham insisted she break the engagement.[8] When Franklin completed his law studies at Mississippi, he took a position in Hawaii, and he proposed to Estelle early in

1918. At her parents' urging, she reluctantly accepted, and they were married in Oxford April 18, 1918. By all accounts, both Faulkner and Estelle were devastated. He went to New Haven with Stone that spring, in part to avoid the wedding, then to Toronto until December; she went into hysterics on the wedding-eve before resigning herself to the ceremony.[9]

Estelle and Cornell's daughter Victoria, called Cho-Cho, was born in Hawaii ten months later, on February 8, 1919, and now, ironically, there began a period when Estelle and Faulkner were frequently together in Oxford. In the first of several extended returns home, mother and daughter spent that summer with her parents.[10] Faulkner was home from Toronto then, and in September 1919 he entered the university himself for the first of three terms as a special student. He withdrew in November 1920, but remained active there, especially with the drama club he had helped found, called The Marionettes.[11] Late that year he wrote and made perhaps seven copies of the illustrated verse play *The Marionettes*, a copy of which he inscribed for Cho-Cho in the next summer. Estelle was in Oxford from May 1921 through the end of that summer, when Cornell joined them briefly. He had not been reappointed to the federal judgeship in Hawaii, and when the family left Oxford it was for his new position in Shanghai.[12] Estelle's returns prompted Faulkner to poetry, and that year, in addition to *The Marionettes*, he wrote and gave Estelle the sequence of poems *Vision in Spring*.[13] When she left for Shanghai that fall, Faulkner went East again to New Haven and New York, but at Phil Stone's urging he returned before Christmas to take up a position that Judge Oldham arranged for him as university postmaster, which he held until 1924.[14]

Two years later, on December 3, 1923, Estelle and Cornell's son Malcolm was born in Shanghai, and a year after that, in December 1924, Estelle brought Malcolm and Cho-Cho to Oxford with their Chinese amah, Nyt Sung. It was Estelle's first visit in three years, and the first of two very long ones, this extending nearly eleven months into November 1925 before she returned to Shanghai.[15] Ben Wasson would remember such visits as a "constant open house" at the Oldhams' with tea and tennis and drinks.[16] Faulkner saw her there in late February 1925 on a brief return from New Orleans, where he had taken up residence in January. He gave Cho-Cho the poem "If Cats Could Fly" then for her sixth birthday and, back in New Orleans on March 6–7, with Estelle on his mind, he wrote the short newspaper essay "What Is the Matter with Marriage," arguing there that marriages based on "The first frenzy of passion" are doomed to fail.[17] He also met and courted Helen Baird that spring. He wrote the New

Orleans sketches published in the *Double Dealer* and the *Times-Pica-yune*, and in mid-February he began *Soldiers' Pay*.[18] He saw Estelle in Ox-ford in June on his way to Pascagoula, where he finished typing the novel, and again in July, just before he left for six months in Europe.[19] From Eu-rope in November 1925 he sent Odiorne's Paris photograph of him to Es-telle in Shanghai.[20] At home in Oxford in January 1926, he inscribed *May-day* for Helen and rebound *Vision in Spring* for Estelle, who must either have mailed him the book from Shanghai or left it for him the previous fall. Whether or not she actually traveled with it, her attachment to the book of poems and its author is clear. In mid-March 1926 Estelle and her children were in Oxford for a fourth time, this six-month visit constitut-ing what amounted to a trial separation from Franklin. Faulkner, mean-while, had Helen Baird on his mind as well as Estelle. At Pascagoula that June, while Helen was in Europe, he put together the sonnet sequence *Helen: A Courtship* and spent the summer working on *Mosquitoes*, which is dedicated to her. Estelle spent the summer of 1926 at Monteagle, Tennessee, and she had left for Shanghai by October when Faulkner hand-printed and -bound for her the manuscript book *Royal Street: New Orleans*.[21] Her marital situation then may have prompted the gift; her absence when it was made raises the question of whether or not he in fact gave her the book of vignettes with its bitter, misogynistic tailpiece, "Hong-Li."[22]

According to this reconstruction, Estelle was in Oxford from Honolulu in 1918–1921 for approximately eight months, from June through Sep-tember 1919 and from May through the end of summer 1921, and she was in Oxford from Shanghai in 1924–1926 for seventeen months, from De-cember 1924 through summer 1925 and February through September 1926. As these four extended absences from her husband in the first seven years of their marriage suggest, Estelle's marriage was in trouble. Before she returned to Shanghai in fall 1926, she and her parents discussed a di-vorce with Oxford lawyer Bob Farley. The only ground for divorce in Mis-sissippi then was adultery, and so it was tentatively arranged that she would file in Shanghai and wait out a probationary period in Honolulu.[23] Estelle apparently was in Shanghai that fall only long enough to discuss the divorce with her husband, for she was back in Oxford by the first of the year 1927. Cornell followed that January with his own list of griev-ances, charging Estelle with excessive gambling, drinking, and lying. Ac-cording to one source, he also charged that Malcolm was not his child.[24] She again returned to Shanghai with Cornell that winter, began divorce proceedings there, and was back in Oxford by mid-March, 1927, this time for good.

In the fall and winter of 1926–1927, while *Mosquitoes* was edited and prepared for publication, Faulkner shared an apartment with Bill Spratling in New Orleans.[25] For her birthday in February, he gave Cho-Cho the hand-bound story *The Wishing Tree*, where she is portrayed as Dulcie and the mother in the story is modeled on Estelle.[26] That summer and fall he worked steadily on *Flags in the Dust*. Liveright's rejection of the novel in November was a bitter disappointment, but by late winter or early spring 1928 Faulkner had begun *The Sound and the Fury*. He saw Estelle regularly: he wrote to his Aunt Alabama McLean about her that spring, ambiguously pairing her "utter charm" with her "utter shallowness,"[27] and they visited Estelle's mother-in-law Mrs. Hairston in Columbus together. As their anxiety about her divorce and their future increased, so according to Blotner did autobiographical elements of *The Sound and the Fury*.[28] In New York from September to December 1928, Faulkner and Wasson negotiated a contract with Harcourt, Brace for *Sartoris*, which Wasson would revise from the *Flags in the Dust* manuscript. By October Faulkner had a draft of *The Sound and the Fury*,[29] and he was writing and submitting stories to *Scribner's* and *The Saturday Evening Post*—among them "Miss Zilphia Gant," a psychological tale of desertion and sexual repression, and a story which may have originated with Estelle called "Selvage" ("Elly"), about repression and murder.[30] *Sartoris* was published in January 1929. In Oxford from January to May 1929, Faulkner made final revisions in the manuscript of *The Sound and the Fury* and wrote the original *Sanctuary*, dating the completed typescript May 25, 1929. Estelle's divorce was granted April 29, and sometime that spring, perhaps in late February or early March when he was fully engaged with both books, he wrote Hal Smith for a five-hundred-dollar loan. "I am going to be married," he wrote. "Both want to and have to."[31]

That letter suggests to Blotner Faulkner's mixed state of mind when he wrote it: his love for Estelle, his lingering bitterness over broken promises, and his defiant pride in himself as a worthy suitor. Equally, it suggests the nature of his long relationship to her as he saw it retrospectively then—and, in the light of present imperatives, as he saw himself.

THIS PART IS CONFIDENTIAL, UTTERLY. For my honor and the sanity—
I believe life—of a woman. This is not bunk; neither am I being sucked in.
We grew up together and I dont think she could fool me in this way; that is,

make me believe that her mental condition, her nerves, are this far gone. And no question of pregna[n]cy: that would hardly move me: no one can face his own bastard with more equanimity than I, having had some practice. Neither is it a matter of a promise on my part; we have known one another long enough to pay no attention to our promises. It's a situation which I engendered and permitted to ripen which has become unbearable, and I am tired of running from devilment I bring about. This sounds a little insane, but I'm not in any shape to write letters now. I'll explain it better when I see you.[32]

The letter is openly theatrical, written in heightened language that draws upon other, earlier performances, not least his presentation of himself in New Orleans and elsewhere as the father of bastard children.[33] Ostensibly it portrays him facing up to his responsibilities as a man—but only ostensibly. Certainly the promises he claimed he and Estelle had learned to ignore included her broken promises to him in 1918, the pain of which he denied but clearly still felt. Indeed, the situation the letter describes and appears to resolve is the same that Horace Benbow enters when he marries Belle Mitchell under similar circumstances in *Sartoris*, the novel Faulkner had just published, and from which Horace so urgently flees in *Sanctuary*, the novel he was writing when he wrote the letter. Still, writing a thing made it real for him and formed the basis of actions and writing yet to come. Whether in answer to this appeal or not, on May 6, 1929, Cape and Smith sent a two-hundred-dollar advance with a contract for an unnamed novel; Faulkner sent Smith *Sanctuary* in June, but it was more than a year before the novel was set in galleys.[34] On June 20, against Judge Oldham's wishes but with his reluctant approval, Faulkner and Estelle were married in a private ceremony outside Oxford at the College Hill Presbyterian Church.[35]

Faulkner had continued to court Estelle after her marriage to Franklin in 1918, both in person, when she was in Oxford, and in the personal poems and gift books he made for and gave her, and he portrayed them both in the novels he had written in the two years since her permanent return in 1927. The wedding trip that now followed was as unconventional and disrupted as the long, uneven courtship that preceded it. They took Malcolm with them to Pascagoula on June 21, and a servant of Estelle's former mother-in-law Mrs. Hairston, who joined them herself later that summer with Cho-Cho.[36] At Pascagoula Faulkner was involved almost at once with the galleys of *The Sound and the Fury* as well as with his new family, and unlike Estelle he was on familiar ground and among friends. Reportedly, both he and Estelle drank heavily that summer: at one point she reportedly attempted to drown herself.[37] Summarizing her situation in the summer of 1929, at the end of an eleven-year period when she had chosen Franklin over Faulkner, borne two children, watched her first marriage deteriorate into divorce, and then married the man she had rejected, Blotner writes:

> She faced an uncertain future. She was living now [in Pascagoula] in a run-down house with one servant—borrowed like the silver they ate with. And it was clear that the life she had known in the Far East could never be duplicated in Oxford. But Cornell's money would provide for the children, and Faulkner had always been so loving that she could feel well assured that they would suffer much less than most children of broken homes. Some of her distress could have come from a feeling that she and her bridegroom had been forced into the marriage, or that they had been motivated by a sense of duty or pride or both. They loved each other, and he, now a mature man, could be a passionate lover. But they were separated by a dozen years and widely different experiences from the people they had been in the early period of their relationship.[38]

There was more. Among their visitors when they returned to Oxford in the autumn were Cornell Franklin and his new wife Dallas.[39] Cornell was paying child support, which Faulkner shared with the Oldhams, where Malcolm went to live.[40]

The marriage matter of *Sanctuary* derives in large part from Faulkner's long relationship with Estelle and its irregular movement toward this situation. The problem he faced with the novel, and struggled through the many revisions in both versions to resolve, was representing the destructive potential of the matters at hand without smothering the book in personal detail or revealing too much of himself.

ii. A Dark Twin of the Man

As Richard Poirier has it, such a project involved the artist's keeping "within and yet in command of the accumulations of culture that have become a part of what he is."[41] The Faulkner-Estelle chronology details the ebb and flow of an ongoing courtship in which their lives periodically

veered apart and came together again without either party being over-
whelmed by or entirely losing interest in the other. *Sanctuary* was written following the second climax in that relationship, Estelle's separation
and divorce, which resulted in their marriage. Read against the background of their periodic separations and reunions, the book regains something of the immediacy it must have had for Faulkner when he wrote it
in 1929 and again when he revised it in 1930. And for Estelle, when she
read it.

He had written of courtship and marriage matters for years, in poetry
and increasingly in fiction, and most often in both genres in relation to
her. Poem XI of *Vision in Spring* (1921), for example, is a portrait of Estelle at her piano, playing for Franklin or, perhaps, for Faulkner himself.
Whether the setting of the poem is Hawaii or the Oldham house in Oxford, the unidentified gentleman a husband or a lover, it is clear that both
the man and the woman are troubled by their relationship. Her memory
of "a certain spring / That blossomed in shattering slow fixations, cruel
in beauty / Of nights and days" (VIS, 72) evokes Estelle's April 1918 marriage, and the concluding lines portray the unresolved sexual tension between the two people.

> He stands and watches her mount the stair
> Step by step, with her subtle suppleness,
> This nervous strength that was ever his surprise;
> The lifted throat[,] the thin crisp swirl of dress
> Like a ripple of naked muscles before his eyes.
> A bursting moon: wheels spin in his brain,
> Shrieking against sharp walls of sanity,
> And whirl in a vortex of sparks together again.
> At the turn she stops, and shivers there,
> And hates him as he steadily mounts the stair.
>
> (VIS, 74–75)

Faulkner and Estelle had been married for four years and were living at
Rowan Oak in 1933 when he published a version of Poem XI in the collection *A Green Bough*, and their marriage may have motivated a small
but significant revision. There the poem is titled "Marriage," with the
last line revised, though still not unambiguously, to read, "*Nor watches
him* as he steadily mounts the stair" (GB, 15; emphasis added).

Occasionally, when circumstances suited, Faulkner gave poems written for one woman to another. Sonnet XV from the 1926 manuscript book *Helen: A Courtship*, for example, may originally have been written for Estelle, or from an immediate memory of her. The poem opens on a retrospective note of lost love: "Knew I love once? Was it love or grief / This young body by where I had lain?" (HAC, 126). It dates from March 1925,[42] the month when Faulkner returned to New Orleans from a visit with Estelle in Oxford and wrote the newspaper prize essay "What Is the Matter with Marriage." Estelle's (to him) precipitous marriage in 1918 and her increasing marital problems are obliquely analyzed in the marriage essay, which blames broken unions on "The first frenzy of passion" in partners too short-sighted to see that lasting relationships are built not on lust but on love, which the essayist calls the "fuel which feeds its never-dying fire." Faulkner advised the prospective lover there "To take what he has at hand and to create from it his heart's desire."[43] If this sounds very much like subsequent statements of his aesthetic, he appears to have taken what he himself had at hand then of love and grief and written it into his sonnet, which concludes with the classic literary formulation that the lover's love lives on his the poem:

> Though warm in dark between the breasts of Death,
> That other breast forgot where I did lie,
> And from the stalk are stripped the leaves of breath,
> There's yet one stubborn leaf that will not die
> But restless in the wild and bitter earth,
> Gains with each dawn a death, with dusk a birth.
>
> (HAC, 126)

Sonnet XV was well suited for inclusion in *Helen: A Courtship* in 1926, when Faulkner was working through the loss of Helen Baird,[44] but the March 1925 date implicates Estelle, as well. This poem, too, was included in the 1933 volume *A Green Bough*.

Biography was the frame of reference for courtship and marriage relationships in Faulkner's early fiction, as well. He wrote in *Mosquitoes* (1926) that "A book is the writer's secret life, the dark twin of a man: you can't reconcile them" (MOS, 251). This and the accompanying statement that "fact and fallacy gain verisimilitude by being in cold print" (MOS, 251) were truths to which he had come early in his writing, reinforced when he was writing *Soldiers' Pay* in the spring of 1926 by Sherwood Anderson, with whom these sentiments are associated in *Mosquitoes*. In *Soldiers' Pay* Cecily Saunders's broken engagement to Lt. Mahon and April elopement with George Farr constitute an unhappy scenario of what might-have-been for Faulkner and Estelle in April 1918. The bride's name and the elopement are borrowed from Jack Falkner's secret marriage in September 1922. Margaret Powers's marriage to the dying Mahon is a melodramatic version of the same might-have-been, this based on Faulkner's presentation of himself in Oxford in 1919 as a suffering, if not dying, war veteran.

Marriage matters take the form of self-parodic melodrama in *Elmer*, the unfinished, deeply autobiographical novel Faulkner wrote in Europe in 1925. Elmer Hodge's memory there of his relationship with a woman named Ethel draws upon aspects of Faulkner's experience in 1918–1921[45] and on his relationship with Estelle in the early 1920s, to which he returned in *The Sound and the Fury* and later. Carvel Collins has reported that a friend of Faulkner's in Paris—almost certainly William C. Odiorne—read a manuscript of Faulkner's about a family of three brothers and a sister that Collins theorized was an early version of the Compsons. Together with the repeated and destructive contrasts between reality and Elmer's naive idealism, the brother-sister relationships in the manuscript between Elmer and his sister Jo-Addie and between Elmer and Ethel, who calls him her brother (Elmer, 433), suggest that what Odiorne read might rather have been *Elmer*.[46] Like Caddy Compson, Ethel marries another man when she discovers she is pregnant with Elmer's child, and sends Elmer away to war with the Canadian Expeditionary Forces. The last pages of the unfinished manuscript are taken up with their renewed courtship from the retrospective point of view of an accidental meeting in postwar Houston. Ethel is glad to find Elmer unmarried; Elmer expects that "their former relations would naturally be resumed. . . . from his natural inclination and his former experience with her, he trusted her to take care of details" (Elmer, 439). In his imagination of things, Ethel will forsake her husband, Elmer will acknowledge and reclaim his child as his own, and the family will be reconstituted as it should have been from the beginning. However, the child turns out to be a spoiled five-year-old, Ethel insists that they were no more than "children together" who did "childhood things" (Elmer, 445), and when they part, unlike the situation of *Vision in Spring*, "He did not even watch her as she crossed the room and mounted the stairs" (Elmer, 446).

Thomas McHaney has rightly called *Elmer* "a comical portrait of the artist as a young American"; "A Portrait of Elmer," the story Faulkner extracted from the manuscript of the novel in the mid-1930s, has been characterized as an instance of literary self-criticism.[47] Recalling that Faulkner several times met Estelle and her children and husband in Oxford after his return from Canada, and that his reunion with Estelle in March 1925 was complicated by his having fallen in love with Helen that spring, the melodramatic reunion Elmer dreams in the novel and the ending Faulkner appended to "A Portrait of Elmer" constitute a compound, self-critical performance. Like Faulkner's with Estelle, Elmer's reunion with Ethel is complicated by his meeting another woman, Myrtle Monson, whom he follows to Europe along the route Faulkner took with Spratling in 1925. In a comic scene added to the short story, Elmer effectively purges himself of her and perhaps all women: sitting in a water-closet at his (and Faulkner's) apartment on the Rue Servandoni in the throes of diarrhea, he "seems to see his life supine before the secret implacable eyeless life of his own entrails like an immolation" as he onomatopoetically whispers her name, "Myrtle. Myrtle. *Myrtle*" (USWF, 640, 641).

Flags in the Dust, which was written in the months immediately preceding and following Estelle's permanent return to Oxford in 1927, incorporates a more anxiously troubled mix of fact and fiction. Belle Mitchell's tennis party in *Flags* accords with Ben Wasson's memory of Estelle's parties at the Oldham house in the mid-1920s—the Oldhams had a tennis court in the backyard as do the Mitchells—and Belle's entertaining Horace with piano music and a furtive kiss is based on a particular party Wasson describes.[48] Horace's intimacy with the married but soon-to-be-divorced Belle reflects the material change in Faulkner's relationship to Estelle occasioned by her changed marital status in 1927; it is balanced in the novel by his frustrated love for his sister, itself a retrospectively based representation of Faulkner's relationship to Estelle in 1918 which, in the Ur-*Sanctuary*, extends to Horace's absenting himself as Faulkner did from a wedding too painful to attend. The Horace-Narcissa relationship reinscribed in *Sanctuary* from *Flags* echoes Quentin's love of Caddy and his objections to her marriage (both Bayard Sartoris and Herbert Head are called "blackguard" by the brother). This is part of a recurring pattern in the fiction of the 1920s involving women and miscarried marriages. Caddy is thrown out by Sydney Herbert Head; Narcissa and Margaret Powers are widowed within a year of marriage, and Margaret remarried and widowed again. The instability of these women's unions is matched by the mixed attraction and repulsion in men, especially to once-married women who, like Estelle, have children. Narcissa tells Horace that Belle is "dirty" (Flags, 190), Caddy tells Quentin she is "sick" (TSATF, 112), and Jason claims Caddy has "leprosy" (TSATF, 207). Both Caddy and Narcissa (in "There Was a Queen") bathe waist-deep in a stream after illicit sex, Caddy with Dalton and Narcissa with the Jewish government agent. The explicitness of such marriage matters in the Ur-*Sanctuary*, and their echoing actual situations and events, suggest that Faulkner felt something of the same ambivalent attraction toward Estelle during the years of her marriage to Franklin, especially in the months immediately preceding and following her divorce and their marriage.

The extent to which Faulkner saw marriage to a divorcee as potentially unmanning is suggested by Horace's sense of himself as cuckold, both in *Flags* in 1927, when Estelle returned permanently to Oxford, and in the Ur-*Sanctuary* in 1929, when her divorce was imminent. That aspect of second marriage haunts the reflexive darkness of *Sanctuary*. The book has been called "a bleak epithalamion,"[49] and justifiably so, yet the Ur-*Sanctuary* is not an *epi-* but a *prothalamion* that looks forward not backward to the marriage that took place June 20, 1929. What the original version depicts—or *predicts*, since it is set ten years in Faulkner and Estelle's future—are the dark attractions and manifest dangers for Horace of marriage to a woman with children. That "ten" is a significant number. Revising *Sanctuary* in 1930, some months after his marriage, Faulkner *added* to the book a passage in which Horace tells Ruby, "When you marry your own wife, you start off from scratch . . . . maybe scratching. When you marry somebody else's wife, you start off maybe ten years behind, from somebody else's scratch and scratching" (SR, 16).[50] If that attitude colored Faulkner's first year of marriage to Estelle, the anxiety it represents was not soon allayed. In *Light in August* two years later, Hightower advises Byron Bunch, "the husband of a mother, whether he be the father or not, is already a cuckold. . . . It's not fair that you should sacrifice yourself to a woman who has chosen once and now wishes to renege that choice" (LIA, 316).

The recurring theme suggests that the 1931 version of *Sanctuary* is as dark in its way as the original from which it was revised. Concerns about marriage proliferate in both: in the dilemmas of unmarried, married, and remarried characters, parents and stepparents, and parented and parentless children, and in the forms of the novel that subvert nuptial rituals and the language used to express all of these. The Ur-*Sanctuary* opens with the Negro wife-murderer singing of his impending execution; at the other extreme of the social spectrum, Narcissa inadvertently mixes marriage with murder when she reads to Miss Jenny from newspapers about "arson and adultery and homocide" (SO, 44). Gowan proposes marriage to Narcissa, is refused, and leaves her for an "engagement" with Temple (SO, 39; SR, 27) that leads them to the Old Frenchman place. What amounts to an abduction is presented as a mock-elopement: Temple is once called a "whore" (SO, 97; SR, 49), twice a "slut" (SO, 105, 121; SR, 59, 95), and twice Gowan's "wife" (SO, 91, 94; SR, 42, 46); her disappearance is subsequently represented by Clarence Snopes as "One of them companionate marriages" (SO, 157; SR, 176). At the Frenchman Place on May 12, Goodwin puts the unconscious Gowan in bed with Temple, where Popeye begins the sexual assault he finishes in the barn with a corncob. Temple remembers herself on this macabre nuptial night as a bride in a coffin (SO, 216; SR, 219), and her unconscious allusion to the fate of Emma Bovary echoes Horace's associating Popeye's "blackness" with Mme. Bovary's death throes (SO, 25, 60; SR, 7).[51] Temple's figurative elopement with one man ends in a rape by another that begins a still worse wedding trip to Miss Reba's, where the impotent bridegroom she will call "Daddy" (SO, 227, 231; SR, 231, 236) gives her away to Red, whose power to consummate the union proves him the literal as well as figurative best man. Finally, Temple's leaving the Jefferson courthouse is staged as a wedding procession with her brothers as groomsmen, and her trip to France as yet another wedding trip, this with her actual daddy, Judge Drake, who reclaims her from Popeye.[52]

Faulkner's preoccupation with marriage, desertion, and divorce forms the stuff of a dark comic strain that extends in the novel from Memphis into Yoknapatawpha County. The first prostitute Virgil Snopes and Fonzo Winbush see in Memphis shocks them by entering the outhouse-like "lattice-work false entry" of the brothel with a "husband" (SO, 186, 187; SR, 191, 192),[53] and they assume from overheard love-making that all Reba's "daughters" are "married" (SO, 189, 190; SR, 194, 195). Even if figuratively, these are the only women in the novel who are married. Miss Jenny and Narcissa are widowed, Jenny's husband having died "on the second anniversary of her wedding-day" (SO, 44); Belle is still legally married to Horace, but she, Miss Reba, Minnie, and, in the revised *Sanctuary*, Popeye's syphilitic mother and his grandmother are abandoned women, the grandmother for the second time. Ruby Lamar's first lover is shot trying to elope with her, and she and Lee Goodwin pointedly are unmarried, a fact that subverts her testimony before the jury of "good men, . . . fathers and husbands" (SO, 275; SR, 285) at Lee's trial. None of these is a candidate for remarriage. In a direct reversal of Estelle's expectations of Faulkner in 1929, Narcissa refuses to marry anyone, although Gowan like Franklin proposes, Horace like Faulkner in 1918 approaches her with "the chaotic emotions of a bridegroom of twenty-one" (SO, 38), and her son Benbow in one photograph is dressed as a groomsman (SO, 44). Horace might have been expressing Faulkner's own anxieties about marriage when he thinks, in the Ur-*Sanctuary*, "that if there were no other women in the world a man would not quit his wife for more reasons than one. It was marriage they were trying to quit, since any woman makes a better mistress than she does a wife. And for the man who marries his mistress there is but one excuse: she was the woman of the two" (SO, 66). In the revision a year after his marriage to Estelle, the passage was cut.

Not only the details of personal experiences but also the times in Faulkner's life when these occurred contribute to the grim self-presentations that shape the novel. The present time of *Sanctuary* is May and June 1929, but the fictional present conflates a period ten years in the past, when Estelle married Cornell Franklin, with another, ten years in the future, in which Faulkner imagined himself married to her.[54] In the Ur-*Sanctuary* these are embedded together in the stream-of-consciousness passages where they conjoin as parts of Horace's collective experience, including the experiences of 1919–1920 detailed in *Flags in the Dust*; in the revised *Sanctuary*, especially, the careful juxtapositions of the Temple-Horace stories maintain the sense of simultaneity in time. Conflations like these of times and characters gave Faulkner a stable yet flexible field for performing really daring self-presentations and provided a solution to the long-term artistic problem of controlling troublingly rebellious personal materials.[55] In the two versions of *Sanctuary*, Faulkner's own experience and that he foresaw for himself shape both Horace's experience and that of the several counterparts in the novel in whom Horace recognizes himself. Estelle is represented across time palimpsestically: the virgin of 1918 in Temple and the Narcissa whom Horace recalls from *Flags*, the separated divorcee of 1927–1929 in widowed Narcissa and the Belle Mitchell of *Flags*, and the remarried Estelle of the future in the disinterested Belle of the novel's present. Existing more-or-less all at once in *Sanctuary*, as they do, these avatars overlie, overlap, and intersect one another in ways that engage the fictional Horace at every climactic stage of the actual Estelle's courtships and marriages.

With her slim figure, red hair, and love of dancing, Temple Drake clearly evokes the young Estelle, who like Temple was a judge's daughter courted both by town boys—Faulkner foremost among them—and by an older, more urbane university suitor. Something of Faulkner's pain in his late teens, when Estelle was at the university and he was a high school dropout and bank clerk, is suggested in his brief portrait of Doc, the frustrated suitor from the town who watches Temple and Gowan at the university dance. Doc displays what he claims is her step-in, but in competition with Gowan, who has money, a car, and a degree from the University of Virginia, his only resort is to outdrink him. In the attempt, he sets in motion Temple's ordeal and Gowan's disgrace. Biographically understood, these are outcomes that constitute acts of authorial revenge on the characters' living counterparts, Franklin and Estelle. So, in a sense, does the portrait of Narcissa in *Sanctuary*. Widowed for ten years and with a ten-year-old son, she is a particularly nasty version of Estelle in 1929. Narcissa's "stupid serenity" (so, 39), elsewhere described as the "serene and stupid impregnability of heroic statuary" (sr, 107), alters and diminishes the Narcissa of *Flags*, but it accords with Faulkner's description of Estelle in the letter to Alabama McLean in spring 1928, a year before they were married. "I have *something*—someone, I mean—to show you," he wrote. "Of course it's a woman. I would like to see you taken with her utter charm, and intrigued by *her utter shallowness. Like a lovely vase. . . .* Thank God I've got no money, or I'd marry her."[56] As was his usual practice, Faulkner tried to keep family genealogies and the ages of his characters consistent from book to book. Estelle's son Malcolm was six when Faulkner wrote *Sanctuary* and so younger than Benbow Sartoris. Cho-Cho was ten, the same age as Little Belle in the fictional 1920 of *Flags*, when Belle divorces Harry Mitchell to marry Horace. In *Sanctuary* Faulkner has Belle married to Harry for nine years, as was Estelle to Cornell Franklin before filing for divorce. Belle's subsequent ten-year marriage to Horace reflects Faulkner's own concern in 1929 about marrying another man's wife. Looking back in a passage where he plays with this arithmetic, as Faulkner was looking bleakly forward, Horace muses that Harry always has been an absent presence in his own life with Belle. "They had lived in [the stucco house] seven of their ten years of the nineteen years she had been Harry Mitchell's wife. She had been married to Harry nine years, and Horace thought how it had required Harry's wife's promiscuity to render him [Horace] the affirmation of her chastity" (so, 18). This passage also was cut from the revised novel, but Horace's cuckold anxiety here recalls his recognition in *Flags in the Dust* that his marriage to Belle has failed because "She had ghosts in her bed" (Flags, 347).

The conflation of the actual with the fictional also is the basis of the novel's dark prophecy of repetition and betrayal of and by women. Faulkner made Temple eighteen in *Sanctuary* (so, 275; SR 285), the age Estelle was when she entered the university in 1915 and accepted Franklin's fraternity pin. By combining his and Estelle's past, present, and imagined future in Horace and Belle's past and present, he made Little Belle Temple's age—the same troubling age Caddy is when she marries Herbert and roughly the same that Cho-Cho would be in another ten years. Like Caddy's, Little Belle's and Temple's careless courtships exaggerate and distort Estelle's past as capricious and portray her marriage ten years earlier as precipitous; equally, Horace's frustrated relationships with Little Belle and Temple depict something of what Faulkner had experienced in 1918 and feared he one day might have to repeat as Cho-Cho's stepfather. In his inscription to *The Marionettes* in 1921, he calls Estelle's infant daughter "A TINY FLOWER OF THE FLAME, THE / ETERNAL GESTURE CHRYSTALLIZED," implying that her mother's and Marietta's sexuality is her destiny, as it proved to be when Cho-Cho precipitously married Claude Selby at eighteen. In subsequent years Faulkner and Cho-Cho became genuinely fond of each other, but the disturbing pattern of a young girl's maturation and potential for harm remained on his mind and in his imagination as late as *The Town* and *The Mansion*. Whatever else Gavin Stevens inherits of Horace's, his anxious relation to Linda Snopes is apart. "Thank God she is no flesh and blood of mine," Horace says of Little Belle in a long letter expressive of this concern near the end of the Ur-*Sanctuary*. "I thank God that no bone and flesh of mine has taken that form which, rife with its inherent folly, knells and bequeaths its own disaster, untouched" (so, 282). Faulkner cut this passage from the revised *Sanctuary*, as well, but retained one very like it in which Miss Jenny comments in another way on Horace's mixture of cynicism and masculine anxiety. She says of Gowan's leaving Narcissa for an engagement with Temple, "What is it that makes a man think that the female flesh he marries or begets might misbehave, but all he didn't marry or get is bound to?" (so, 148; SR, 166).

More public and more shocking contemporary events also provided Faulkner models for the marital situations and forms of expression in *Sanctuary*, and he grafted them freely to his own self-presentations. Carvel Collins first hinted in 1951 that Temple's story is based on that of a

Memphis woman who was raped in the way Temple is in the novel.[57] As Collins's records show, the woman he calls Ruby N. and the Memphis gangster Popeye Pumphrey are two of several people on whom Faulkner drew for the brutalities of *Sanctuary*, and several characters in the novel share aspects of their and others' experiences across the span of the 1920s. Probably Faulkner heard the story from a woman named Dorothy Ware at Reno DeVaux's gambling clubs in the Memphis Tenderloin around 1925–1927. According to Dorothy Ware, Ruby N. once told Faulkner part of her life story, including an incident at a "still house" outside Memphis where Popeye and three other men had gone "to fantastic extremes" in the rape of four women. Like his fictional namesake, Popeye Pumphrey did not drink, was impotent, and was peculiar about sex; Dorothy Ware herself, like Ruby Lamar, had been in love with a man shot by her father and brothers.[58] The Ruby N. material is complemented by Blotner's accounts of a university coed molested on a baseball outing[59] and charges of "seduction and breach of promise" brought against Governor Lee Russell in spring 1922 by a woman named Frances Burkhead. At the sensational trial in Oxford in December, it was charged that Russell had offered Miss Burkhead medicine to abort their unborn child and "an instrument she was to use if the medicine failed." The Russell trial jury in 1922 found in favor of the defendant, leaving "a nauseating stench in the nostrils of many Mississippians," but like Lee Goodwin's jury they settled the case in a matter of minutes.[60] In 1920 when Faulkner was a student there, Lee Russell had been hanged and burned in effigy on the university campus for closing fraternities, and Lee Goodwin may owe him both his given name and his own burning by the town.

A second trial that influenced the novel is the 1919 trial of Memphis gangster Allen McNamara for the rape of the seventeen-year-old orphan Mary Thompson.[61] McNamara attempted to force Mary Thompson to perform "an unnatural act," according to the *Commercial-Appeal*, then raped her. The newspaper referred to the crime as "the assault revel in Wolf River Bottoms" and called it "one of the most sensational ever committed in Shelby County." Details of the crime were "unprintable," but descriptions of the trial proceedings suggest their close similarity to the trial in the novel. Asked by the prosecution, "What did he do," the *Commercial-Appeal* reported, Mary Thompson "hung her head. When finally she answered, men, too, hung their heads. It is doubtful whether such an answer has ever gone into a criminal court record even in Shelby County." Unlike the fictional Goodwin trial, where Horace virtually abandons his client by refusing to cross-examine Temple, McNamara's lawyer was fierce with the victim. On the second day, the paper reported, "The crowd had gathered early expecting in its morbid way to breathe again the disgusting air of the courtroom, made more disgusting by the terrific cross-examination of Miss Thompson the day before." This account closely accords with a passage in the Ur-*Sanctuary* in which Horace plans his defense of Goodwin: "He would sub-poena Temple; he thought in a paroxysm of raging pleasure of flinging her into the court-room, of stripping her" (SO, 255). Collins was certain that Faulkner could not have been unaware of the McNamara trial in 1919, and that when he heard the story of Pumphrey from other sources, it must have come to his mind as a complementary episode with integral fictional possibilities. The fictional adaptation of such public events, and Faulkner's grafting them to private realities of his life, have much to say about the complex and various relationships between the real and the imaginary as he came to understand them and the usefulness of the one to the other.

iii. The Poor Players of *Sanctuary*

From its inception, *Sanctuary* was a darkly personal book, and the marriage matter represented there troubled all stages of its composition and revision, as to a degree such personal material also did in contiguous work of the later 1920s and 1930s. Intimate self-presentation—in letters and private gifts but especially in a book to be published—called for distancing and disguise. In the case of *Sanctuary*, it called forth from Faulkner performances of various kinds and intensities touching on several fronts. This is manifested in the strenuous revisions of both versions of the novel, in which passages were added and deleted, and whole blocks of material relocated; in the dramatic juxtapositions of scenes the revisions achieve; in the specifically theatrical conception of characters as players on the various stages of their own and others' making; and in the language of theatre that conveys them.

More than any Faulkner work since *The Marionettes*, to which it is related by similarities of character, situation, and personal resources, *Sanctuary* is theatre, and it was natural, when Faulkner returned to Temple Drake two decades later in *Requiem for a Nun*, that he chose for that novel the overtly dramatic form of a three-act play with prose prologues. *Requiem* is first mentioned in a letter of October 1933 in which Faulkner

said only that "it will be about a nigger woman" and that he liked the title
(SLWF, 75). He returned to the woman and the title in 1950, but there is
no evidence of a substantive relation of that first *Requiem* to Temple and
Sanctuary. *Sanctuary* began, apparently, in 1925 as a prose poem of "2000
words about the Luxembourg gardens and death" (SLWF, 17), and it well
may be, as Polk claims, "the matrix in which the great explosion of 1927–
1932 was born."[62] Faulkner is at the center of the fiction of that period
and Horace Benbow is at either boundary. Starting with *Flags in the Dust*,
and colored by his self-presentation in Quentin in *The Sound and the
Fury*, Faulkner completed in *Sanctuary* a compound portrait of the wordy,
frustrated lawyer–aesthete—the last and most thorough before his transformation into Gavin Stevens in *Light in August* (1932). The Gavin in that
novel and Faulkner's subsequent versions of him owe a great deal more
to Phil Stone than does Horace. Expanded upon in *Intruder in the Dust*
(1948) and *Knight's Gambit* (1949), the Gavin of *Requiem* (1951) is very
different from the Horace of the late-1920s—just how different is suggested by Horace's contempt for Gowan Stevens in *Sanctuary* and Faulkner's making Gavin Gowan's uncle in *Requiem*.

Stone characteristically claimed himself as the model for Horace, but
aside from drawing on his own experience then, Faulkner's primary debt
may have been to Ben Wasson, the lawyer, literary agent, and lifetime
friend who edited *Sartoris* from *Flags in the Dust* in 1928 and placed it
with Harcourt, Brace that fall when he and Faulkner were together in
New York. Specifics of Wasson's experience inform Horace's in *Flags*, and
it was natural that Faulkner should turn again to Wasson as a means of
distancing himself from related but disturbingly intimate matter in *Sanctuary* the following winter and spring.[63] A vase-maker, as Faulkner would
claim to be in the introduction to *The Sound and the Fury*, the Horace of
Flags acts out his love of his sister in his art, apostrophizing both vase and
Narcissa as "Thou still unravished bride of quietude" (Flags, 162), and in-
scribes it in the nearly unintelligible letters he writes her.[64] In *Sanctuary*
his performances still are lodged in the excesses of his language, including the written, but with the addition of his fretful sense of himself as
poor player, acting out his uncertainties and obsessively explaining his
failures.

Behind this evolution of character lies Faulkner's increased anxiety in
1929 about his relation to Estelle. Polk speculates that he revised the
novel so heavily because he found Horace's interior life "intolerably
close."[65] He distanced himself by deleting some details—Horace's mus-

ings on Harry's presence in his and Belle's marriage (SO, 18) and his reconstruction of his invalid mother and other "nightmares of his own
childhood" (SO, 142) are examples—and by transferring others to Popeye, especially in passages added in Chapter 31 of the 1931 novel about
Popeye's unmanning childhood illness and devotion to his own invalid
mother. There were, of course, purely aesthetic revisions, as well, some of
them necessitated by deletions of personal matter.[66] In the Ur-*Sanctuary*,
Horace writes to Belle asking for a divorce on June 2, the day before he
finds Temple at Miss Reba's and hears her story. That date, of course,
charged with special Faulknerian significance, is the day of Quentin's suicide in *The Sound and the Fury*, when he agonizes over Caddy's sexuality. Horace's letter on that day is prompted by the sexuality of young
women Caddy's age—at the end of Chapter 17, when Clarence Snopes an-
nounces that Temple is in a Memphis brothel, Horace looks into his photograph of Little Belle and experiences an upsurge of incestuous desire for
her (SO, 204).[67] In the revision the connection to Quentin is downplayed
by the changed date, but Horace's motivation for a divorce is increased
and clarified by his writing his letter on June 4, at the beginning of Chapter 26, the morning *after* he hears Temple's story on June 3, associates her
with Little Belle, and is overcome by nausea in Chapter 23. The intervening chapters 24 and 25, set two weeks later, intensify Temple's dramatic
effect on Horace by compressing subsequent, thematically related events
into the narrative space between her story and his letter. Temple's graphic
scenes with Popeye and Red at the Grotto in Chapter 24 rejustify Horace's
shocked despair, and Uncle Bud's vomiting at the brothel after Red's funeral in Chapter 25 comically counterpoints Horace's sexual self-disgust.

Although some of the language of theatre was sacrificed in revisions,
especially in excisions of more personal matter, much that is performative was retained. Horace acts out his anxieties in a world that, to him, is
virtually all stage. The house he flees in Kinston is a hall of mirrors where
his stepdaughter's avidity for the college boys she brings home is the obverse of his wife's sexual disinterest in him. The Old Frenchman place is
figured as a theatre complete with the double-visaged symbol of tragic and
comic drama, here represented in Popeye's grimacing "mask carved into
two simultaneous expressions" (SO, 22; SR, 5). The ruined mansion evokes
for Horace "another world, another time" (SO, 22), populated with imaginary "broughams and victorias . . . bearing women in flowered muslin
and chip bonnets . . . flanked by riders in broadcloth and wide hats" (SO,
26), all of which he recognizes as "part of the vanished pageantry of a

dream," the costumed "lost puppets of someone's pomp and pride . . . leaving not so much as the print of a slipper on the dusty stage" (SO, 51). No more than Quentin is Horace the "real man" depicted in *Sanctuary*, where Ruby uses that term to describe Lee Goodwin to Temple (SO, 105; SR, 59) and Temple to describe Red to Popeye (SO, 227; SR, 231). Like the Harvard undergraduate and virgin of *The Sound and the Fury*, the runaway husband of *Sanctuary* is a poor player, vainly acting the parts of the sexually active men he encounters. Quentin constructs a scene to confront Dalton Ames ("Ill give you until sundown to leave town") out of Western movies Faulkner would have seen in New Haven in 1918 and later in Oxford,[68] then faints (TSATF, 159, 161); at the wedding he imagines shooting Herbert *"through the floor of Caddy's room"* but with only his voice (TSATF, 105). At the Old Frenchman place with the underworld toughs, Horace significantly phrases such masculine competition in terms of theatrical performance, thinking "of how, having blundered into that reality which he thought he was so hot for, his efforts to establish himself as a factor in it had been like those of a boy watching other boys do things he cannot or does not dare attempt, and who performs the dwarfed mimicry of their skill or daring with a sort of raging importunity: Look at me! Look at me!" (SO, 65). Horace's obsessions in *Sanctuary* may or may not have been Faulkner's, but his roles of second husband and stepfather were ones Faulkner took on in Oxford in the years between the composition and the revision of the book. Horace's being a graduate of "Oxford," in this context, acquires certain ironic point.

As Oxford, Mississippi, was the scene of Faulkner's courtship of Estelle, so Horace's Jefferson is "a stage upon which tragedy kept to a certain predictableness, decorum" (SO, 142). There are other stages there, as well, among them the reopened Benbow house, where Horace surprises Narcissa and himself "in a thousand forgotten pictures out of the serene fury of their childhood" (SO, 61), and the courthouse, where not the truth but the play is the thing. A director of sorts, Horace rehearses Ruby in her trial testimony but fails to speak his own proper lines there, though he twice is cued to speak by the judge. Memphis, too, is a scene of tragic and comic performances. Miss Reba's brothel is described as a shadow-theatre where Temple struts and frets before her mirror in a variety of costumes, including "a spurious Chinese robe splotched with gold dragons and jade and scarlet flowers" (SO, 226; SR 230) that specifically recalls the wardrobe Estelle brought from Shanghai.[69] Faulkner's preference as a young man for tightly tailored suits (see Fig. 2) is reflected in the town boys' and Popeye's costumes ("What river did you fall in with that suit on? Do you have to shave it off at night?") and his appreciation later for the more casual attire of New England universities (see Fig. 3) in Horace's "gray flannel trousers" and "tweed coat" (SO, 98; SR, 50, 3). Facing one another across the pool, Popeye and Horace are costumed as opposed aspects of the author, one with a gun in his pocket and the other with a book.

In the Ur-*Sanctuary*, and somewhat less so in the revision, characters are associated specifically with puppet-theatre in ways reminiscent of *The Marionettes*. Horace's description of the "lost puppets" of the past was deleted in revision, but Miss Myrtle's nephew Uncle Bud, limp-kneed and dangling in Minnie's hand (SO, 253; SR, 259), is an ironic modern avatar. The shaggy Tommy in bare feet and overalls recalls a Raggedy Andy doll, and red-headed Temple, if not Raggedy Ann, still is a "doll-faced slut" (SO, 105; SR, 59), the volitionless marionette with "legs straight before her, her hands limp and palm-up on her lap" to whom "Something is happening" in the barn (SO, 140; SR, 102). With his "doll-like hands" (SO, 23; SR, 5) and face "like a wax doll set too near the fire" (SO, 23; cf. SR, 5), Popeye is both puppet and her puppet-master. He is described gripping Temple by the back of the neck as a puppeteer might his hand puppet (SO, 164, 166, 167; SR 138, 141) and "lifting her slowly erect by that one hand" (SO, 166; SR, 141). There is no saving Temple from this usage by men. At the courthouse she is again a marionette, her face "quite pale, the two spots of rouge like paper discs pasted on her cheek bones, her mouth painted into a savage and perfect bow, also like something both symbolical and cryptic cut carefully from purple paper and pasted there" (SO, 275; SR, 284). Cringing, shrinking, "her body arching slowly" in her father's grasp (SO, 279; SR, 289–290), she departs the trial the creature Popeye made her at the Old Frenchman place and Miss Reba's, as helpless in the hands of her father and brothers as she was "arching slowly backward" in the throes of desire at the Grotto (SO, 234; SR, 238). The underlying drama of each of these scenes is a product of male sexuality and female fear,[70] and the characters who act out these roles are themselves what Horace calls "lost puppets." Yawning into her mirror in the Luxembourg Gardens at the end of the novel, Temple might say with Marietta, in her garden at the end of *The Marionettes*, "I desire—what do I desire?" (Marionettes, 54).

In one sense Faulkner's return to the novel in the 1930 galleys constituted a self-confrontation that set in motion strategies of disguise and avoidance in the revision. This is reflected in the characters' seeing or refusing to see themselves as they are and it accords with the pervasive pattern of stage acting in the book. Temple may be called a whore and appear to Ruby to be a "doll-faced slut," but as Ruby also says, she is only "Playing at it" (SO, 106; SR, 60–61); Reba tells Horace, "She wasn't born for this kind of life" (SO, 218; SR, 220). Playing at whoredom, nonetheless, creates an audience and makes her the focus of voyeurism in the novel: nearly everyone watches her performances, from the town boys at the dance to the bootleggers to Clarence Snopes and Popeye, who turns the brothel into a "peep-show" (SO, 249; SR, 255). In fact, Temple's imprisonment at Miss Reba's, with its culminating account of her night at the Old Frenchman place, is one extended moment of theatre. In the twilight confines of the brothel, Temple's room is her stage. In that contracted space, desire intensifies. Alone there, she rehearses before a mirror in which linger "spent ghosts of voluptuous gestures and dead lusts" (SO, 179; SR, 155); in bed with Red, she performs sexually for Popeye as an audience of one. At the Grotto she simulates their love-making in public scenes with Popeye and Red. Red's funeral in the following chapter, and the madams' postmortem at Reba's, are burlesque theatre, complete with jokes about monkey glands and copulation as a spectator sport. Reba's description of Temple and Red "nekkid as two snakes, and Popeye hanging over the foot of the bed without even his hat took off, making a kind of whinnying sound" prompts Miss Lorraine's line, "Maybe he was cheering for them. . . . The lousy son of a bitch" (SO, 252; SR, 258–259).

The threat of the real—the recognition that all of this acting is not play, imagination, a bad dream—hovers about Temple all through the novel, and it generates her most imaginative and, for Horace, terrifying performance. Horace recognizes in Temple's story of her night at the Old Frenchman place "one of those bright, chatty monologues which women can carry on when they realise that they have the center of the stage," and he realizes that "she was recounting the experience with actual pride, a sort of naive and impersonal vanity, as though she were making it up" (SO, 213; SR, 216). What she describes is not only Popeye's assaulting her in her room on that night but also, and in more compelling detail, her own desperation now as then to deny the reality of the rape she pointedly does not describe. Her power over Popeye is the power of the fabulator, if only that, and she invents for herself a full repertoire of roles by which to counter and forestall him—a boy with a phallus, a princess in a chastity belt, a dead bride in a coffin, a middle-aged teacher, an old man with a beard. At the penultimate moment, however, all artifice fails her and self-presentation ceases. Unable to confront the reality of her nightmare, both on that night and now in her telling of it, Temple stops consciousness and story together: "Then all of a sudden I went to sleep. I couldn't even stay awake until his hand got there. I just went to sleep" (SO, 217; SR, 220).

Role-playing reveals as it conceals the performing self, and it was typical of Faulkner's married life with Estelle—their daughter remembers that "Living with Ma-ma and Pappy was like living on a stage-set. Everybody was playing a role. . . . they were standing back and watching themselves play this particular part."[71] As a device of fiction, as well as a strategy for living, role performance disguises the self and distances reality, but it substantively alters neither one. In Temple's case, her real terror is communicated to Horace by its elision from her tale.[72] Her avoidance and the un-narrated rape generate the confusion, tension, and horror of the book. As he would do in the drafts of the introduction to *The Sound and the Fury* two years hence, Faulkner consciously excised some self-revealing details of his own experience from the *Sanctuary* galleys, rewrote and reinscribed others. Those revisions highlight areas where he saw in 1930 that he had presented himself most personally, but there is internal evidence in both versions of the novel that he was concerned for the painfully personal nature of his project early as well as late. Painful, that is, for him.

A helpful way of reading Faulkner's simultaneous self-presentation and distancing is a strategy John T. Matthews describes for rendering history in *The Sound and the Fury* and calls the "rhetoric of containment." It applies, as well, to the 1929 and 1931 versions of *Sanctuary*. Matthews argues from the work of Frederic Jameson that history—"the real"— "must be conceived as non-textual." He writes,

> Novelistic discourse mobilizes both narrative structure and fictional language to conceal history's conditioning of its apparent free play. To glimpse historical reality, the reader must be prepared to look in the gaps that open in all texts. These pits of contradiction may be read as the points at which history has been given textual form without becoming wholly neutralized. History and its representation abide in a dissonant relation.[73]

Matthews describes a way in which social and cultural meaning is generated in first-person narratives by its very elision. Thus Quentin's anxieties about the Southern class system, racial and economic reversals, and the collapse of his culture show through his narrative at points where his forgetting or repressing history in the face of a subjective obsession makes history present to the reader—in short, when he is playing a role.

If "history" implicitly conditions the apparent free play of narrative, so to a degree must personal history. The undisguised self of the author—the "real" historical personage—is just as slippery as is history in Matthews's model, and as with historical representation, Faulkner's actual history can be glimpsed in *The Sound and the Fury* and, especially, in *Sanctuary* through analogous "pits" or "crevices of contradiction"[74] where personal matter likewise "is given textual form without becoming totally neutralized." This Faulkner accomplished by the inversions, divisions, and conflations of situations, characters, and times in the novel. The 1930 revision took place, of course, after his marriage, when some of the mounting tensions of 1927–1929 had been resolved and anxieties allayed. He and Estelle owned Rowan Oak then and Estelle was pregnant with their first child. But if this was reason to tone down the book, the revisions did less to erase than to disguise the life history of the author. Like the pointed elision of history in Matthews's model, such devices of self-presentation and the patterns formed by their recurrence express as they attempt to conceal the historical person.[75]

Not every revealing personal fact, of course, is elided, especially not those relating to Estelle. Certainly Faulkner chose not to change the June 20, 1929, date of Lee Goodwin's trial, which also was the date of his wedding. In the 1931 *Sanctuary* the sentence reads, "The trial was set for the twentieth of June" (SR, 267; cf. SO, 260). In *Sanctuary* Horace Benbow is in flight toward a hill, as he says, from a history of broken ideals, both personal and cultural, that repeats itself in the present and drives him into despair. The sharply drawn line of his descent was not compromised in revision. In the reflexive darkness of *Sanctuary*, Faulkner presented in Horace both his own past sexual disappointments and the future as he bleakly envisioned it in early 1929. The "realities" of those times haunt Horace's flight. He holds them at bay, if barely, from the moment he confronts Popeye across the spring at the Old Frenchman place until Temple's story and her likeness to Little Belle in Chapter 23 bring him abruptly to face his lost ideal of himself and he vomits in disgust.

Temple prompts his darkest musings—on death and the logical pattern of evil—and his memory of her confession produces his darkest tropes of self-contemplation. He sees his own repressed desire in two figures standing face to face in an alley mouth, "the man speaking in a low tone unprintable epithet after epithet in a caressing whisper, the woman motionless before him as though in a musing swoon of voluptuous ecstasy" (SO, 218; SR, 221); he recognizes his own empty ideals in the remembered "eyes of a dead child, and of other dead: the cooling indignation, the shocked despair fading, leaving two empty globes in which the motionless world lurked profoundly in miniature" (SO, 218; SR, 221); and he discovers his own stillborn ambition in "the chemical agony of a world left stark and dying above the tide-edge of the fluid in which it lived and breathed" (SO, 219; SR, 222). Returning across the square toward home at 3:00 A.M. on June 4, he seems to meet himself leaving for Oxford in search of Temple at 3:00 A.M. on May 25 (SR, 167). It is "as though there had not been any lapsed time between," and he thinks of the intervening days as "a dream filled with all the nightmare shapes it had taken him forty-three years to invent" (SO, 219; SR, 222). With Temple's tale in his mind, and Little Belle's picture in his hand, he vomits up his visions. The revision of the novel establishes the more lasting impact of this crisis: on the following morning, in the original version, Horace digs himself "back into that world he had vomited himself out of for a time" by eating breakfast (SO, 255); in the revision, he writes to ask Belle for a divorce, "feeling quiet and empty for the first time since he had found Popeye watching him across the spring four weeks ago" (SR, 260).

Horace's self-knowledge at this climactic point in the Ur-*Sanctuary* is unaltered in the revision. It is rooted in related representations of threatened identity in *The Sound and the Fury* and anticipates those in *As I Lay Dying*. Its representation in *Sanctuary* is significantly indebted to Faulkner's reading, especially of T. S. Eliot. Like Quentin, who lies "neither asleep nor awake looking down a long corridor of gray halflight . . . thinking I was I was not who was not was not who" (TSATF, 170), Horace imagines those at the Old Frenchman place "Removed, cauterised out of the old and tragic flank of the world. And I, too, now that we're all isolated; thinking of a gentle dark wind blowing in the long corridors of sleep" (SO, 218; SR, 221). Like Darl Bundren, who confronts the question of "what I am" as he lies "beneath rain on a strange roof, thinking of home" (AILD, 80), Horace, in his extremity, recalls "lying beneath a low cozy roof under the long sound of rain" (SO, 218; SR, 221). On the night of his drowning, Quentin walks the empty corridor at Harvard in the footsteps of all the "sad generations seeking water" (TSATF, 173); Darl recalls going at night to the water bucket, seeing in "the still surface of the water a round orifice in nothingness," and his eyes, therein, like "a star or two" in the void (AILD, 11). Horace's self-confrontations begin when he leaves the Jefferson highroad "to seek water" (SO, 21), sees Popeye's hat superimposed on his own reflection as in a distorted mirror, and squats facing him for two hours across the spring.[76] That scene looks backward in Faulkner's writing to Pierrot's self-confrontation with the Shade in the final drawing of *The Marionettes* and forward, later on in *Sanctuary*, to

Horace's vision of himself in the toilet bowl, where he relives Temple's rape and ascends with her in imagination into the void to "swing faintly and lazily in nothingness filled with pale, myriad points of light. Far beneath her she could hear the faint, furious uproar of the shucks" (SO, 220; SR, 223). That passage, in turn, recalls the language of Temple's first, foreboding vision at the brothel and anticipates *As I Lay Dying*, where it is virtually quoted in Darl's description of the water bucket: like the fascinated subject of a fortune telling, Temple watches "the final light condense into the clock face, and the dial change from a round orifice in the darkness to a disc suspended in nothingness, the original chaos, and change in turn to a crystal ball holding in its still and cryptic depths the ordered chaos of the intricate and shadowy world upon whose scarred flanks the old wounds whirl onward at dizzy speed into darkness lurking with new disasters" (SO, 176; SR, 151).

Faulkner's reading of Eliot is suggested by similarities between Horace's dilemma and that described by the speaker in "Gerontion," who confronts the perverse rituals of a diminished present asking, "After such knowledge, what forgiveness?"[77] Faulkner knew Eliot well, and the parallels are instructive, even to the poem's epigraph from *Measure for Measure*, which is also descriptive of the conflation of real times on which Horace's fictional experience is based: "Thou hast nor youth nor age / But as it were an after dinner sleep / Dreaming of both." The central passage of the poem, in which Gerontion imagines History as the body of a woman, is especially to the point.

<blockquote>

Think now

History has many cunning passages, contrived corridors
And issues, deceives with whispering ambitions,
Guides us by vanities. Think now
She gives when our attention is distracted
And what she gives, gives with such supple confusions
That the giving famishes the craving. Gives too late
What's not believed in, or if still believed,
In memory only, reconsidered passion. Gives too soon
Into weak hands, what's thought can be dispensed with
Till the refusal propagates a fear. Think
Neither fear nor courage saves us. Unnatural vices
Are fathered by our heroism. Virtues
Are forced upon us by our impudent crimes.
These tears are shaken from the wrath-bearing tree.

</blockquote>

The poem is a virtual gloss on the novel. In passages of the Ur-*Sanctuary*, Horace twice imagines darkness as a woman's body as Gerontion does history, thinking of "the smooth belly of the dark" (so, 143) and "the body of night, darkness" (so, 148), and his groping in the literal and figurative darknesses of the book leads him to conclusions like those of the blind historian–prophet of the poem. Horace is witness to unnatural vices and impudent crimes, from which neither fear nor courage saves him or, for that matter, Temple, Lee Goodwin, and Ruby Lamar. It is his part to know but not act to effect, to see without doing. His moral paralysis at the end of the book is a matter of passions endlessly rehearsed and reconsidered. He, too, loses "beauty in terror, terror in inquisition," and he returns to Kinston and Belle like Gerontion, a windy, disillusioned "old man driven by the Trades / To a sleepy corner." Windy Horace certainly is—and prophetic. His climactic vision of Temple floating "in nothingness filled with pale, myriad points of light" is very like Gerontion's vision of the abused women of the poem. Unlike mythic Calisto, who was raped by a god and placed in the sky as the constellation Ursa Major, Gerontion's De Bailhache, Fresca, and Mrs. Cammel will be "whirled / Beyond the circuit of the shuddering Bear / In fractured atoms."

Faulkner was perfectly capable of adapting Eliot's poem to his own subject matter in 1929—Poem xi of *Vision in Spring* (1921) is a loose adaptation of Eliot's "Portrait of a Lady"—and of extending the oracular in the poem to personal visions of his own.[78] A good part of Horace's self-knowledge, and of the prophetic understandings that haunt him and bring him to self-confrontation, derives from his looking into the photograph of Little Belle as into a mirror or a reflecting pool, both of which the photograph evokes. Little Belle is introduced very early in the Ur-*Sanctuary*, in a scene where she calls Horace "Shrimp! Shrimp!"—the appellation derives from his own secret self-recognition in *Flags*—then flings herself upon him in "myriad secret softnesses beneath firm young flesh and thin small bones" (so, 15). In a variation on the drawing at the end of *The Marionettes*, Horace and Little Belle embrace at the house in Kinston between two mirrors, permitting him to see "her secret, streaked small face watching the back of his head with pure dissimulation, forgetting that there were two mirrors" (so, 15). What he pointedly omits to describe is his own *self*-contemplation—the fact that he also must see *his* face as she does hers.

This is the only time in the novel Horace physically touches his stepdaughter, but the conscious coquetry of her performance, and his unstated longing for her, are reenacted in the photograph he removes from its frame and takes with him from Kinston.[79] Unframed, it figuratively is unbound from strictures of family and society: it makes Little Belle available to Horace in imagination as she is not at home, and it acquires for him a life and significance of its own. The difference is explicit: "*Within* the frame the small, soft face mused in sweet chiaroscuro," prompting Horace's self-fashioning as her "counsellor, handmaiden, and friend" (SO, 19; emphasis added); *unframed*, "the soft, sweet, vague face" prompts consideration of his mortally "aging flesh . . . an accumulation of hours, breaths, temporarily in a single impermanent clot" (SO, 59). In Jefferson, subsequently, when the Negro wife-murderer's "clot of knuckles" in the jail window releases "a shape out of the nightmares of his own childhood" (SO, 142), Horace projects upon the photograph repressed desires only temporarily held in check by "the narrow imprint of the missing frame" (SO, 143). In the half-light of his room, Little Belle's face becomes "blurred and faded" (SO, 145), a "sweet veiled enigma" (SO, 146), and he imagines his crumbling decorum, camera-like, as threatened by darkness, "that agent which destroys the edifice with which light shapes people to a certain predictable behavior, as though by the impact of eyes" (SO, 145). Half obscured in the imperfect light as in a bath of developer, the face that emerges from the photograph now is subjectively shaped by his emerging desire for her, which flouts the decorous, "predictable behavior" of a young woman's self-styled "counsellor, handmaiden, and friend."

> Again the face blurred into the highlight, yet the familiarity of the face's planes enabled him still to see it, as though beneath disturbed water or through steam, and he looked down at the face with a sort of still horror and despair, at a face more blurred than sweet, at eyes more secret than soft. He reached for it so quickly that he knocked it flat, whereupon once more the face mused tenderly behind the rigid travesty of the painted mouth.
> (SO, 146)

Horace imagines Little Belle's photographic face developing sexuality in precisely the way Faulkner developed his forebodings about Cho-Cho in the novel. Later in the Ur-*Sanctuary*, the shadow of Horace's body lies portentously upon the photograph and it seems to him that Little Belle's face is "looking up out of the shadow with a crass brazenness, a crass belief that the beholder were blind" (SO, 205).

Much of this material, again, was excised from the published novel, arguably because it was redundant. And too personal. Faulkner certainly

was concerned in 1929 with being stepfather to a girl he imagined growing up like her mother, as Little Belle does Belle in the novel. The alteration of Little Belle's photograph, like the serial changes exhibited by the
drawings of Marietta in *The Marionettes*, may also proceed from changes
Estelle underwent in her marriage to Franklin and from Faulkner's baffled
longing for her then. As she became wife and mother, living in exotic
lands, he was leading a Boy Scout troop in Oxford and working as a small-
town postmaster. He sent Estelle photographs of himself after her marriage, and he certainly owned such a photograph of her. Indeed, he had
only her photograph when she was in Hawaii and Shanghai.

If excisions in the Ur-*Sanctuary* blunt somewhat the psychological
force of Horace's desire, desire was not erased by revision. On the night
Horace meets Temple in the revised novel, Little Belle's photograph
comes alive in his hands. The language of the scene is drawn from the just
previous description of two figures Horace sees in a Memphis alley, the
man caressing the woman with "unprintable epithet after epithet," the
woman before him "in a musing swoon of voluptuous ecstasy" (SO, 218;
SR, 221). As so often in Faulkner, the heightened language signals a personal performance that draws upon deep emotional resources.

> Communicated to the cardboard by some quality of the light or perhaps by
> some infinitesimal movement of his hands, his own breathing, the face ap-
> peared to breathe in his palms in a shallow bath of highlight, beneath the
> slow, smoke-like tongues of invisible honeysuckle. Almost palpable enough
> to be seen, the scent filled the room and the small face seemed to swoon
> in a voluptuous languor, blurring still more, fading, leaving upon his eye a
> soft and fading aftermath of invitation and voluptuous promise and secret
> affirmation like a scent itself. (SO, 220; SR, 222–223)

In just this way, by the "infinitesimal movement" of his own hand and
pen on the blank manuscript page, Faulkner brought to life in his novel
the young woman he loved and had lost; in just this way over the years of
their separation, her photograph had communicated to his own eye "a
soft and fading aftermath of invitation," her image returning to him in-
ferent of just such "voluptuous promise and secret affirmation." The addition of the honeysuckle that so troubles Quentin's sense of Caddy and
himself only reinforces and strengthens Faulkner's compound authorial
self-presentation in Horace and the collective authorial experience inscribed in the novels of 1927–1932.

iv. Weddings

Faulkner dared in *Sanctuary* nothing less than the public revelation of his inmost emotional life. Personal history conditions the apparent free play of the structure and language of the book and, though disguised, is never wholly neutralized by the fiction, even in revision. For Faulkner, the writing and revising were paired aspects of an artistic performance at once self-expressive and purgative. Leading Lee Goodwin to the flames, Popeye to the hangman, Temple to Europe, and Horace back to Belle, the novel led Faulkner back from the fictional marriage matters he inscribed there to his actual marriage with Estelle, on which they were modeled. As was so often the case when art intersected with life, what he had written and, often too, what he had read exerted as powerful a continuing force on his imagination as what he had lived.

He would portray a number of married couples in his seventeen novels but only four weddings: Caddy's in *The Sound and the Fury*, Nathaniel Burden's in *Light in August*, Ellen Coldfield's in *Absalom, Absalom!*, and, in the late 1950s, Linda Snopes's in *The Mansion*. Of the three novels written in close proximity to *Sanctuary* and to his and Estelle's wedding, two contain clear self-presentations. Faulkner was away from Oxford in New Haven when Estelle married Cornell Franklin in April 1918, and he portrayed Caddy's wedding as he might have darkly envisioned Estelle's then, not in the concrete detail of a direct witness but rather in the series of subjective images that anguish Quentin—the wedding invitation, for example, and Caddy's *"running out of the mirror the smells roses roses the voice that breathed o'er Eden"* (TSATF, 81). Mr. Compson's more detailed account of Ellen's wedding night, in Chapter 2 of *Absalom, Absalom!*, expands upon some facts of Estelle and Franklin's wedding, exaggerates and inverts others, and strikes directly, even again vengefully, at the actual bride and groom. Mr. Compson does not become narrator of the Sutpen story until ten pages into the chapter, precisely at the point when Sutpen comes courting Ellen in April 1838. His Sutpen is a brigand from Haiti rather than a lawyer from Hawaii, as Franklin was, but Ellen's hysteria at the rehearsal recalls Estelle's on the night before her wedding, as Blotner reports it, when she insisted she loved Faulkner not Franklin.[80] Like Estelle's actual wedding, Ellen's fictional one is traumatic: the mud and filth thrown at the fictional groom perhaps reprises Faulkner's attitude in 1918 toward Franklin, his outrage projected in the novel through the townspeople of Jefferson. Miss Rosa's comment on divorce in Chapter

1 constitutes another retrospective judgment of Estelle: she says of Ellen's marriage to Sutpen, "This occurred before it became fashionable to repair your mistakes by turning your back on them and running" (AA!, 19).

Mr. Compson shares Rosa's regard for ceremony, especially in marriage matters, and his comments on the consequences of ceremonial impropriety evoke personal marital concerns of the kind that inform both versions of *Sanctuary*. Faulkner and Estelle were married quickly and privately in 1929 in an informal ceremony at the College Hill Presbyterian Church by Dr. W. D. Hedleston, with the minister's wife and Estelle's spinster sister Dot as the only witnesses.[81] Several details of that wedding are incorporated into a passage in Chapter 2, where Mr. Compson turns to the importance of the marriage ceremony. "[Y]ou will notice," he tells Quentin, "that most divorces occur with women who were married by tobacco-chewing j.p.'s in country courthouses or by ministers waked after midnight, with their suspenders showing beneath their coattails and no collar on and a wife or spinster sister in curl papers for witness" (AA!, 37). If the passage lacks clear point in the novel, it registers a marital crisis that was developing in Faulkner and Estelle's life about the time it was written, in June 1935. In Hollywood, Faulkner soon would begin a relationship with Meta Carpenter, to whom he would give the manuscript of the novel two years later. In October 1935, Estelle filed for divorce in Los Angeles on grounds of desertion.[82] Given this conjunction, and the pattern of unhappy marriages it culminates, Mr. Compson may speak for the author as well as Sutpen and Ellen, and for such unhappily married predecessors as Caddy and Horace, when he concludes, "it did, indeed, rain on that marriage" (AA!, 45).

Faulkner's reading is strangely implicated in this conjunction, as well, providing a literary source and an allusive dimension to these self-portrayals. As several commentators have noted, there are significant parallels between Jay Gatsby's American Dream in *The Great Gatsby* and Sutpen's design,[83] but the marriage matters in Fitzgerald's famous book also are arrestingly familiar. Reading the novel in 1925, Faulkner could hardly not have found eerie similarities between Estelle's hysteria on her wedding-eve in 1918 and Daisy Fay's receiving a letter from Gatsby the night before her marriage to Tom Buchanan, when she gets drunk and tells Jordan Baker to "Tell 'em all Daisy's change' her mine." Daisy is persuaded out of her prenuptial reluctance by Jordan as Estelle was by Dorothy Oldham and marries Tom the next day "without so much as a shiver,"[84] as Estelle married Franklin. The Buchanans even honeymoon

in the South Seas as had the Franklins in Hawaii. *Gatsby* is likewise a resource in some scenes based on the same personal circumstance in *The
Sound and the Fury*.[85] Like the Gatsby of fact and rumor, Caddy's first
lover Dalton Ames is a mysterious stranger who has *"been in the army . . .
killed men"* (TSATF, 148), and Daisy's reunion with Gatsby "Under the
dripping bare lilac trees," as Nick describes it, with "A damp streak of
hair . . . like a dash of blue paint across her cheek"[86] contributes its imagery to Quentin's memory of Caddy's talking about Dalton, *"the smell of
honeysuckle upon her face and throat. . . . like a thin wash of lilac colored paint"* (TSATF, 147–148). Returning to marriage matters and weddings in novels from *The Sound and the Fury* to *Absalom, Absalom!*,
Faulkner found in such reading as well as his own writing an accretive
means of expression for very personal matters in his life. Mirroring his
personal circumstances in the startling ways that it does, *The Great
Gatsby* became a means of performance for successive self-presentations.

Sometime between the completion of the original *Sanctuary* and revision
of the galleys—the date is not certain—Faulkner drafted a preface for *Sartoris*, in which he said that he had created the characters in that book
"partly from what they were in actual life and partly from what they
should have been and were not. Thus I improved on God, who, dramatic
though He be, has no sense, no feeling for theatre."[87] Like the earliest
drafts of the introduction to *The Sound and the Fury*, which also were
written after *Sanctuary*, this piece is rough and inconsistent, but like
those drafts, it also is openly personal. Faulkner's sense of his *Sartoris*
characters as "shady visions" and a "host which stretched half formed"
into a "teeming world" yet to be written,[88] echo in the Ur-*Sanctuary*,
where Horace moves among actual shadows and imagines the darkness
"filled with that yawning sense of teeming and accomplished space" (SO,
148). Indeed, Faulkner might have been speaking of *Sanctuary* as well as
of *Sartoris* at the end of his preface, where he wrote of himself as a creature of his fictional creation. "I speculated on time and death," he said
there, "and wondered if I had invented the world to which I should give
life or if it had invented me, giving me an illusion of quickness."[89] Both,
perhaps, are true of *Sanctuary*.

IV. Who's Your Old Man?

I do the best I can, much as I can get my

mind on anything, but durn them boys.

As I Lay Dying

---

i. Guides and Sponsors

Consonant with his reimagining himself and the world in his work, Faulkner fashioned his life under the guidance of other men, rejecting some as models and adopting others at need, usually temporarily. Probably there is justification in arguing, as Richard Gray and others before him have done, that "Faulkner never thought of his actual father as his father figure."[1] Yet Murry's failings are only part of the story. Lacking an authoritative father in Murry, Faulkner had created him so in his letters in 1918–1925; in the years before his marriage he also enjoyed a sponsored independence, seeking out as substitutes for Murry the series of older male companions who aided and guided him: Phil Stone in Oxford and in New Haven, Stark Young in New York, Sherwood Anderson and William Spratling in New Orleans, Spratling and William C. Odiorne in Europe. He freely made himself a dependent of his editors, as well. At the height of his enthusiasm for *Flags in the Dust*, he drew a two-hundred-dollar draft on Horace Liveright, and he called on Hal Smith to finance his marriage. Writing to William Stanley Braithwaite in 1927, he depicted himself to the famous anthologist as a powerless victim of the literary establishment: "It never occurred to me that anyone would rob a poet," he said. "It's like robbing a whore or a child" (SLWF, 35). These were men associated with the arts, if not all were literary, and most of them generously advanced his development as an artist in practical ways, directing his reading, handling his personal affairs, finding him employment, providing him time to write. By the time of his marriage, nearly all of these relationships had been broken or were in abeyance.

In Phil Stone's case by then, the pattern of dependence was virtually reversed. When the Bank of Oxford failed in December 1930, Stone and his father were bankrupted.[2] *Sanctuary* was published to considerable if mixed notice in February 1931, and Stone began capitalizing on Faulkner's new acclaim and their long friendship by offering his own signed copies of *The Marble Faun* to bookstores and collectors for seventy-five dollars apiece. Typically, and with justification in the case of *The Marble Faun*, to which he had contributed his own money, Stone claimed a proprietary interest in the author. "I was the one who lent him books, and encouraged him," he wrote E. Byrne Hackett, proprietor of the Brick Row Book Shop in June. "I read all of his stuff, advised and criticised, furnished him with money off and on and generally carried him forward until he was self-sustaining both financially and artistically." To a book collector from Wilmington, Delaware, he wrote in July, "As for the book itself and its verses it is not worth much. It is just about the average first book of poems. Its value lies in its rarity and in its autographs." In November 1931 he wrote Faulkner, in New York, asking him to find buyers for *The Marble Faun*. "Look around too," he added, "and see if you cannot find some sort of hack work I can do in the way of writing, book reviews or advertisements. I simply must add to the amount of money which I am making."[3] In the fiction of the 1920s Faulkner had exaggerated to effect the physical trials and emotional turmoil from which Stone's and others' sponsorship had partially relieved him, presenting himself in the "philoprogenitive" Quentin Compson and the fatherless stepfather Horace Benbow who dreads the self-reliance he propounds. In the months following Stone's appeals, Faulkner began writing Stone into fiction as Gavin Stevens. In *Light in August* the Harvard-educated county attorney improbably explains the course of Joe Christmas's flight from jail in demeaningly racist terms as a conflict between his black and his white blood (LIA, 448–449). Two years later Stone wrote and sold a study of Faulkner, the short-lived three-part series, "William Faulkner, the Man and His Work," published in the *Oxford Magazine* in April, June, and November 1934.[4]

Sherwood Anderson guided Faulkner in a different way but to the same end. The only well-established fiction writer of the group, Anderson is a recurring point of reference in Faulkner's statements about his growth as an artist, but he too was written into Faulkner's fiction and out of his life. In New Orleans in 1925, Faulkner lived from January until March with Elizabeth Anderson and Anderson's teenage son Bob. Elizabeth mothered them both, housing and feeding them and even keeping their money.[5] Anderson in 1925 was a genial literary companion and, briefly, a collaborator in the "Al Jackson Letters," in which he and Faulkner contended for honors as most outrageous liar. The storytelling apparently was begun as a game on the Lake Ponchartrain boat trip on which *Mosquitoes* is based. Faulkner subsequently wrote two surviving letters, the first about Al Jackson's sheep herding in the Tchufuncta River swamp and the second about Andrew Jackson's horse-alligators at the Battle of New Orleans, and Anderson wrote at least one in answer. They are comic tall-tale performances. The brief series ended there, but Faulkner used parts of all three letters to characterize Anderson in *Mosquitoes*, and in reviews and essays he wrote in 1925 and 1953 he applied to Anderson himself Anderson's tale of Flu Balsam's attempt to trade his horse for a night's sleep.[6]

Anderson also was a literary sponsor of considerable influence. Faulkner's New Orleans letters make clear that Anderson read *Soldiers' Pay*, introduced him to Horace Liveright, and recommended that Liveright publish his first novel. He also was the writer who confirmed Faulkner in the inherent fictional possibilities of self-presentation and performance. "What really happens," he said of Anderson's portrayal of him as David in the story "A Meeting South," "never makes a good yarn. You have got to get an impulse from somewhere and then embroider it. And that is what Sherwood did in this case" (TofH, 194–195). It is of some consequence that Anderson portrays Faulkner as the troubled war veteran he had portrayed to Anderson when they briefly met in 1924. What Faulkner suggests were embellishments were real enough self-presentations, but Maud Falkner would not have been pleased by a published account of her son as an excessive drinker who falls asleep in a brothel. In the same letter he cautioned her, "I am now giving away the secrets of our profession, so be sure not to divulge them." Describing Anderson's *Tar: A Midwestern*

Childhood (1926) there, he said, "He is now writing a book about child-hood, his own childhood; and I have told him several things about my own which he is putting in as having happened to him" (TofH, 195). Such comments amount to an early statement of fictional aesthetics that Faulkner was quick to apply in his work on *Soldiers' Pay* (1926) that spring and the following year in *Mosquitoes* (1927), where Anderson is portrayed with other figures from Faulkner's life in New Orleans in 1925–1926.

Although he parodied Anderson's style in the foreword to his and Spratling's *Sherwood Anderson and Other Famous Creoles* (1926), he also named him as an important influence and model in an early draft of the 1930 introduction to *The Sound and the Fury*,[7] and he said in 1953 that his most abiding debt to the older writer lay in Anderson's turning him homeward, and ostensibly inward, to his own lived experience. What Faulkner claimed Anderson had called "that little patch up there in Mississippi"[8] became Yoknapatawpha County; *Sartoris* (1929), the first Yoknapatawpha novel and the one most closely modeled on Faulkner's paternal family, is dedicated "To Sherwood Anderson / *through whose kindness I was first published, with the belief that this book will give him no reason to regret that fact.*" He had publicly broken with Anderson then, as he would with his other father-figures as his work gained in power and he became more independent, but the older writer's influence in New Orleans in 1925 remained an aspect of his experience that generated and shaped fictional self-presentations.

A case in point is the 1931 short story collection *These 13*. Faulkner still was writing for Anderson's publisher in 1927 when he announced to Liveright that he was working on *Flags in the Dust* and "a collection of short stories of my townspeople" (SLWF, 34). The collection published four years later by Cape and Smith might have borne the same inscription, and it, too, might have been dedicated to Anderson. After 1919 no collection of American short stories about life in a small town could help but recall Anderson's successful and influential *Winesburg, Ohio*, and by 1931 Faulkner was well equipped to follow Anderson's *Winesburg* example. His home place, not to mention his own experience of it, was a well-established resource for his fiction then, and the Short Story Sending Schedule he kept in 1930–1931 shows that he had on hand nearly two dozen stories that could qualify as "short stories of my townspeople."[9] What Anderson provided Faulkner in *These 13* was a personal focal point and precedent for the subject matter of the book and a model for its form. In *These 13* six stories about townspeople are framed by four about World

War I in the opening section and three at the end of the collection set in other times and places. The contents page reads:

Part I	Part II	Part III
Victory	Red Leaves	Mistral
Ad Astra	A Rose for Emily	Divorce in Naples
All the Dead Pilots	A Justice	Carcassonne[10]
Crevasse	Hair	
	That Evening Sun	
	Dry September	

Like Anderson's retrospective collection of stories about his youth in Clyde, Ohio, *These 13* recalls significant details of Faulkner's experience a decade and more earlier. The aviators of the war stories "Ad Astra" and "All the Dead Pilots" recall early Faulkner personae; "Victory," "That Evening Sun," and "A Justice" draw on specific aspects of his wartime and childhood experience; the narrators of "Mistral" and "Divorce in Naples" describe events from his walking tour of Europe with Spratling in 1925. The subject matter of Part II spans Yoknapatawpha and Lafayette County history from Indian times in "Red Leaves" and "A Justice" to the present in stories written and set in 1930–1931.[11]

There was reason enough in Faulkner's life in 1931 for the unlucky number "13" in the title and for the frustration and defeat most of the stories express. The book's dedication "To Estelle and Alabama" recalls some of that, yet most of the stories were written before Estelle's difficult pregnancy, Alabama's birth and death, and Faulkner's accordant financial difficulties. None draws on issues or events in his life specific to the immediate present. In fact, the stories are less a perspective on a present situation than another kind of autobiographical retrospect (with *The Sound and the Fury* and *Sanctuary*) on the period 1918–1927, which began in dislocation and dependence on friends and sponsors and concluded in self-confidence with his first successes as a novelist. It was a period that might well have been called to his mind again by the challenges of marriage and prospective fatherhood, set forth in *Sanctuary*, and the personal losses of 1931.[12]

At one level the contract for a book of stories offered an opportunity to bring into print work he had been writing and trying to sell to magazines for two years. He needed the money the book would bring. But writing for Faulkner meant performance. It was a means of acting in the world against the circumstances and contingencies of his existence.[13] Publication, equally, was a mode of public self-presentation. Indebted to *Winesburg* for their selection and arrangement, the stories were significantly affected by materials and methods of self-presentation with which Faulkner had experimented in *The Sound and the Fury* and *Sanctuary*. Two stories have Quentin as their narrator; "All the Dead Pilots," "A Rose for Emily," "Hair," "Dry September," Mistral," and "Divorce in Naples" turn in one way or another on rites of courtship and marriage; "A Rose for Emily," "A Justice," and "That Evening Sun" are stories of paternal inefficacy and injustice. Ranging from the figuratively dead pilots of the opening section to the aspiring artist of "Carcassonne," the stories from first to last exhibit Faulkner's imaginative allegiance to images of himself developed in his twenties, still powerfully influential.

One of these self-images Anderson already had documented in "A Meeting South." In November 1924, barely a week after he and Faulkner met in New Orleans, Anderson wrote the story about his adopting for an evening a wounded R.A.F. aviator and poet he called David. Based on that familiar Faulknerian persona, "A Meeting South" was published in the *Dial* the following April, when Faulkner described his and Anderson's fictional method to his mother. He parodied Anderson in *Mosquitoes*, where the *Dial* is described as "a home for old young ladies of either sex" (MOS, 209).[14] In March 1931, two months after the death of Alabama and two months before he signed the contract for the collection that became *These 13*, Faulkner wrote the answering piece to Anderson's story about him. In "Artist at Home" he presented himself as a tubercular poet who seeks the patronage of a famous writer at a Virginia retreat based on Anderson's Ripshin Farm, makes love to his wife, then dies, leaving one poem to commemorate the love affair. Roger Howse sponsors Blair and arranges the posthumous publication of his poem. As Anderson had in his 1924 story about Faulkner, Howse records these events in an autobiographical book of his own. In Faulkner's story Anne Howse mothers John Blair as Elizabeth had Faulkner in New Orleans and Roger embroiders the incidents he witnesses as Faulkner told his mother Anderson had done, writing "Word for word, between the waiting spells to find out what to write down next, with a few changes here and there, of course, because live people do not make good copy, the most interesting copy being gossip, since it mostly is not true" (CSWF, 644). Here Faulkner virtually quotes his own letter, reinscribing in fiction the aesthetic principle Anderson had taught him six years before.

"Artist at Home" was not included in *These 13*, but among the several levels of self-presentation in the story, two bear particularly on the form of the stories in the collection. First, as he would do two months later in his collection, Faulkner looked back in the story to a period of his creative life when he was turning from poetry to fiction, affirming in the person of John Blair his own early aspirations, his limited achievement, and his ultimate end as a poet. Second, he, too, was an artist at home in Oxford, Mississippi, when he wrote the story, and by portraying Anderson as a writer writing from life in a maritally and financially troubled home, he also made an oblique, confessional gesture to the present circumstances that prompted both this story and the collection that followed.[15] In this distancing of the personal, he presented himself as simultaneous actor and onlooker, both suffering performer and voyeur-writer. If the Howses' apparent reconciliation seems to put forth Faulkner's hope that his marriage might likewise resume and prosper after the death of Alabama, however, the circumstances of the poet's death strike a contrary note. Blair dies from standing in the rain outside Anne's window, evoking in this context of short stories and collections the death of Michael Furey in Joyce's "The Dead" and the devastating implications of that for Gabriel Conroy's marriage. Things are not "all right" with the Howses, as is ironically claimed at the conclusion: rather, Roger's longing for "Christmas soon, and then spring; and then summer, the long summer, the long days" (CSWF, 646) brings into Faulkner's story the concluding scene of Joyce's collection about his Dublin townspeople and Gabriel's sense after the Christmas party that snow is general all over Ireland.[16]

Whether "Artist at Home" stimulated Faulkner's thinking about Anderson and *Winesburg* in 1931 or was stimulated by it, the story is a significant link to his revisiting his past in *These 13*, where Anderson's most famous book is a strongly felt presence. Anderson described his *Memoirs* as "my rambling house of a book, a book of people."[17] Faulkner found just such loose structure in *Winesburg* and a model for his own collections of "stories of my townspeople." He described such collections to Malcolm Cowley in 1948 as "single, set for one pitch, contrapuntal in integration, toward one end, one finale."[18] The stories in *These 13* are arranged and presented in the manner of the war experiences of "All the Dead Pilots," as a "series of brief glares" approximating a photographic "composite" (CSWF, 512). Several of the isolated characters are Andersonian grotesques, Emily Grierson, Minnie Cooper, and the barber Hawkshaw among them, and the young Quentin Compson, like George Willard, is a troubled dreamer, ineffectual confidant of marginalized townspeople like Nancy in "That Evening Sun" and Sam Fathers in "A Justice." With the young narrator of "Mistral" and the peripheral first-person narrators of "A Rose for Emily," "Hair," and "Divorce in Naples," whose accounts contribute to the composite form, Quentin brings to the collection something of George Willard's sense of the half-perceived mysteries Anderson saw lying "beneath the surface of lives."[19] Quentin senses as much at the end of "A Justice," where he says, "I was just twelve then, and I would have to wait until I had passed on and through and beyond the suspension of twilight. Then I knew that I would know. But then Sam Fathers would be dead" (CSWF, 360).

This subject matter and mode of telling evoke a time between youth and maturity, represented in "Carcassonne" by the space between waking and dreaming occupied by the tramp-poet of that enigmatic and emblematic story of the artist's condition. The fragmentary prose poem, in its evocation of artistic aspiration and human frailty, is reminiscent of Faulkner's several statements about the tenuous relation of visionary ideal and failed expression, but "Carcassonne" never fully opens itself to interpretation outside its own internal referents. An unemployed tramp (or poet, or both) beds down in a rat-infested garret at Rincon beneath a roll of tarred roofing paper and imagines himself riding to immortality on a buckskin pony *"with eyes like blue electricity and a mane like tangled fire"* (CSWF, 895). His visions are populated by figures from Faulkner's reading— the Christian Crusaders Tancred and Godfrey of Bouillon, Shakespeare's Hamlet, Homer's dying Agamemnon, and Christ—and he fumbles for expression in composite, allusive passages that recall both the most intense mindscapes of Faulkner's novels and the most oblique rhetorical experiments.

> Mrs Widdrington owned the rats too. But wealthy people have to own so many things. Only she didn't expect the rats to pay for using her darkness and silence by writing poetry. Not that they could not have, and pretty fair verse probably. Something of the rat about Byron: allocutions of stealthful voracity; a fairy pattering of little feet behind a bloody arras where fell *where fell where I was King of Kings but the woman with the woman with the dog's eyes to knock my bones together and together*[.] (CSWF, 898)

At the end of the story, in a passage drawn from A. E. Housman,[20] the tramp-poet's skeleton warns him that "the end of life is lying still" (CSWF,

899), but he rejects the proposition, and imagines himself rising instead, sea-changed, to shape his imaginative vision in the "soundless words" (CSWF, 899) so often associated in Faulkner with writing.[21] His aspiration is *"to perform something bold and tragical and austere"* (CSWF, 899), and the story concludes with such a performance, both his and Faulkner's. The rider-writer is ascendant now, revived and strong: "Steed and rider thunder on, thunder punily diminishing: a dying star upon the immensity of darkness and of silence within which, steadfast, fading, deepbreasted and grave of flank, muses the dark and tragic figure of the Earth, his mother" (CSWF, 900).

The Andersonian contexts of the inception and composition of *These 13* suggest something of Faulkner's intention for this story. Indeed, the concluding passage of "Carcassonne" is a standard strategy in portraits of the outsetting young artist. *Winesburg* concludes in the same way with George Willard departing on a westbound train to follow "his growing passion for dreams. . . . when he aroused himself and again looked out of the car window the town of Winesburg had disappeared and his life there had become but a background on which to paint the dreams of his manhood."[22] In addition, the placement of Faulkner's story, the description of the writer as divided man, and some specifics of imagery make "Carcassonne" a kind of "Anti-Book of the Grotesque" in which the writer is portrayed as a young man at the end of a collection rather than an "old writer . . . [with] a white mustache" at the beginning.[23] That placement coincides with Faulkner's residence in garret rooms in New Orleans and Europe at the end of his apprenticeship in 1925–1926, when he found in Anderson a literary guide and surrogate father. In the famous headpiece to *Winesburg*, Anderson distinguishes artistic vision from craftsmanship in the persons of the old writer "filled with words," dreaming his "dream that was not a dream,"[24] and the old carpenter who rebuilds his curious bed, raising it so he can see the town from his window. Visionary and carpenter are distinctions Faulkner adapted to his own uses in Darl and Cash Bundren in *As I Lay Dying* the year before *These 13*. Like the tramp-poet of "Carcassonne," who conjures Crusaders and ignores the advice of his mortal bones, Anderson's old writer in his bed conceives of his imagination as "a woman, young and wearing a coat of mail like a knight."[25] This, too, is an image Faulkner adopted in 1930—for the draft preface to *Sartoris*, where art is compared to "mammalian" reproduction, a feminine bringing forth of "something alive begotten of the ego and conceived by the protesting unleashing of flesh."[26] "Carcassonne" was written earlier, during the time Faulkner and Anderson were friends: his Tancred and Godfrey derive from Anderson's Joan of Arc, products like her of that associative vision that for Anderson's old writer produces a procession of figures driven by the "young thing," and for Faulkner's young writer extends to encompass Homer, Shakespeare, and Christ—"*the Resurrection and the Life*" (CSWF, 897), literal embodiment of divine vision, the Creator's Word made Flesh. If the tramp-poet aspires to a poetry he does not write, neither does Anderson's old writer publish his dream-book, which the first-person narrator of "The Book of the Grotesque" reads and, perhaps, reproduces as *Winesburg*—he, too, sponsored like Faulkner by a surrogate father and figurative "old man." [27]

ii. Fathering

That marriage meant fatherhood, Faulkner of course knew, but his own role as father initially was exasperatingly ambiguous, shortly became tragic, and in the long term was frustratingly diverse and demanding. He became a stepfather immediately by virtue of Estelle's children, Cho-Cho, who was ten when her mother remarried, and Malcolm, who was six. Both called him Billy, and both retained the name Franklin. Cho-Cho lived with her mother and stepfather in their apartment in Oxford and then at Rowan Oak, but Malcolm lived into early adulthood with Estelle's parents, Judge and Lida Oldham, who were named their grandchildren's custodians in the divorce decree. From the outset the Oldhams received, and shortly were forced to live on, the child-support payments Cornell Franklin sent from Shanghai. [28] Faulkner and Estelle's first daughter Alabama was born in January 1931 but lived only nine days. Jill Faulkner was born in June 1933, four years after her parents' marriage, and it was she who first called Faulkner Pappy, the name by which he was thereafter known to the children. Following Murry Falkner's death in 1932, Faulkner took his father's place with his brother Dean, who was ten years younger than he, and when Dean and Louise's daughter Dean was born in 1936, four months after Dean's death, she and her widowed mother became Faulkner's responsibility, as well. Cho-Cho married that year, and when she was deserted by her husband Claude Selby in September 1937, Faulkner brought her and her newborn daughter Vicki to Rowan Oak, where they lived for a time during World War II with Cho-Cho's second husband William Fielden. [29] By age forty Faulkner was the family patriarch, supporting in addition to these people his widowed mother in her house in Oxford, his brother John and his wife and two sons at Greenfield Farm, and servants he inherited from his grandfather and father, among them Mammy Caroline Barr and Ned Barnett, who moved to Rowan Oak with him and Estelle in 1930.

By all accounts, Faulkner loved and respected this extended family and he honored his obligations to them for many years. Yet the patriarchal responsibilities he assumed were uniquely demanding on a man who lived by and for writing. Given the number of people at Rowan Oak during the 1930s, the time he spent in Hollywood to support them, and the work he set himself to accomplish then, it would be astonishing if his duty to his family had not interfered, at times, with his art. In a now famous letter to Robert K. Haas in May 1940, he wrote:

> Every so often, in spite of judgment and all else, I take these fits of sort of raging and impotent exasperation at this really quite alarming paradox which my life reveals: Beginning at the age of thirty I, an artist, a sincere one and of the first class, who should be free even of his own economic responsibilities and with no moral conscience at all, began to become the sole, principal and partial support—food, shelter, heat, clothes, medicine, kotex, school fees, toilet paper and picture shows—of my mother . . . [a] brother's widow and child, a wife of my own and two step children, my own child; I inherited my father's debts and his dependents, white and black without inheriting yet from anyone one inch of land or one stick of furniture or one cent of money; . . . I bought without help from anyone the house I live in and all the furniture; I bought my farm the same way. I am 42 years old and I have already paid for four funerals and will certainly pay for one more and in all liklihood two more beside that, provided none of the people in mine or my wife's family my superior in age outlive me, before I ever come to my own.[30] (SLWF, 122–123)

For the resolution of such a dilemma, he had few satisfactory models to turn to. Like him, his own father was a first son, and never well-to-do, but Murry never was asked to assume responsibilities beyond his immediate family and, in fact, remained more or less dependent on his own father for much of his life. By the time his son acknowledged the outrage to his father's principles "at having been of a bum progenitive" in the 1932 introduction to *Sanctuary*, Faulkner already was providing bread at need for a brood of his own, bums or not.

The character who most closely resembles Faulkner's situation as patriarch in the decade of the 1930s, and displays the attitude he expressed in his 1940 letter to Haas, is not a father at all but a guardian. Jason Compson characterizes himself as being burdened with an illegitimate niece, idiot brother, hypochondriac mother, manipulative uncle, and, as he says, "six niggers that cant even stand up out of a chair unless they've got a pan full of bread and meat to balance them" (TSATF, 180). He has witnessed, if not paid for, the funerals of his brother and father and his mother will shortly make a third. But even Jason is not mean-spirited enough to obscure the justice of some of his claims against Mr. Compson, and Maud Falkner recognized her husband in Faulkner's portrait of him.[31] Like Murry's, Jason's destiny is the hardware store rather than Harvard, and his bitterness about it is just plausible.[32] Jason's behavior as father-surrogate to his niece ties him also to Faulkner's self-presentations in Horace, a stepfather with whom Jason shares an invalid mother (remembered in the Ur-*Sanctuary*) and pride of name, and characters such as Popeye, with whom Jason shares sexual impotence, familiarity with the brothels of Memphis, and a mortal aversion to alcohol. As Temple does Popeye, Lorraine calls Jason "daddy" to grim purpose (TSATF, 193).[33] Whereas Horace suppresses his desire for his stepdaughter by fleeing Little Belle, Jason both lusts after and despises the niece he self-destructively drives into fleeing him.

An early draft of the introduction to *The Sound and the Fury* identifies Jason as loving Caddy "with the same hatred of [sic] jealous and outraged pride of a father."[34] This is a particularly mordant self-projection. More violent than Quentin's frustrated desire for Caddy, Jason's for her daughter is threateningly overt. Based on the single, subjective standard of Jason's "what I say" (TSATF, 180), his chapter is framed as a bleak morality play or allegory of incestuous temptation and sexual disgust in which he acts the part of an avid Pluto to Miss Quentin's shabby Persephone.[35] Reminded that she is his own flesh and blood, he responds, "that's just what I'm thinking of—flesh. And a little blood too, if I had my way" (TSATF, 181). He casts her variously as a circus clown, a seductress, a whore; calls her a "dam little slut" (TSATF, 185); tells her, "You dont look all the way naked, . . . even if that stuff on your face does hide more of you than anything else you've got on" (TSATF, 187). Obsessed with costumes and dress, he fixates on "her kimono slipping off her shoulder. . . . unfastened, flapping about her, dam near naked" (TSATF, 183, 184), and compares her to women on Gayoso and Beale Streets in Memphis, "who dress like they

were trying to make every man they passed on the street want to reach
out and clap his hand on it" (TSATF, 232). The forty dollars he steals of the
fifty dollars Caddy sends Quentin for an Easter dress repays the cost of the
forty-dollar dress he bought Lorraine (TSATF, 193–194). Jealous of the circus man—"I'll make him think that dam red tie is the latch string to hell,
if he thinks he can run the woods with my niece" (TSATF, 241)—Jason offers himself as a substitute lover in a thinly veiled invitation at the dinner table. "'Did you get a good piece of meat?' I says. 'If you didn't, I'll try
to find you a better one'" (TSATF, 257). Mrs. Compson calls Jason "the
nearest thing to a father you've ever had," but as Quentin justifiably says,
"he won't let me alone" (TSATF, 259).

Part of Jason's attraction and revulsion, certainly, lies in Quentin's il-
legitimacy, a generative theme for Faulkner introduced first in *The Sound
and the Fury* and investigated from a variety of angles in subsequent fiction. It derives from his uncertain relationship with his own father and
from uncertainties like Jason's and Horace's about fathering other men's
children. These matters led him to a related issue, based likewise in personal experience: the complexities of identity for the child with no father.
In *The Sound and the Fury* and following he created a category of sen-
sitive young men self-consciously attuned to family proprieties and conventions, the literal and figurative sons of Mr. Compson: Quentin and
Horace foremost, Darl Bundren, Gail Hightower, Henry Sutpen, and Isaac
McCaslin. Among and sometimes against these he set a group of characters of unknown or questioned paternity who challenge or belie standards
held to by the first: Miss Quentin, born too soon after Caddy's wedding
for Head to believe she is his, and Popeye, whose lack of a surname symbolizes what his biography in the revised *Sanctuary* affirms, that his
mother, like Caddy, married too late. They were joined in consecutive
novels of the 1930s by Jewel Bundren, Joe Christmas, Jackie Shumann,
and Charles Bon and by minor characters such as Nathaniel Burden's son
Calvin II, whose legitimacy is established after the fact by Nathaniel and
Juana's marrying; by Lena Grove's son "Joey," Wash Jones's unnamed
great-granddaughter by Sutpen, and, arguably, by Sutpen's own grandson
Charles Etienne St. Valery Bon and Charles Etienne's son Jim Bond. Their
immediate heirs are the first black McCaslins of *Go Down, Moses*, Tomy
and Turl, whose descendants are called by the maternal surname Beauchamp, and Roth Edmonds's unnamed son by James Beauchamp's granddaughter. Whether named or unnamed, *identity* in every case is from
the father. Legitimacy is paternally determined. In her extremity Temple

Drake, who has no mother in the novel and no female models except whores, clings like Quentin Compson to a paternal ideal, repeating as a mantra, "My father's a judge. My father's a judge" (SO, 99; SR, 51).

iii. The Inturned Vision of *Pylon*

"No one can face his own bastard with more equanimity than I," Faulkner told Hal Smith in 1929. In 1925 he let Sherwood Anderson understand that he had illegitimate children in Mississippi, and at least one cadet in Toronto believed the same.[36] The evidence of the biography is that his bastards were inventions. Nonetheless, the paternal identity and legitimacy of his children and dependents were issues from the beginning. The fictional locus is *Pylon* (1935), where those personal issues are undisguisedly set forth in Laverne's triangular relationship with Roger Shumann and Jack Holmes and in her son Jackie Shumann, of whom in various forms first she and then Jiggs, the Reporter, and Doctor Shumann all demand, "Who's your old man?" (Pylon, 46, 16, 18, 318).[37] The love triangle derives from what Faulkner conceived as his own triangular relationship to Estelle and her husband after she married Franklin. That prompted the hopeless love relationships that form around Margaret Powers in *Soldiers' Pay*, Narcissa Benbow in *Flags in the Dust*, and Caddy in *The Sound and the Fury*, and generated the motifs of the cuckold and the bastard in *As I Lay Dying*, *Light in August*, and *Absalom, Absalom!*, the last of which Faulkner put aside in 1934 to write *Pylon*. The immediate model for Jackie Shumann and source of his complex circumstances almost certainly was Malcolm Franklin. Faulkner was acutely aware that Estelle's children both were and were not his own. He had written Cho-Cho into *Flags in the Dust* as Little Belle in 1927, and his anxiety about being her stepfather into *Sanctuary* in 1929. His relationship to his stepdaughter became more comfortable in the first years of his and Estelle's marriage, but Malcolm remained enigmatically inside and outside the new family.[38] When the Sutpen story gave him problems in 1934, Faulkner turned again for inspiration to familiar issues from his fiction and his role as stepfather, this time to Estelle's son.

Malcolm was born in 1923 and spent nearly half of his first four years away from Cornell Franklin with his mother and sister in Oxford, where Estelle moved permanently in 1927. They lived then with the Oldhams. She and the children frequently saw Faulkner, whom the children called

"Billy" or "Mr. Bill" then,[39] and Malcolm often visited his paternal grandmother, Mrs. Hairston. He spent part of the Faulkners's sometimes difficult honeymoon at Pascagoula with his mother and her new husband.[40]
Whatever confusion there was about fathers was compounded in the autumn of 1929, shortly after they returned, when Cornell Franklin and his
second wife Dallas visited Oxford to see the children.[41] Jackie Shumann's
unsettled life with Laverne is similar in a number of details. Like Malcolm, whose paternity Cornell Franklin briefly called into question when
Estelle filed for divorce,[42] Jackie's paternity is uncertain, his surname decided by a roll of the dice. He is six in the novel, as Malcolm was when
Estelle married Faulkner, and his sense of identity is uneasily suspended,
as Faulkner must have seen Malcolm's then, between his mother's two
lovers. After Estelle's divorce Malcolm was sent to live with his Oldham
grandparents, filling a gap in their lives created in 1916 when their nine-
year-old son Edward died. Jackie, similarly, is left after Roger's death with
the elder Shumanns, who call him "Roger" and "our boy" (Pylon, 320,
322). The Oldhams received child support payments from Cornell, and
Dr. Shumann and his wife are provided money by the Reporter and Jiggs.
Laverne is pregnant then with Holmes's child; Estelle became pregnant
within a year of her marriage to Faulkner.

Pylon is no thinly veiled family biography, however, but is based like
several preceding books in ironic self-presentations and still more outrageous performances. On the surface, and in its insistence on depthless surfaces, both spatial and temporal, the novel seems a radical departure from
the fictional agenda Faulkner set in motion with Flags in the Dust. It neither is set in Yoknapatawpha County nor draws upon the steadily expanding cast of characters Faulkner developed and returned to in stories and
novels for nearly a decade. Like some other of Faulkner's books, notably
Sanctuary, it draws upon times and events in his past, here conflated and
compressed into a few days in 1934. In Pylon Faulkner looked back to
his immediate experience of New Orleans, in February 1934 when he attended the air show at Shushan Airport during Mardi Gras, and through
that visit back beyond it to 1925 and 1926 when he was a twenty-eight-
year-old like the Reporter, supporting himself in newspaper city rooms
while he worked at what the copy boy in Pylon calls "the beginning of literature" (Pylon, 323). The connection was no doubt strengthened by
Faulkner's reunion with his Times-Picayune editor Roark Bradford and
his wife, with whom he briefly stayed that February.[43] Uncertain about the
long historical novel he had begun by calling "Dark House," and with de-

tails of the Shushan Airport adventure freshly in mind as subject matter and stimulus, there came back to Faulkner that fall the old familiarity with the settings and scenes of his extended stays in New Orleans, and with these a full measure of the speed and self-confidence he had found then writing *Soldiers' Pay*. All of this conspired to ease the way of the novel he began in October and finished in December while *Absalom, Absalom!* was on hold.

Whatever adhered to the book from his personal experience of the city—and there is a great deal—the city itself was a first and inestimable resource. The Reporter recognizes this for himself near the end of the novel when he envisions New Valois moving with him in the night, a presence as important to him as it proved to be also to Faulkner, essential and inescapable in space as well as in time. Driving toward Feinman Airport, he realizes:

> He was not escaping it; symbolic and encompassing, it outlay all gasoline-spanned distances and all clock- or sunstipulated destinations. It would be there—the eternal smell of the coffee the sugar the hemp sweating slow iron plates above the forked deliberate brown water and lost lost lost all ultimate blue of latitude and horizon; the hot rain gutterfull plaiting the eaten heads of shrimp; the ten thousand inescapable mornings wherein ten thousand airplants swinging stippleprop the soft scrofulous soaring of sweating brick and ten thousand pairs of splayed brown Leonorafeet tigerbarred by jaloused armistice with the invincible sun: the thin black coffee, the myriad fish stewed in a myriad oil—tomorrow and tomorrow and tomorrow; not only not to hope, not even to wait: just to endure. (Pylon, 291–292)

New Orleans is everywhere present in *Pylon*, of course, and Faulkner drew broadly on his own remembered experience for significant details. The Reporter's apartment in the French Quarter is very like the one Faulkner and Spratling shared in 1926 on an upper floor of a building in Cabildo Alley, between Orleans Alley and Saint Peter St. behind Jackson Square.[44] Spratling drew the alley and adjoining buildings for the frontispiece of *Sherwood Anderson and Other Famous Creoles*, with an arrow pointing the location of Le Petit Theatre du Vieux Carre around the corner. It is Orleans Alley that "rang more than once to the feet of the pirate Lafitte" (Pylon, 96) and was renamed Pirate's Alley for just that reason after Faulkner left the city. It runs the length of St. Anthony's Garden at the rear of St. Louis Cathedral, where the bells ring the hours as they do in the novel

(Pylon, 283, 286), and Faulkner rented rooms from Spratling there in 1925 with a newspaper advertising salesman named Lewis Piper. He wrote his mother then about "a colored Lady yclept Eleanora" (TofH, 190), who appears in the novel as the splay-footed maid Leonora. The Reporter's obscure reference to "the church annex where the boy scouts are tripping one another up from behind" (Pylon, 99) is explained by another 1925 letter about the cathedral garden, in which Faulkner told Maud, "Between masses the little choir boys in their purple robes and white surplices play leap frog in the garden, yelling and cursing each other, then go back inside and sing like angels" (TofH, 188).

Faulkner's first Mardi Gras, in 1925, provided images of the city confirmed and expanded by events of 1934. Writing to his mother on February 20, 1925, he said, "Carnival began last night, with floats and masques and colored fire. The street was hung with colored lights and all traffic stopped for three hours. A people! gosh. I got caught on the wrong side and thought I'd never get home." He added, "A plane with a wing-walker has been over here" (TofH, 185); perhaps this memory, jogged by the 1934 air show, also helped join the two times in his imagination. He was flying himself in 1934, of course, but he had thought of and presented himself as an aviator for years, seldom more so in 1925 than when he wrote to thank Sherwood Anderson for his gift of an R.A.F. necktie. "I looked in at the British Service Club last evening," he told Anderson, "and an Australian ex-air mechanic recognized it at once."[45] Soon after that letter, he began *Soldiers' Pay*, in which Cadet Lowe idolizes the wounded airman named Mahon. The Reporter's hero worship of the homophonically named airman Roger *Shumann* is a version of the same, as is the newspaper copyboy's admiration for the Reporter, all of which with some other details of sponsorship and substitute fathering may have been generated by another personal relationship with a fatherless boy in 1925. Faulkner said of Lewis Piper then, "He is quite young—he tells me about his mother, and how old he is, and how he likes New Orleans. He is from Illinois, only child. His father is dead. Funny kind of a boy. He has the strangest admiration for me. Makes me feell [sic] like I ought to do something quite grand for his sake" (TofH, 197). As the copyboy pastes together the Reporter's eulogy for Shumann, recognizing it as "the beginning of literature," so Piper was one of two volunteers who retyped Faulkner's first novel, *Soldiers' Pay* (TofH, 208). Like Piper (and Faulkner), both Julian Lowe and the Reporter are their mothers' boys.

If the unnamed Reporter is based upon Faulkner's friend Herman

Deutsch, the tall New Orleans newspaperman who reported the Shushan dedication in 1934,[46] it is worth noting that the Reporter's reluctance to report facts is based on the far shorter Faulkner, whose Mirrors of Chartres Street pieces for the *Times-Picayune* were exclusively feature stories, never news. In an interview with Bruce Kawin, Howard Hawks remembered Faulkner's writing *Pylon* "through the eyes of a drunken reporter— who was Bill himself."[47] But the Reporter is not Faulkner—live in his house, work at his avocation at the same age, and share in his admirations and some of his fantasies though he does. Rather, he is compounded of a decade of actual and imagined experience and produced by the inward-looking imagination that Faulkner associated with self-presentation and described in a passage in *Pylon* as a quality of Jiggs's intoxication: "quiet waiting and tranquil; and bemused too, the inturned vision watching something which was not even thought supplying him out of an inextricable whirl of halfcaught pictures, like a roulette wheel bearing printed sentences in place of numbers, with furious tagends of plans and alternatives" (Pylon, 126). In fact, there are as many half-caught aspects in the novel of Faulkner's own inturned, occasionally intoxicated vision as there are mirror images of his characters. Virtually every New Valois scene is one Faulkner knew in New Orleans, and every setting is theatre, every activity a performance.[48] The air show and ground show are the pylon-like axes of events, the airmen and the masked characters of the Mardi Gras floats are performers, and the groundlings their audiences. Indeed, every lamppost in New Valois is adorned with bunting and reproductions of the comic drama mask Faulkner calls "cryptic shields symbolic of laughter and mirth" (Pylon, 86). The Reporter lives around the corner from a theatre, and his room is furnished "from a theatrical morgue" and divided by "an old theatre curtain" (Pylon, 89–90).

Significantly for the self-presentations and performances of the novel, this actual setting from Faulkner's life in New Orleans is the place of the Reporter's own extraordinary intoxication and the focal point of his own inturned imaginative visions.[49] The apartment is both the literal scene of Roger and Laverne's sexual performance and the locus of a multiple sexual fantasy in which performers and audience act as one. When the Reporter confesses his desire for Laverne to Shumann in the fifth chapter, titled "And Tomorrow," he describes himself as a voyeur for whom the imagined is more real than the real. "You see," he says, "it don't matter where I would be. I could be ten miles away or just on the other side of that curtain, and it would be just the same. . . . Because maybe if I was to even sleep with her, it would be the same" (Pylon, 177–178). That night Roger makes love to Laverne in the Reporter's bed behind the curtain, and the Reporter in his newsroom across the city fantasizes the scene, thinking *"Now she will be . . . ."* (Pylon, 206), "Yair. Now she will be. . . . . ." (Pylon, 207), "Yair. *She will be . . . .*" (Pylon, 209). But the act of love generates such fantasies in lovers as well as dreamers. In the Reporter's bed with Laverne, Roger reimagines simultaneously and in exquisite detail her making love to him in the cockpit of his plane and her parachute jump that in turn generated the deputy's vision of "the ultimate shape of his jaded desires [falling] upon him out of the sky, not merely naked but clothed in the very traditional symbology—the ruined dress with which she was trying wildly to cover her loins, and the parachute harness—of female bondage" (Pylon, 200). To sexual actor and voyeurs alike, Laverne is a love fetish.[50] At the height of these actual and vicarious sexual performances with Laverne, when the Reporter says of his night's work, "I aint through here," the proofreader replies, "you better finish it in bed" (Pylon, 209).

The Reporter's stage is not his bed but the printed page. He sees in Laverne what Faulkner saw for so many years in Estelle, "the bright plain shape of love" (Pylon, 240), and like Faulkner he writes about her marriage and her child. Or he may. When she and Jack Blair take Jackie to the Shumanns, the Reporter momentarily becomes the drowned Roger at the bottom of the lake, "having to lie there too and look up at the wreath dissolving faintly rocking and stared at by gulls away, and trying to explain that he did not know. 'I didn't think that,' he cried. 'I just thought they were all going'" (Pylon, 309). His empathetic identification with his hero finds written expression as "the beginning of literature" in his first obituary, which also, in the context of this transposition of actor and audience, is a dramatic *self*-presentation, a eulogy for himself.[51] What he did not know but learns from his vision is what Faulkner knew from experience with Estelle and Malcolm—that, as the Reporter writes in his second, ironic obituary, "their six year old son will spend an indefinite time with some of his grandparents" (Pylon, 324). Under the spell of his inturned vision, the Reporter also may write the story of Laverne's return to Myron, Ohio.[52] Inserted in the narrative of his return to the newspaper office, the story is introduced with the deliberate ambiguity of a dream, as if it also is written from the lake bottom:

again it tasted, felt, like so much dead icy water, that cold and heavy and lifeless in his stomach; when he moved he could both hear and feel it sluggish and dead within him as he removed his coat and hung it on the chair-

back and sat down and racked a sheet of yellow paper into the machine. He
could not feel his fingers on the keys either: he just watched the letters
materialise out of thin air, black sharp and fast, along the creeping yellow.
(Pylon, 310)

At this point, the 13-page text of the Myron, Ohio, story is transcribed
and the narrative returns to the newspaper office: "When the city room
began to fill that evening a copyboy noticed the overturned wastebasket
beside the reporter's desk and the astonishing amount of savagely defaced
and torn copy which littered the adjacent floor" (Pylon, 322). That amount
of copy may well include the discarded story of Jackie's abandonment;
certainly it is more than enough for the two-paragraph eulogy the copyboy pastes together.

    Ohio was Sherwood Anderson's home place as well as Roger Shu-
mann's, and the story-in-a-story of Jackie and the Shumanns may constitute another expression of Faulkner's admiration for Anderson in New
Orleans in 1925 and for the stories of the buried life in his *Winesburg,
Ohio*. There is a sense, after all, in which *Pylon* is not only a return to
New Orleans but a summing up of significant aspects of Faulkner's experience there through the lens of his life and his writing since then. This
involved, in addition to self-presentations, reinscribing and adapting in
the novel his own work and his reading of others'. The bootlegger Pete and
his restaurant are reintroduced from *Mosquitoes* as part of the New Orleans milieu in the chapter "Night in the Vieux Carre," and there are
echoes and extensions of many other Faulkner texts.[53] Jiggs's account of
Laverne's seduction by her brother-in-law, for example, returns to and extends Jason's abuse of his niece Miss Quentin, whose flight with a circus
man is brought forward in Laverne's flight to an air circus with a daredevil
pilot. As Quentin Compson is unhoused, so the Reporter literally is unnamed by his mother's many marriages, the most recent (and painful) to
a Mr. Hurtz, and is represented in *Pylon* by allusions to Joyce's Odysseus-
NoMan-Bloom. Faulkner experimented with Joycean techniques both in
Soldiers' Pay, which was written in New Orleans, and in *Mosquitoes*,
which is set there, and his stylistic experiments and extensive adaptations
in *Pylon* from the Aeolus chapter of *Ulysses* mark another instance of his
return to the imaginative milieu of the earlier time.[54]

    The mixture of self-presentation and performance in *Pylon*, finally,
is the kind of self-conscious play that permitted Faulkner at once to acknowledge such contemporaries as Anderson, Eliot, and Joyce and to place

himself as an equal among them. Editor Hagood names Lewis, Hemingway, and Tchekov as having no place on a newspaper staff, where what is wanted "is not fiction, not even Nobel Prize fiction, but news" (Pylon, 48), but it is just such fiction that Faulkner, like the Reporter, aspired to write in 1925.[55] Like Faulkner, though to a considerably lesser degree, Hemingway followed Joyce's example in *The Sun Also Rises*, where the journey motif and allusions to Circe and Elpenor recall Homer's *Odyssey*. Starting with the fact that like Bloom and Jake Barnes the Reporter is a newspaperman, Faulkner accommodated the work of both novelists to *Pylon*. Indeed, his parody of "hemingwaves" in *If I Forget Thee, Jerusalem* (Jerusalem, 82) in 1939 may have been suggested as much by his prior use of Hemingway in *Pylon* as by Harry and Charlotte's residence in Chicago near Oak Park.

Carnival is the central fact of *Pylon* as of *The Sun Also Rises*, Mardi Gras and the Festival of San Fermin providing the Christian-pagan background against which both writers portray a lost generation. Air racing is the American equivalent of bullfighting—Jake Barnes, the aficionado, is a wounded aviator—and Roger Shumann is the analogue of Pedro Romero. Faulkner's New Valois like Hemingway's Paris is an "Unreal City" indebted to Eliot's poetic representation of the modern urban nightmare. Masked celebrants parade through both books, and in each a woman is raised up as a sexual icon—Brett Ashley as the anti-Virgin and Laverne as the shape of love.[56] Both have an entourage of drunken partners and admirers who, Circe-like, they turn into figurative swine; both dress and act the part of men; each is accompanied by a wounded or sexually frustrated lover. In some measure, however, *The Sun Also Rises* was Faulkner's subject as well as a source, a script he rewrote and recast as darkly ironic and parodic. Pamplona and the Basque country are echoed in the "Spanish jar" and "Pyrenæan chamber pot"[57] (Pylon, 60, 61) at the Hotel Terrebonne, a house of "teared Q pickles of one thousand worn oftcarried phoenixbastions of rented cunts" (59) like Brett's shady Hotel Montana in Madrid. The Terrebonne is headquarters of the air show, where officials and judges conduct financial deals rather than the spiritual examinations of the Hotel Montoya, and none of the businessmen there possesses *aficion*.[58]

As this range of conjunctions between art and life reveals, *Pylon* is thickly palimpsestic. But the point is not only *what* Faulkner did in the book but *how* he did it, how easily he could call up Anderson and Hemingway and Joyce in 1934 from a repertoire astonishing for its dimension and depth.[59] Faulkner's inturned vision of his family and financial situation, of his double-layered past in New Orleans, and of his own reading and writing, provided him a version of Jiggs's "tagends of plans and alternatives" for characters and plot in the novel and the narrative techniques to present them. Writing, for Faulkner, was an act of self-presentation, and *Pylon* exhibits the solid, seemingly chaotic yet controlled symmetries of personal experience. Writing also was a self-validating performance. It was a way of saying both "I am" and "See what I am!" The Reporter experiences a sense of this near the end of the sixth chapter, "Love Song of J. A. Prufrock," when he realizes he has become the actual physical extension of the aftermath of a love-making he only imagined: "it was himself who was the nebulous and quiet ragtag and bobend of touching and breath and experience without visible scars, the waiting incurious unbreathing and without impatience" (Pylon, 289). It is just such a conception, similarly phrased in *Absalom, Absalom!*, that enables Quentin and Shreve to create "(. . . between them, out of the rag-tag and bob-ends of old tales and talking, people who perhaps had never existed at all anywhere, who, shadows, were shadows not of flesh and blood which had lived and died but shadows in turn of what were (to one of them at least, to Shreve) shades too) quiet as the visible murmur of their vaporising breath" (AA!, 243).[60]

iv. Charles Bon, Charles Good

It is tempting to speculate that his own family circumstances underlie Faulkner's descriptions of *Absalom, Absalom!* to Hal Smith in 1934. He was calling the novel "Dark House" in February when he said, "It is the more or less violent breakup of a household or family from 1860 to about 1910" (SLWF, 78). By August it was *Absalom, Absalom!*. He called it "the story . . . of a man who wanted a son through pride, and got too many of them and they destroyed him" (SLWF, 84).[61] Family difficulties he certainly had in 1934–1935, as the marriage matter of the novel suggests, but no sons of his own. When he returned to *Absalom Absalom!* in March 1935, resuming the design of his fictional world with the story of Sutpen's design, he compounded the father-son situation of *Pylon* by recasting it across time in the fuller context of racial identity, brother-sister incest, and multiple families. Focused in Charles Bon's quest for paternal identity, the question "Who's your old man?" resonates throughout the novel as a cognate of social standing and identity in the South, even in the frontier Mississippi of the 1830s. Sutpen is distrusted in Jefferson because he is a "stranger" (AA!, 23) with aspirations and mysterious assets but no apparent antecedents—he is "not even a gentleman," according to Rosa (AA!, 11). His account to General Compson of the history of his design turns upon being rejected at the home of the Tidewater planter he adopts as a model and his own subsequent rejection of the identity the planter sees in him and his kind: "cattle, creatures heavy and without grace, brutely evacuated into a world without hope or purpose for them" (AA!, 190). Sourceless, he gains nominal acceptance in Jefferson by marrying the daughter of Goodhue Coldfield, "the two names, the stainless wife and the unimpeachable father-in-law, on the [marriage] license, the patent" (AA!, 39). Quentin, conversely, is a third-generation Jeffersonian. According to Mr. Compson, who values social ceremony and family name, Rosa Coldfield chooses him as her champion because of who his grandfather was.

Of course narrative authority is at issue in paternal identity, as well: what Mr. Compson learns from General Compson, Quentin learns from his father and recasts still more plausibly with Shreve, who "sounds just like father" (AA!, 147). Quentin's and Shreve's accounts focus on the identities of Sutpen's sons, Henry and Charles Bon, and on the relationship between them that begins, according to Mr. Compson, in college rooms at Mississippi like theirs at Harvard where, in The Sound and the Fury, Quentin is first preoccupied with what "Father said." Bon's obsession with paternal acknowledgment evolved from such circumstances of fathering. Faulkner's return to Absalom, Absalom!, then, was a return not only to the novel's fictional sources in The Sound and the Fury but also, as the marriage matter of Absalom, Absalom! suggests, to the personal sources of the earlier book too. When he chose Mr. Compson to narrate Henry's meeting Bon at the University of Mississippi in 1858, he was drawing again upon memories of living in Phil Stone's rooms in New Haven in 1918 and on issues and imperatives that haunted him then. That was a time for Faulkner not only of disappointed love but of personal insecurity, manifested in the father he recreated as a stable presence in letters and in his grateful acceptance of and allegiance to male substitutes and sponsors, some of whom he elevated to heroes. He created Quentin and the world-weary Mr. Compson from such states of mind in The Sound and the Fury and used Quentin in Absalom, Absalom!, he told Smith, for "his bitterness which he has projected on the South" (SLWF, 79). The source of that bitterness, again, is Mr. Compson, whom he elevated to the narrator of Chapters 2, 3, and 4.

Alone of the Compson children in The Sound and the Fury, Quentin

listens to and venerates his father's words, clinging to them to his own destruction. In *Absalom, Absalom!* there is much that Mr. Compson does
not know—Bon's race, Sutpen's motives for forbidding Judith's marriage,
and Henry's reasons for shooting Bon are examples; and some of what he
learns, Quentin himself supplies—the secret of Bon's race, for example.
But much of what he tells Quentin in Chapter 4 about the relationships
among Henry, Judith, and Bon are things Quentin learned from experience
in Jefferson and at Harvard in *The Sound and the Fury*—and Faulkner before him in Oxford and at Yale. Quentin understands with Mr. Compson
the "single personality with two bodies" (AA!, 73) that binds Henry and
Judith; he shares with Henry what Mr. Compson calls Henry's "fierce provincial's pride in his sister's virginity" and his consciousness that virginity "must depend upon its loss, absence, to have existed at all" (AA!, 76–
77); and he knows, because Mr. Compson teaches him in both novels,
that "no battle is ever won. . . . They are not even fought. The field only
reveals to man his own folly and despair, and victory is an illusion of phi-
losophers and fools" (TSATF, 76).

   Absalom, Absalom!, that is, is grounded in understandings and as-
sumptions that evolved with Quentin as he evolved, among them the implications for identity of mixed race in the South. Citing his own father
and grandfather as authority in this, Quentin says of Sutpen,

> Father said he probably named him himself. Charles Bon. Charles Good. . . .
> he would have insisted on it maybe, the conscience again which could not
> allow her and the child any place in the design . . . the same conscience
> which would not permit the child, since it was a boy, to bear either his name
> or that of its maternal grandfather, yet which would also forbid him to do
> the customary and provide a quick husband for the discarded woman and so
> give his son an authentic name. He chose the name himself, Grandfather
> believed, just as he named them all—the Charles Goods and the Clytem-
> nestras and Henry and Judith and all of them—that entire fecundity of drag-
> ons' teeth as Father called it. (AA!, 213–214)

It is the plight of the unacknowledged son, as Mr. Compson sets it forth,
both to be and to not be. To this cultural understanding Quentin grafts his
own experience of father substitutes and hero worship as he and Shreve
shape the relationship of Henry, Judith, and Bon and its outcomes.

   According to Shreve, Bon sees in Henry's face in 1858 *"my father's, out
of the shadow of whose absence my spirit's posthumeity has never es-*

caped" (AA!, 254). Mr. Compson imagines Henry seeing in Bon an urbane older man from a larger world and an older culture. And much more:

> this man handsome elegant and even catlike and too old to be where he was, too old not in years but in experience, with some tangible effluvium of knowledge, surfeit: of actions done and satiations plumbed and pleasures exhausted and even forgotten. So that he must have appeared, not only to Henry but to the entire undergraduate body of that small new provincial college, as a source not of envy because you only envy whom you believe to be, but for accident, in no way superior to yourself: and what you believe, granted a little better luck than you have had heretofore, you will someday possess;—not envy but of despair: that sharp shocking terrible hopeless despair of the young which sometimes takes the form of insult toward and even physical assault upon the human subject of it. (AA!, 76)

The despair of the young that Mr. Compson describes here draws on his description of the unattainable in the earlier novel. It is based in *Absalom, Absalom!* in the perception of impossible personal aspirations— not the truer-than-truth *"might-have-been"* that underlies Rosa's telling (AA!, 115), nor the "have to be" of love posited by Shreve (AA!, 258), but an unattainable *never-to-be*.

In Henry's relation to Bon, Faulkner exaggerated and compounded his own circumstances and states of mind in New Haven in 1918 as he had earlier in Quentin, both times through Mr. Compson, who here is an actual narrator as well as a remembered voice. The dark side of hero worship as Mr. Compson defines it is congruent with his self-confounding sense of the past as a heroic time lost to the diminished present, and it is the underlying source in both novels of Quentin's despair. In *The Sound and the Fury* it is the root of Quentin's hopeless attack on Gerald Bland, whom he associates with Pluto and Shreve with Jove, and the basis of his suicide; in *Absalom, Absalom!* it drives him to that premonitory moment of self-recognition when he knows that "I am older at twenty than a lot of people who have died" (AA!, 301). Shreve says of Quentin as they re-create history together, "Dont say it's just me that sounds like your old man," and Quentin thinks, *"Yes, we are both father. Or maybe Father and I are both Shreve, maybe it took Father and me both to make Shreve or Shreve and me both to make Father or maybe Thomas Sutpen to make all of us"* (AA!, 210). This is philoprogeniture with a will! The thought that prompts that speculation, and the famous analogy of the pebble in the umbilically connected pools that accompanies it, constitutes the formula of patterned authorial self-presentation and performance by which Faulkner reprised and reenacted roles from novel to novel. *"Maybe nothing ever happens once and is finished,"* Quentin thinks in *Absalom, Absalom!*, where, despite what he calls a *"different molecularity of having seen, felt, remembered,"* not only the Sutpen story but issues and imperatives of earlier novels move in him at *"the original ripple-space, to the old ineradicable rhythm"* (AA!, 210).

Clearly Henry Sutpen's despair, as Mr. Compson defines it, also evolved from Quentin's in the earlier book. In the last half of *Absalom, Absalom!* Quentin associates himself with Henry particularly, and he and Shreve imagine Henry and Bon in a quite complex relation for which Faulkner's sponsored relationships are again the emblematic model. Nearly every preceding novel pairs literal or figurative sons of Mr. Compson with older men in relationships characterized, like Faulkner's own, by mimicry, role-playing, and performance. In widely varying situations but to similar, often despairing ends, young men like Quentin and Henry are fascinated with larger-than-life men who are their guides and, often, objects of their envy: aviators (Cadet Lowe with Donald Mahon, the Reporter with Shumann), artists (Mr. Talliaferro with Gordon), lovers (Quentin with Ames, Head, and Bland), forefathers (Gail Hightower with his grandfather), aristocrats (Byron Snopes with Bayard Sartoris), and outlaws (Horace with the bootleggers). The categories and some of the characters were personally based imaginative extensions of Faulkner's relationships to R.A.F. aviators in New Haven and Canada and men like his flying instructor Vernon Omlie; to Sherwood Anderson and Stark Young; to Phil Stone's family and his own socially and financially prominent Falkner ancestors, including especially his great-grandfather; to bootleggers in New Orleans and to Memphis gamblers like Reno DeVaux; and to urbane ladies' men, including especially the successful suitors of women he loved, Cornell Franklin in particular.[62] If Faulkner's muse was Estelle—or his mother, or his grandmother, Damuddy Butler, or any of the other women who attracted him, encouraged him in his vocation, or inspired his work[63]—the heroes and blackguards of his life and his fiction were men such as these and Charles Bon, some of whom generated in him, as in Henry, that "terrible hopeless despair of the young."

Probably Faulkner had no single idealized person before him in 1918 when he wrote to his mother about enlisting in "the English Army" (TofH, 63). In his letters from New Haven, he names well-known members of the Lafayette Escadrille who were in the news then and war veterans whom he knew at Yale and especially admired. His brother Jack had enlisted in the Marine Corps in May, and Faulkner could expect to be drafted into the infantry in September, but he had been eight weeks in the larger world and older Eastern culture of New Haven then, and there were enough heroes there to bring a provincial Mississippi factory clerk close to the kind of despair he describes in *Absalom, Absalom!*. It was Stone's opinion that Faulkner had been going to seed in Oxford,[64] but New Haven in its way was no better. "At the rate I am living now," Faulkner wrote Maud in June 1918, "I'll never be able to make anything of myself" (TofH, 63–64). The war he described was a war of his own invention, safely removed from reality, and his account of his projected enlistment was a clear exhibition of romantic self-fashioning. He would enlist "as a second year Yale man," apparently on no other basis than his residence with Stone, and be recommended for a commission at once. "The chances of advancement in the English Army are very good," he declared. "I'll perhaps be a major at the end of a year's service." He said nothing of British mortality rates in France but compared his anticipated service, ironically, to the dangers of serving under "an inexperienced officer" in the U.S. Army. "The English officers are the best yet," he concluded, "take better care of their men and weigh all chances for them. So I shall learn war in the best schools, where the elimination of risk is taught above every thing" (TofH, 63). He posed for the enlistment photograph then in the soft-collared shirt and loose-fitting coat and cravat he had said Yale men favored (see Fig. 3), invented English antecedents for himself, and probably practiced British pronunciations, as Stone later claimed, with an Englishman named Bernard Reed.[65]

This was personal theatre of a kind familiar in Faulkner's life and letters then, and it carried into *Absalom, Absalom!*, where the narratives are subjectively shaped by narrators who perform for and with one another. From Rosa's description of Sutpen and his architect and slaves as a "raree show" (AA!, 12) in Chapter 1 to Mr. Compson's concluding vision of her in Chapter 9 replaying life in *"that place or bourne where the objects of the outrage and of the commiseration also are no longer ghosts but are actual people to be actual recipients of the hatred and the pity"* (AA!, 301–302), the narrators of the novel are persistently and pervasively theatrical.[66] Mr. Compson thinks of Sutpen and Ellen as playing parts they wrote for themselves but guided, nonetheless, by "fate, destiny, retribution, irony—the stage manager, call him what you will" (AA!, 57). Rosa's chapter-long soliloquy in Chapter 5 is characterized, like Shegog's sermon, by the heightened language of performance and by her roles as auditor and self-portrayed object of Bon's courtship of Judith. With justification she declares herself *"all polymath love's androgynous advocate"* (AA!, 117), for she is both witness to and site of the Sutpen drama—"*O furious mad old man,*" she tells Sutpen when he proposes, "*I hold no substance that will fit your dream but I can give you airy space and scope for your delirium*" (AA!, 135–136). Clearly, she shares Faulkner's sense of art in the South as spectacle.

Quentin shares Rosa's and his father's dramatic imagination, and he shares Faulkner's experience of love and loss and male friendship which he dramatizes for and with Shreve in their Harvard rooms. At the end of Chapter 5 Quentin restages the scene he cannot pass—Henry's confronting Judith after his murder of Bon—and he returns to it at the beginning of Chapter 6 when he envisions Henry's "gaunt tragic dramatic self-hypnotized youthful face like the tragedian in a college play, an academic Hamlet waked from some trancement of the curtain's falling and blundering across the dusty stage from which the rest of the cast had departed last commencement" (AA!, 142). In this setting, and at this distance in history, the theatric analogy portrays him as well as Henry. The academic imagery is rooted in academic experience that Faulkner knew as a Southern outsider at Yale, and recreated first in Quentin and then Henry from his own fascination and envy and, at Yale very possibly, despair. For Quentin the linked scenes in Chapters 5 and 6 constitute an epiphany of personal failure. In the contexts of Estelle's reluctant marriage to Franklin and Caddy's to Head, and of Faulkner and Quentin's failures to act on their respective behalfs, whether as husband or intercessor, the words Quentin imagines Henry speaking to Judith represent his sudden understanding that what Henry did literally to Bon, Quentin dared not do to Ames and Head.

> *Now you cant marry him.*
> *Why cant I marry him?*
> *Because he's dead.*
> *Dead?*
> *Yes. I killed him.* (AA!, 139–140)

The first movement of the novel ends and the second begins with this scene. It and the equally impressionistic interview between Quentin and

Henry at the end of Chapter 9 frame the second half of the novel, in which Quentin and Shreve reimagine more finely and more dramatically than before Henry's love of Bon and Bon's obsession with his father.

At the middle of Chapter 8, when Quentin and Shreve turn the focus of their narrative to the triangular relationship between Henry, Judith, and Charles, the stories of Sutpen's design and Bon's mother's revenge are behind them. They "overpass to love, where there might be paradox and inconsistency but nothing fault nor false" (AA!, 253), reconstructing in that context scenes that resolve and explain the relationships between father, sister, brother, and lover that Mr. Compson finds "just incredible" (AA!, 80). Henry accedes to incest out of love of Bon when he "authorize[s]" him to write Judith (AA!, 279) at the end of the war;[67] Sutpen raises the stakes when he reveals Bon's racial identity and charges Henry with protecting his sister; and Bon raises them again and brings the theme of "Who's your old man?" to its climax when he insists on the marriage. He forces the murder that will confirm him Sutpen's black son.[68] Despite Henry's despairing insistence that he and Bon are brothers, he is first his father's son, the agent and ironically self-destructive instrument of Sutpen's design. Bon is no less his father's son when he defines himself for Henry in Sutpen's terms as *the nigger that's going to sleep with your sister. Unless you stop me, Henry*" (AA!, 286).

The scenes in the Confederate camp in Carolina bring to closure the issues of paternity and sponsored independence in the Sutpen materials. The words *father* and *son* are used only twice each in Chapter 9, in the passage where Shreve comically characterizes the South as "a kind of entailed birthright father and son and father and son of never forgiving General Sherman, so that forever more as long as your children's children produce children you wont be anything but a descendant of a long line of colonels killed in Pickett's charge at Manassas" (AA!, 289).[69] Mr. Compson's letter to Quentin that opens in Chapter 6 with words Charles Bon acts out his life in vain to hear—"*My dear son*" (AA!, 141)—is completed in Chapter 9 but unsigned. Unlike Quentin's impressionistic imagination of the murder at the Sutpen gate in Chapters 5 and 6, and Wash's report to Miss Rosa in Chapter 4 that "Henry has done shot that durned French feller. Kilt him dead as a beef" (AA!, 106), the scenes between Henry and Bon that climax Chapter 8 are purposely stylized, visually distinguished by the unbroken margins and dashes (restored in the corrected text), and have a nuanced sense of the text as a play or a cinematic script.[70] Scenes are set as they are in film story treatments:—*the winter of '64 now, the army retreated across Alabama into Georgia"* (AA!, 276); characters are objectively described as in stage directions: Henry *"is gaunt and ragged and unshaven; because of the last four years and because he had not quite got his height when the four years began, he is not as tall by two inches as he gave promise of being, and not as heavy by thirty pounds as he probably will be a few years after he has outlived the four years, if he do outlive them"* (AA!, 281);[71] action is similarly described: *"Bon puts the cloak about Henry and goes and takes up his tumbled blanket and swings it about his shoulders, and they move aside and sit on a log. Now it is dawn"* (AA!, 284); and passages of direct dialogue are glossed as speeches in a script: *"Now Henry speaks"* (AA!, 283), *"Bon does not speak"* (AA!, 284), *"Henry doesn't answer"* (AA!, 285). The source of this mode of expression, and of some of the subject matter, is Hollywood cinema.

Faulkner worked with Howard Hawks for three years (1932–1935) immediately before and during the writing of *Absalom, Absalom!*, and what he learned then about writing films he adapted at need to his fiction. Photographic imagery, for example, is frequent and specific in *Absalom, Absalom!*, where Mr. Compson imagines "the way in which [Bon] took the innocent and negative plate of Henry's provincial soul and intellect and exposed it by slow degrees to this esoteric milieu [of New Orleans], building gradually toward the picture which he desired it to retain, accept. . . . watching the picture resolve and become fixed. . . . stroking onto the plate himself now the picture which he wanted there" (AA!, 87–88). In addition he experimented with cinematic techniques, expanding especially his understanding and use of montage.[72] Two films that share significant similarities with *Absalom, Absalom!* are *Today We Live*, which Faulkner adapted for Hawks in 1932–1933 from his *Saturday Evening Post* story "Turn About," and *The Road to Glory*. Bruce Kawin points out that Faulkner "was still working on *Absalom* when he collaborated with Joel Sayre on the script for *The Road to Glory*," and calls the two films "a diptych . . . very much like *The Sound and the Fury* and *Absalom, Absalom!*."[73] Faulkner's initial script of *Today We Live*, subsequently revised, begins with an emblematic childhood event like those that control the lives of Quentin and Sutpen,[74] and both films like the novels are based on love triangles with strong elements of male friendship, in which Hawks also was interested. Hawks called them "two men and a girl" stories. In *Today We Live* it was Faulkner who added the girl and the motif of sublimated incest that also links the film and the novels.[75] Both films are stories of World

War I, which Faulkner had associated with the Civil War in his letters from New Haven and in his fiction since *Flags in the Dust*. Similar to *Absalom, Absalom!*, *The Road to Glory* concludes with the heroine's two lovers going to the Front with the father of one in command.[76]

The last draft of *Today We Live* that Faulkner wrote alone, the second in the process of the film's composition, is especially interesting in that it incorporates slightly altered materials from previous fiction that in turn anticipate *Absalom, Absalom!*. Asked to add a female lead to the story in the second draft, he turned to the love triangle in *The Sound and the Fury*, giving the torpedo-boat driver Ronnie Bryce-Smith a sister, named Ann, and making Ronnie's partner Claude a ward of the Bryce-Smith family. Paternity is made an issue in the film by the death of Mr. Bryce-Smith. Claude, the younger boy, idolizes Ronnie and loves Ann. On his way to join Ronnie at Oxford, Claude tells a military guard, "Ronnie's there already. He's cock of the school. He's the same as my brother. I'm going to marry his sister" (Today, 139). Bryce-Smith's death recalls Murry Falkner's in August 1932 and Claude's hero-worship recalls Dean Falkner's outspoken admiration for his older brother William then. The children's relationship also has several elements of the Henry-Judith-Charles triangle but differently configured, as if the film were an intermediate stage in the extended process of composition by which the Quentin-Caddy-Dalton plot evolved into the pattern in *Absalom, Absalom!*. The academic setting, with its "fag system," casts Ronnie like Henry as the younger admirer of an older student, here a senior who abuses him. Faulkner's script specifies that Oxford University, like Yale in 1918 and the University of Mississippi in 1861, is both a college and a military base, in this case the scene of the Royal Flying Corps Ground School, the place he expected to be assigned when he enlisted in 1918 (TofH, 64). Hero worship in the film is serial. Like Faulkner in 1918, Ronnie and Claude envy veteran officers, note war casualties, and impatiently wait to enlist, fearing the war "will be over before we get there" (Today, 144). Ann loves both Ronnie and Claude, whom she follows to Oxford as Pat Robyn, in *Mosquitoes*, plans to follow her brother Josh to Yale. The American Bogard is introduced at this point as another older man and Oxford student whom Ronnie admires. He introduces him to Ann, creating a second love triangle in which Bogard competes for Ann with Claude, who by now is her lover. As Faulkner pretended he had, Bogard becomes an aviator, and like Faulkner he gets his girl in the end, here when Claude is blinded and dies.

Hawks himself, it is clear, was another of Faulkner's sponsors. Bruce

Kawin speculates that "Faulkner admired the way Hawks told a story" and that he "recognized and respected the understated power, the fun, the seriousness of Hawks's methods."[77] His work for Hawks may account for dramatic effects he worked out in *Absalom, Absalom!* when he returned to the novel from *Pylon* in March 1935. It may also have prepared him to more powerfully represent the imperatives of fatherhood and male sponsorship that had long been implicated in his life and his fiction. In this context self-presentation and performance were inextricably one. Faulkner still was writing himself into being in *Absalom, Absalom!*, presenting himself—whether as the young Southerner who might "enter the literary profession," as Miss Rosa suggests (AA!, 5) or as that past-haunted one "still too young to deserve yet to be a ghost but nevertheless having to be one for all that" (AA!, 4)—for his own contemplation and ours.

Eric J. Sundquist makes this point another way in his comments on the relationship between paternity and literary form, where he says that "Faulkner saw *Absalom, Absalom!* as the preliminary culmination of his own fictional design of Yoknapatawpha. It is his most ambitious, detailed, and complex novel, and he felt compelled to add to it not only a genealogy and chronology but also a map of Yoknapatawpha, which summarized his work to date in visual form."[78] And, one might add, summarized his life in his work.

For better or worse, the father-figures and sons Faulkner created and the roles they perform in the masterworks created him in turn. He said of *Sartoris* in 1930 that he had "improved on God, who, dramatic though He be, has no sense, no feeling for theatre."[79] In 1955 he still claimed to have moved his characters around in his fictional cosmos "like God, not only in space but in time too" (Lion, 255). His immortality was not to be in his own paternity, however: Faulkner fathered no sons of his own and for all of his grief over the daughter he lost in infancy and his love for the daughter who lived, he still could tell Jill, "Nobody remembers Shakespeare's children."[80] The family name would be carried on by John's sons Jimmy and Murry ("Chookie") Faulkner; his name would be on his books and his blood in the "cold impersonal print," as he said in the "Foreword to *The Faulkner Reader*" (1954), by which the artist could "lift up man's heart for his own benefit because in that way he can say No to death." The language of the piece is the language of masculine begetting, of "blood and glands and flesh still . . . strong and potent" (ESPL, 182, 181, 180). The artist, he said there, seeks his immortality "by means of the hearts which he has hoped to uplift, or even by means of the mere base glands which he has disturbed to that extent where they can say No to death on their own account by knowing, realizing, having been told and believing it: *At least we are not vegetables because the hearts and glands capable of partaking in this excitement are not those of vegetables, and will, must endure*" (ESPL, 181–182). The heightened declaration in the foreword is a public performance in itself, as it is also a critique of previous artistic performances, a dramatic assertion that the fiction it introduces and describes retains and conveys the powers of the creator who begot them. When we read *Pylon* and *Absalom, Absalom!*, that is to say, we also, and inescapably, read "Faulkner."[81]

V. Stage Manager

... fate, destiny, retribution, irony — the

stage manager, call him what you

will — was already striking the set and

dragging on the synthetic and spurious

shadows and shapes of the next one ...

Absalom, Absalom!

---

i. The Authorial Sovereign

Reflecting on the overall design of his fictional cosmos in 1955, Faulkner told Jean Stein, "I can move these people around like God, not only in space but in time too" (Lion, 255). That explicitly performative statement is implicit in much that preceded it. The figure of the artist as God had been in his mind at least since the preface to *Sartoris* a quarter of a century earlier, drawn in that case from the final pages of the 1927 typescript of *Flags/Sartoris*, where Miss Jenny muses on the Sartorises.

> The music went on in the dusk; the dusk was peopled with ghosts of glamorous and old disastrous things. And if they were just glamorous enough, there would be a Sartoris in them, and then they were sure to be disastrous. Pawns. But the Player and the game He plays—who knows? He must have a name for his pawns, though, but perhaps Sartoris is the name of the game

itself—a game outmoded and played with pawns shaped too late and to an old dead pattern, and of which the Player Himself is a little wearied. For there is death in the sound of it, and a glamorous fatality, like silver pennons downrushing at sunset, or a dying fall of horns along the road to Roncevaux. (Flags, 369–370)

Parts of that passage, in turn, echo F. Scott Fitzgerald's story "Absolution" (1926), in which Rudolph Miller affirms his identity as Blatchford Sarnemington and "a silver pennon had flapped out into the breeze somewhere and there had been the crunch of leather and the shine of silver spurs and a troop of horsemen waiting for dawn on a low green hill."[1] Both passages display self-authoring: Fitzgerald's story, drawn from autobiographical materials of *The Great Gatsby*, points to his character's imaginative self-affirmation, and Faulkner's novel to his own part as author-cum-Player in a fictional chronicle in which he depicted the glorious and fatal history of his own family.

The authorial self of the *Flags* passage and the figure of the Player-artist carried into a late passage in *Light in August* in which a similarly God-like entity manipulates the lives of Joe Christmas and Percy Grimm. Gavin Stevens's racial theory of Joe's flight from jail is countered there by a narrator who proposes that Christmas acts in "lean, swift, blind obedience to whatever Player moved him on the Board" (LIA, 462). The Player again is the novelist who moves his people around "like God": Christmas, as his fictional creation, *literally* is "not flesh and blood" and it is the author-Player "who moved him for pawn" who *literally* "found him breath" (LIA, 462). Grimm, likewise, is "merely waiting for the Player to move him again" (LIA, 464), and when he rushes into Hightower's house he does so as an agent of the artist's design. In the final paragraph of Chapter 19, the narrator's equally self-referential statement that "the Player was not done yet" (LIA, 464) suggests the extent to which Faulkner was indulging himself as well as his characters in the violence of the murder and castration that follows, imposing a lasting image of the dying Joe Christmas on readers as well as on fictional watchers. He had done this before, and to similar effect, in *Sanctuary*, by withholding details of the crime against Temple until the end of the trial, in Chapter 28. When Eustace Graham produces the blood-stained corncob, the auditors and readers alike sigh "a long hissing breath" (SR, 288) of terrible recognition.

The fateful Player who moves Thomas Sutpen and is called "stage manager" in *Absalom, Absalom!* (AA!, 57) is another such metaphoric

self-presentation, this deriving from Faulkner's more detailed knowledge
of Hollywood in the mid-1930s. Prior to that, of course, he had used theatrical images to describe characters and situations, but his work as a screenwriter expanded his resources of theatrical and performative expression.
An image from *Light in August*, extended in *Absalom, Absalom!*, will il-
lustrate the change. In the earlier novel, Faulkner drew on Aubrey Beardsley, whose drawings he had imitated in *The Marionettes*, to describe
Joanna Burden "in the wild throes of nymphomania, her body gleaming
in the slow shifting from one to another of such formally erotic attitudes
and gestures as a Beardsley of the time of Petronius might have drawn"
(LIA, 259–260). Four years later, he evoked the same source in the expanded theatrical terms in which Mr. Compson imagines the octoroon's
visit to Bon's grave:

> the interlude, the ceremonial widowhood's bright dramatic pageantry. . . . It
> must have resembled a garden scene by the Irish poet, Wilde: the late after-
> noon, the dark cedars with the level sun in them, even the light exactly
> right and the graves, the three pieces of marble . . . looking as though they
> had been cleaned and polished and arranged by scene shifters who with the
> passing of twilight would return and strike them and carry them, hollow
> fragile and without weight, back to the warehouse until they should be
> needed again; the pageant, the scene, the act, entering upon the stage—the
> magnolia-faced woman a little plumper now, a woman created of by and for
> darkness whom the artist Beardsley might have dressed, in a soft flowing
> gown designed not to infer bereavement or widowhood but to dress some
> interlude of slumbrous and fatal insatiation, of passionate and inexorable
> hunger of the flesh, walking beneath a lace parasol and followed by a bright
> gigantic negress carrying a silk cushion and leading by the hand the little
> boy whom Beardsley might not only have dressed but drawn. (AA!, 157)

The scene is a self-assured tableau, typically cinematic in its evocation of
the artificial setting, the quality of light and the mixture of bereavement
and desire projected by the actors. Literally it is stage managed in the manner of a Hollywood movie set.

Faulkner's increasing mastery of the fictional world he had been colo-
nizing since the late-1920s is apparent in his confident enlargement on
such early resources as these and, particularly to the point, in his confi-
dently moving characters and their histories from novel to novel, sometimes, like Horace Benbow, from a peripheral to a primary role and at

other times, as with the Compsons, from one major role to another. His manuscripts reflect this process, as well: the dramatic relocation of materials from the original to the revised *Sanctuary* is only the most striking example in the fiction of this period of the artist's working his will on his work. The freedom to be God, however, was not absolute but carried with it obligations to the emerging cosmos. And to his life as a man. Faulkner had said as much about "the teeming world I had had to create" in the preface to *Sartoris*,[2] and General Compson alludes to the same double sense of art as freedom and obsession when he says of Thomas Sutpen's pursuit of his design that he "lacked not only the money to spend for drink and conviviality, but the time and inclination as well: that he was at this time completely the slave of his secret and furious impatience, his conviction gained from whatever that recent experience had been—that fever mental or physical—of a need for haste, of time fleeing beneath him, which was to drive him for the next five years" (AA!, 25).

Something of the same was true of Faulkner in 1934. In the five years between the publication of *Sartoris* and *The Sound and the Fury* in 1929 and the first notice of *Absalom, Absalom!* (SLWF, 78–79), Faulkner had become both master and slave to his art. He had by 1934 published five novels, written several dozen short stories of which twenty-seven had been brought together in two collections, and published a book of sometimes very personal poems that dated from his early twenties. If he shared something of Sutpen's "secret and furious impatience," it must have been exacerbated by other kinds of obligations and attendant interruptions. For the representation of Sutpen as subject to the will of a stage manager additionally recognizes the circumstances to which both Faulkner's need for the privacy to write and his growing public reputation ironically subjected him then.

To pay his bills in the years immediately following his marriage to Estelle, he had begun to trade fiction writing in Oxford for script writing in Hollywood. At that cultural distance from home and all that home represented of substance and security in his art, the explosive pace of his writing slowed. Just as important, the writing for which he was paid was of a different kind than his art, and what he did of it he characterized as hack work. Still more severely pressed a decade later, in January 1946, he would tell Robert Haas, "What a commentary. In France, I am the father of a literary movement. In Europe I am considered the best modern American and among the first of all writers. In America, I eke out a hack's motion picture wages" (SLWF, 217–218). In this he was doubly the prisoner of his art, caught between his reputation as a writer of great power and the base need to earn money by capitalizing on that. Incapable of supporting the family he had acquired by what he felt he must write, he found himself all but incapable of writing what he must while supporting them and himself as a hack. Both dilemmas are reflected in Mr. Compson's description of the force that undercuts Sutpen's apparently settled design in the years following his marriage to Ellen: "while he was still playing the scene to the audience," Mr. Compson says, "behind him fate, destiny, retribution, irony—the stage manager, call him what you will—was already striking the set and dragging on the synthetic and spurious shadows and shapes of the next one" (AA!, 57). In Faulkner's case in the early 1930s, as the theatrical metaphor affirms, the next scene was the literally synthetic one of movie sets and sound stages at Universal Studios. From that thraldom the imperial achievement that is *Absalom, Absalom!* was doubly hard won.

This sense of the master mastered is not without a related and, for Faulkner, a particularly instructive precedent in American literary history. It is reflected, first, in his retrospective sense of the literary artist's necessary "failure to do the impossible" (Lion, 238), which in Andre Bleikasten's acute analysis places Faulkner squarely in the tradition of Hawthorne, Poe, and Herman Melville. It was Melville's judgment, in his 1850 review of Hawthorne, that "it is better to fail in originality, than to succeed in imitation. He who has never failed somewhere, that man cannot be great. Failure is the true test of greatness."[3] Tracing the implications of this for Faulkner, Bleikasten finds that failure is the informing principle of *The Sound and the Fury*. "Whether the blame falls on the artist or on his medium, language, everything happens as though the writing process could never be completed, as though it could only be the gauging of a lack. Creation then ceases to be a triumphant gesture of assertion; it resigns itself to be the record of its errors, trials and defeats, the chronicle of its successive miscarriages, the inscription of the very impossibility from which it springs."[4] Such reflexiveness, by extension, includes the self-presenting writer with his writing.

The issue of the finite limits to absolute authorial authority calls forth specific resemblances to writers Faulkner admired, both contemporaries he named and important American predecessors, Melville chief among them.[5] Tracing the ironies of creative mastery in Melville's artistic life between the writing of *Omoo* and *Typee* and of *Moby-Dick*, Wai-chee Dimock describes him as an authorial "sovereign . . . a figure whose literary individualism is always imperially articulated." The "mutuality between self and nation" that Dimock identifies in Melville and the "spatial appetites of Truth [that] make the author an 'imperial self'"[6] are instructive in Faulkner's work of the mutual relation between self and region. As his map of Yoknapatawpha County overlies and takes its spatial form from Lafayette County, so his actual life in northern Mississippi supplied the matter of his fiction. The relationship was so close, in fact, that fictional characters and events came to inform Faulkner's biographical accounts of himself, in private letters and later, more openly, in work such as the essay-story "Mississippi." Dimock argues that Melville fully realized his imaginative freedom first in *Mardi*, but he realized subsequently that sovereignty was not without paradoxical difficulties of a kind Faulkner was also to encounter. For imperial "dominion" implies subjection as well as freedom; one's territorial domain comes to represent the boundaries of one's liberty. In the logic of the imperial self, Dimock suggests, "freedom is always part of a complementary formation, set in a landscape of polarized attributes and discrete repositories. Freedom not only entails an obverse; it is itself constituted by that obverse."[7] *Mardi* did not sell well, and writing the "beggarly" *Redburn* and *White-Jacket* that followed it, Melville described himself as an impoverished "dun" of the book-buying public. According to Dimock's scheme, the "poetics of authorial sovereignty" that characterize *Mardi* gave way to a "poetics of authorial subjection," the "textual correlatives" of which trace Melville's attempt in the two despised books "to represent and to give meaning to his imagined powerlessness," "to figure forth the 'persecuted' artist," and "to identify that artistic powerlessness with other forms of powerlessness, to credit it with the same meaning and the same weight."[8]

This condition has a more than metaphoric application to Faulkner's career as it was interrupted by Hollywood in 1934–1935, when he put aside the manuscript he first called "Dark House" to write *Pylon*, then returned to that project, from which he crafted the manifestly imperial *Absalom, Absalom!*. For *Pylon*, like Melville's *Redburn* and *White Jacket* as Dimock describes them, is also a book "haunted . . . by the specters of those for whom powerlessness is anything but metaphor,"[9] and its autobiographical protagonist, like theirs, is a "'loser,' someone who accumulates not capital but deficits," whose labor, like Redburn's, "turns out to bring in no 'lucre' at all. . . . In fact it actually puts him into debt."[10] Faulkner first went to Hollywood in May 1932 and finished *Light in August* there that summer. By 1934, instead of capitalizing on the enlarged imperial powers generated by his writing *Light in August,* he was accumulating artistic rather than financial deficits. He said in July that money-making movie-making had forced him "to put off the novel [*Absalom, Absalom!*] too much already" (SLWF, 83); nine months later, in a March letter to Morton Goldman, he said, "I believe I have got enough fair literature in me yet to deserve reasonable freedom from bourgeoise material petty impediments and compulsion, without having to quit writing and go to the moving pictures every two years" (SLWF, 90). The letter pointedly associates "literature" with "freedom," "moving pictures" with a bourgeois poetics of subjection.

Pylon was published in the same month, on March 25. There Faulkner had presented the Reporter as a fumbling subject prince, if not sovereign, confined by the physical city as by the conventions of journalism and longing for flight as for expression. Exploited, tyrannized, dispossessed by the traveling performers in the air show, the Reporter is no doer but a self-conscious watcher/voyeur in the line of Quentin Compson and Darl Bundren. Like Darl's and Horace Benbow's, the free-ranging imagination that gives him access to others' private lives is a tormenting and frustrating affliction. The Reporter's schemes are as impossible as travel in the city at night; they run into blind alleys, detour, turn back on themselves. In the mazed night-world of *Pylon,* the Reporter struggles to establish vicarious dominion by a kind of writing free of journalistic proscription, but like his account of his troubled progress, writing itself breaks down, being dictated, edited, published in cryptic headlines, forged, torn apart, and pasted together. So with economic accounting in a novel where money is borrowed, misspent, lost, stolen, and burned.

To read *Pylon* from this point of view is to understand that Faulkner was writing the book not *for* a reading public, nor even *against* it as it is argued he sometimes did,[11] but against the immediate circumstances of his life then. For all of the frenetic linguistic experimentation that interrupts communication in the novel, *Pylon* represents Faulkner's flight in imagination from Hollywood to the magical time and place where his writing transformed him from aspiring poet into novelist. It marks a return to the New Orleans where he wrote *Soldiers' Pay* and, a year later, made the city his own fictional domain by writing it and its people into *Mosquitoes.* In his youth there in 1925 Faulkner had surmounted some of the same barriers that confront the Reporter and written what he calls in *Pylon* "the beginning of literature" (*Pylon,* 323). Had he thought of it in Hollywood—and perhaps he did, given the prevalence of allusions to Mel-

ville in the fiction to this time and after—Faulkner might have said with
Ishmael, "Who aint a slave?" and conceived of his captive art then in
terms Ishmael ascribes to imperial Ahab's imprisoned subterranean self,
whose "root of grandeur, his whole awful essence sits in bearded state;
an antique buried beneath antiquities, and throned on torsoes! So with a
broken throne, the great gods mock that captive king; so like a Caryatid
he patient sits, upholding on his frozen brow the piled entabulatures of
ages." [12] *Pylon* revisits a scene of just such generative force in Faulkner's
past life to mock not his buried art but the great gods of the business establishment, including especially Hollywood business, whose standards
and conventions held him temporarily in thrall.

His most critical representation of California is the story "Golden
Land" (1935), which dates from the time of *Pylon*,[13] but the novel, too,
draws upon California subject matter as it also parodies Hollywood aesthetics. As Hollywood was making movies then from his "Turnabout"
and *Sanctuary*,[14] so Faulkner used aspects of the movie city milieu to
make a novel about his New Orleans. He evoked Hollywood in the opening pages by the "faintly Moorish or Californian" airport facade (Pylon,
14); the final words of the novel, the Reporter's "*I am on a credit*" (Pylon,
324), evoke both bar tab and screen credit. Jackie Shumann is born "on a
unrolled parachute in a California hangar" (Pylon, 46), and Editor Hagood
with his roadster convertible, golf clubs, and sporty clothes is far more a
1930s Hollywood cinema director or producer than a New Orleans newspaperman. Like an aging movie star, the Reporter's mother has "the fine
big bosom . . . the broad tomatocolored mouth, the eyes pleasant shrewd
and beyond mere disillusion, the hair of that diamondhard and impervi-
ously recent lustre of a gilt service in a shopwindow, the goldstudded teeth
square and white and big like those of a horse" (Pylon, 91–92); frequently
married, she is honeymooning, at present, at the Hotel Vista del Mar in
Santa Monica (Pylon, 277).[15] The Reporter is dependent financially upon
both Hagood and his mother and imaginatively upon Roger Shumann and
Laverne. She is cast as a movie queen, complete with a male harem. A
small-town beauty discovered by Shumann, she plays a love scene in the
cockpit of his airplane more explicit than anything in Faulkner's fiction
before Hollywood and represents "the bright plain shape of love" (Pylon,
240) not only to the Deputy who witnesses her first parachute jump but
to the Reporter who imagines her in bed with the pilot. The Reporter's
hero worship and his obsession with Laverne, in this context, are the stuff
of a moviegoer's fantasies. Four years later Faulkner would attribute the

same fantasy life to a similarly innocent and this time literal prisoner, writing of the tall convict in *If I Forget Thee, Jerusalem*, "who to say what Helen, what living Garbo, he had not dreamed of rescuing from what craggy pinnacle or dragoned keep when he and his companion embarked in the skiff" (Jerusalem, 126).

In such ways, initially, Hollywood constituted both a barrier to literature and the challenge of new ways of visualizing and telling, and Faulkner addressed both in what he borrowed and parodied in *Pylon*. All artistic acts have precedents, and in new fiction of the 1930s he drew increasingly, as well, on his own prior writing, trying out as in so much of his work the limits of literary originality. As Richard Poirier has asserted in his study of Emersonian influences on modern writing,

> A literary text, any text, generates itself, word by word, only by compliance with or resistance to forms of language already available to it. The impulse to resist, or at least to modify, is necessarily stronger than is the impulse to comply, but the two factors coexist in a sort of pleasurable agitation which often evokes the image of sexual intercourse. Emerson refers to the "oestrum of speech," to "spermatic, prophesying man-making words," to thought being "ejaculated as Logos or Word." [16]

Sexuality provided Faulkner a metaphor in his famous description of the "ecstasy" of writing *The Sound and the Fury*"; [17] it likewise is his metaphor for the struggle to engender original meaning in his fictional world, as in Addie Bundren's attempt through Whitfield "to shape and coerce the terrible blood to the forlorn echo of the dead word high in the air" (AILD, 175). The forms of language most immediately available to him as he wrote were those he had created himself, and it is for that reason that there are so many virtual quotations, paraphrases, and internal allusions from book to book. In conception and execution his work was cumulative, the greatest of it both progressive and collective. As Yoknapatawpha became both a place and a way to tell stories, recurrence verified lines of development that revision redirected. He seldom repeated himself.

Yet he necessarily saw writing not only as an ecstatic performance but as a nearly physical struggle for originality. Darl Bundren says as much in another sexual context in *As I Lay Dying* when he gives clear expression to Cash's "fumbling" description of Jewel's nightprowling. "When something is new and hard and bright, there ought to be something a little better for it than just being safe, since the safe things are just the things that folks have been doing so long they have worn the edges off and there's nothing to the doing of them that leaves a man to say, That was not done before and it cannot be done again" (AILD, 132). At such moments Faulkner conceived of language much as Poirier says Emerson conceived it, "Language not as a transparency but as an obstruction, language not as inherently mobile but as static and resistant, unless made momentarily otherwise. . . . The necessity that one must *struggle* with language in the effort to appropriate its otherwise hidden powers." [18]

Contention of this sort also is inherent in the complementary relation of artistic sovereignty and subjection, and it complicates Faulkner's work precisely because of the matter of precedence. Because each novel in combination with the preceding ones exerts a visible force on the next, the challenge to resist, to modify, to be "original" increases at each new stage of literary creation. This is clearly manifested in the experimentalist fictions of which *Absalom, Absalom!* is the crowning achievement and can be traced in the steady formal transformations of those books by what is modified and what retained. The four-part structure of *The Sound and the Fury*, for example, becomes openly Cubist in the fifty-nine chapters of *As I Lay Dying*, and implicitly Cubist juxtapositions thereafter order the counterposed third-person narratives of the revised *Sanctuary* and *Light in August*.[19] The originality of *Light in August*, however, lies not only in the extension of formal experiments but also in its introduction to the canon of the new subject matter of race, religion, and, especially, history. Historical representation was a particular challenge, which Faulkner addressed there by separate internal narratives: the six chapters (6–11) beginning "Memory believes before knowing remembers" (LIA, 119), in which Joe relives his life chronologically from his years in the orphanage to the present; the scene at the end of Chapter 11 in which Joanna Burden tells Joe her family history; and the long flashback that is Chapter 20 in which Hightower impressionistically recreates his past from the tales of his grandfather's slave woman and thereby confronts his present and future. *Light in August* was originally titled "Dark House," as was *Absalom, Absalom!* two years later (SLWF, 78), when Joanna Burden's dark house took the altered form of the dark house of history at Sutpen's Hundred.

Hollywood hack work and the new historical subject matter combined to temporarily close Faulkner's access to *Absalom, Absalom!*. In his experience of Hollywood to that time, movie-writing had meant mostly frustrating collaborations between screenwriters, actors, and directors to the end of producing outsized visual images of larger-than-life heroes and heroines for an audience in another sort of dark house. As he told Jean

Stein in 1955, "a moving picture is by its nature a collaboration and any collaboration is compromise" (Lion, 240).[20] He had used that sense of compromise in his treatment of journalism in *Pylon*,[21] which he set in an absolutely pastless present where no character has a history longer than a few years. His own past as an aspiring artist in New Orleans was both scene and subject of the novel, and he parodied his own love of linguistic performance there in the language excesses of the book.

The differences are instructive. In *As I Lay Dying*, to take one example, even the most subjective logic has metaphoric point. Darl proves his *is*-ness when he empties himself for sleep by reference to the empty coffin that "complete, . . . now slumbered lightly alive, waiting to come awake" (AILD, 80). At another juncture, Tull describes the coffin in unconscious puns that portray Addie's reason for dying (boredom) in the condition of her corpse (bored), Anse's self-pity (Bundren's burden), and Cora Tull's self-righteousness in bearing up to and facing her own burdens—all of this with kindly good nature.

> And the next morning they found [Vardaman] in his shirt tail, laying asleep on the floor like a felled steer, and the top of the box *bored* clean full of holes and Cash's new auger broke off in the last one. When they taken the lid off they found that two of them had *bored* on into her *face*.
>
> It's a judgment, it aint right. Because the Lord's got more to do than that. He's bound to have. Because the only *burden* Anse *Bundren*'s ever had is himself. And when folks talks him low, I think to myself he ain't that less of a man or he couldn't a *bore* himself this long.
>
> It aint right. I be durn if it is. Because He said Suffer the little children to come unto Me dont make it right, neither. Cora said, "I have *bore* you what the Lord God sent me. I *faced* it without fear nor terror because my faith was strong in the Lord, a-bolstering and sustaining me." (AILD, 73; my emphasis)

By contrast to such subtle and effective word play, the language of *Pylon* is sometimes static, derivative, characterized often by slangy word games and obscenities for their own sake.[22] Newsboys with Brooklyn accents out of Moviescenes newsreels cry, "Boinum boins" and "Laughing Boy in fit at Woishndon Poik" (Pylon, 53, 55). Jiggs transforms the Reporter's "Tiered identical cubicles of one thousand rented sleepings" (Pylon, 56) into a caustic dirty joke—"Teared Q pickles. Yair; teared Q pickles of one thousand rented cunts if you got the jack too. I got the Q pickle all right.

I got enough Q picklefor one thousand. And if I just had the jack too I wouldn't be teared" (Pylon, 56). The Reporter puts the vulgar situation of the Hotel Terrebonne into the same vulgar language, when he describes the Roger-Laverne-Jack triad—"'Yair,' he thought, 'teared Q pickles of one thousand cuntless nights. They will have to hurry before anybody can go to bed with her'" (Pylon, 61). The point is not only that the language is offensive, although Smith and Haas clearly knew it would be and edited it accordingly; it is almost pointlessly so. There are sexual forces enough in Faulkner's fiction prior to his work as a screenwriter, but none so explicit.

After *Pylon* Faulkner came to see collaboration as a potential resource of narrative rather than as a barrier. As a form of collaborative storytelling, cinema writing might complement his familiar southern tradition of "old tales and talking" (AA!, 243) and extend his experiments with multiple narration. He was finding ways to manage a form of expression that had resisted him earlier, and he returned to *Absalom, Absalom!* with a larger sense of how fictional history might be written and historical figures represented. Cinema proved a complement, as well, to his experience of still photography.

In *Pylon* there are numbers of news photographers but no photographs. *Absalom, Absalom!*, conversely, is photographic in a number of ways [23] and specifically cinematic in some of its consequent effects, as in the closing pages of Chapter 8. Still photography is a mode of characterization in the novel, as when Mr. Compson imagines Bon's initiating Henry to New Orleans as a photographic process, and of historical representation, as in the portrait of the Sutpens that emerges from Rosa's telling, arranged for Quentin "into the conventional family group of the period, with formal and lifeless decorum" (AA!, 9). Although Mr. Compson imagines the Sutpens as possessing "a sort of lifeless and perennial bloom like painted portraits hung in a vacuum" (AA!, 59), his obsession with a larger-than-life past moves him to represent history by a more dynamic metaphor. Father, brother, sister, and lover emerge from his reconstruction of history in Chapter 3 like actors enlarged upon a screen, "in this shadowy attenuation of time possessing now heroic proportions, performing their acts of simple passion and simple violence, impervious to time and inexplicable" (AA!, 80). Here and elsewhere in the novel, the word "shadowy" is specifically evocative of cinematic images. [24] In the final pages of Chapter 9, the dormitory window in the growing dawn becomes for Quentin a kind of screen on which is projected the as yet unread page of his father's letter:

"he could not tell if it was the actual window or the window's pale rec-
tangle upon his eyelids, though after a moment it began to emerge." What
emerges from the letter here, as at the outset of Chapter 6, is not only the
writing on "the once folded sheet" but the pictured scene of its writing,
"out of Mississippi attenuated" (AA!, 301), which, of course, is the very
scene of the history Quentin and Shreve have been collaboratively nar-
rating. This seems a distinctly cinematic use of photography and letters,
a means by which history moves again because it is life, and it is differentiated in the novel from still photography that documents a historical
moment, often ambiguously. Examples are the imaginary Sutpen family
portraits and, perhaps especially, Judith's photograph of Charles Bon, "A
picture seen by stealth" that validates Rosa's dream image of a man she
never saw: "even before I saw the photograph," she says, "I could have
recognised, nay, described, the very face" (AA!, 118).[25]

Faulkner's sense of authorial sovereignty when he returned to *Absalom, Absalom!* on March 30, 1935, is apparent in one other form of collaborative historical telling, this openly self-reflexive. The short story
"Wash" is retold twice in *Absalom, Absalom!*. It was written in the summer or autumn of 1933 and appeared in *Harper's* in February of 1934 and
again in *Doctor Martino and Other Stories* in April, by which time Faulkner was at work on the Sutpen material that this story and some others
were beginning to unlock.[26] In late 1935 "Wash" was incorporated into
Absalom, Absalom!. In Chapter 6 Faulkner abandoned the tightly closed
form of the published story in order to integrate the new subject matter
into Sutpen history and address imperatives of the novel, chief among
them Wash and Milly's place in Sutpen's design. Spurred by his father's
letter announcing the death of Rosa Coldfield and by Shreve's urging that
he *"Tell about the South"* (AA!, 142), Quentin gathers the strands together, recalling to himself Sutpen's return from the war, his seduction of
Milly, his murder by Wash, and the manner of Judith's life at Sutpen's Hundred thereafter. Like Faulkner, he is reflecting on stories that he knows
and considering to himself the ways in which they might fit his tale.

Near the end of Chapter 7, when he breaks in on Shreve's "playing"
with these facts, he focuses his previous reflections. Recounting the story
of Wash Jones that he heard from his father, he selects and arranges his
material to give it expressive historical form in the new context. If that
form is not precisely the same as the closed form of "Wash" (given the demands of the now much expanded subject matter), the story that Quentin
tells Shreve and attributes to his father in Chapter 7 still is essentially the

same as that published two years before the novel by William Faulkner, and the process by which Quentin shapes it is analogous to that by which his own creator and spiritual father crafted the novel. This is not to say that Quentin *is* William Faulkner, or even his spokesman. He is, however, a reflexive emblem of the artist, his maker—the fictional teller and reteller of Faulkner's own fictions who shapes his tale from "the rag-tag and bob-ends of old tales and talking" (AA!, 243)—including Faulkner's old tales.

Faulkner's oblique self-presentation in Chapters 6 and 7 of *Absalom, Absalom!* was part of a different kind of performance in the years 1934–1936 that was more extended and still more self-involved. This was the physically and imaginatively demanding act of writing two novels quickly in succession in a little over a year. Faulkner wrote *Pylon* in November and December 1934 without substantial revision. He sent Hal Smith consecutive chapters from November 11 to December 15 (SLWF, 86–87), he read galleys in January, and the book was published on March 25, 1935. He returned to full-time work on *Absalom, Absalom!* right away and that writing also went well, the chapters coming in regular succession in June, July, August, and October.[27] Even the most serious personal interruptions did not slow or stop him. In October Estelle filed for divorce in Los Angeles County Court on grounds of desertion, on November 10 Dean died in an airplane crash, and late that year Faulkner began a liaison with Meta Carpenter. Yet he was able to write chapters 6–9 in December and January, much of it in Hollywood. The completed manuscript is dated January 31, 1936. In a matter of months he had turned again to Mississippi and to Quentin and his father who, with Rosa and Shreve, collaboratively recreate the Southern history in which their lives are implicated. "Quentin Compson, of the Sound & Fury, tells it, or ties it together," he had told Hal Smith; "he is the protagonist so that it is not complete apocrypha. I use him because it is just before he is to commit suicide because of his sister, and I use his bitterness which he has projected on the South in the form of hatred of it and its people to get more out of the story itself than a historical novel would be. To keep the hoop skirts and plug hats out, you might say" (SLWF, 79). Drawing in this way on his precedent work for a present conception, he reasserted artistic freedom then and authorial sovereignty over his fictional domain. He reaffirmed it that spring by adding to the manuscript a chronology and genealogy of the novel, and he drew a map of Yoknapatawpha County on which he declared himself "Sole Owner and Proprietor."[28]

ii. Paradox and Inconsistency

The process by which *Absalom, Absalom!* came into being was never so schematic as a genealogy, chronology, and map appended to the published novel might suggest. The book grew from a writing situation far from ordered or even very orderly, and the fictional world that resulted is considerably less than seamless. As with so much of Faulkner's work, the "rag-tag and bob-ends" (AA!, 243) of resources from which it came approximated not a filing case, as he later said, so much as a junk box or lumber room (FU, 116, 117). He conceived of his fiction as life fixed in another dimension where, by his art as by Shreve and Quentin's narration, "there might be paradox and inconsistency but nothing fault nor false" (AA!, 253). In a body of fiction given to speculation and uncertainties, inconsistency is as necessary as it is natural, and in *Absalom, Absalom!* it is not hard to find. There are anomalies of omission in the novel—Goodhue Coldfield's wife, who dies giving birth to Rosa in 1845, is nowhere present at her older daughter Ellen's wedding in 1838. There were errors of commission—factual contradictions in the published novel between the text Faulkner finished in January 1936, and the genealogy and chronology he appended to the novel later that spring.[29] And the map of Yoknapatawpha is in error—though it locates as yet unwritten or unpublished events from *The Hamlet* and *The Mansion*, it mistakenly places Tull's farm in *As I Lay Dying* on the opposite side of the Yoknapatawpha River from the Bundrens's farm. These inconsistencies Faulkner abided precisely because the work was fiction, alive, in motion, a domain of truths rather than Truth. Editorial errors were another matter.

His imperiousness is everywhere apparent in comments on the *Absalom, Absalom!* galleys, where he struggled not with his own language but the editor's inability to master its complications. Faulkner's attention to detail is indicated in marginal fuming about a mis-transcription early in Chapter 6: "this word 'thinking' is NOT italics. There is no period after it. Look at the mss."[30] Erroneous additions and clarifications of the text likewise trouble the galleys and he addressed them with increasing annoyance. The delicate sense of a passage later in Chapter 6 was disrupted by the editorial addition of the word "thinking" to the lines, "'Suffer the little children to come unto Me': and thinking what did He mean by that?" Faulkner canceled the addition and wrote, "My God, cant you leave it alone? See copy as I wrote it before I inherited this collaborator. It was the Bible that said 'Suffer the little children': not Gen. Compson."[31] In

Sutpen's account of going to the West Indies in Chapter 7, in the sentence beginning, "I had had some schooling during a part of one winter, enough to have learned something about them," an editor substituted "women" for the word "them." Faulkner wrote in the margin, "them. them. Jesus Christ, he means the West Indies, just like he told you 17 words before this. What in the name of God would this 14 year old boy [need] believe himself to need to know about women? and how in hell would he learn it in the 3rd grade? My God, man! Please see the *type written* script."[32] Even when the errors were humorous, he was not amused. Parenthetic inserts in Chapter 6 confused Ellen with Judith. The galley reads, *"who to know what moral restoration she (Ellen) might have contemplated"*; Faulkner canceled the parenthesis and wrote in the margin, "If you must have a 'come the dawn' here, do you object to the correct one? Judith!! JUDITH! JUDITH!!! Damn damn damn."[33] To the italicized portion of the phrase, *"Because there was love* Mr Compson said," an editor appended the words *"between Ellen and Bon,"* to which Faulkner responded, "Kindly delete, please. One reason is, Ellen was Judith's mother. At this time she has been dead about 20 years. Thanks for the tip, tho; I have now pierced my collaborator's disguise: it's Elinor Glyn."[34] A concluding gloss that sums up his attitude to such interference reads, "By transposing this parenthetic clause (see mss) you have broken the continuity between here and here [connecting lines]. If you want it this way, all right. I know what it means because I wrote it. I gave this mss in its original form to 11 people, some of whom took longer than 1 day to return it and none of whom found it confusing, which is more than can be said (based on the evidence of this editing) for who ever the hell it was that improved it."[35]

A gloss on another of the galleys serves as a reminder of the *immediacy* of much of Faulkner's work. Even in hard times, Estelle was often careless of money. In June 1936, having discovered that she had charged one thousand dollars worth of goods in Oxford and Memphis stores, Faulkner had placed ads in the Memphis *Commercial Appeal* and the Oxford *Eagle* stating that he no longer would be responsible for her debts.[36] He may have had her extravagant shopping in mind in Chapter 3 of *Absalom, Absalom!*, written the previous July, when he described Ellen Sutpen's shopping from her carriage "against her background of chatelaine to the largest, wife to the wealthiest, mother of the most fortunate" in Jefferson (AA!, 54). In these years following her marriage, Mr. Compson says there, Ellen "bloomed, as if Fate were crowding the normal Indian summer which should have bloomed gradually and faded gracefully through six or eight years, into three or four, either for compensation for what was to come or to clear the books, pay the check to which his wife, Nature, had signed his name" (AA!, 54). Like Fate, Faulkner had found himself overdrawn for similar reasons, and the financial embarrassment of the past June was brought back to him that mid-August by further editorial confusion at this point in the galleys. An editor proposed changing the terminal "his" to "her," making it Nature's rather than Fate's name on the check. Faulkner's gloss rejecting the change directly reflects his angry experience with Estelle two months previously: "His! His! didn't your wife ever sign your name to a check and buy a dress with it so the landlord or the grocer could call you a sonofabitch?"[37]

This, too, is a veiled self-presentation, the more remarkable for crossing into writing of this kind, where a marginal note influenced by one financial embarrassment glosses a passage from the novel based on others. Such immediacy is indicated in the fiction, often, by a novel's being set in the present time of its writing, or by its contemporaneous subject matter, or by both. The Ur-*Sanctuary* is set when it was written in the spring of 1929 and the marriage matter there directly derives from Estelle's imminent divorce and Faulkner's accordant anxiety. In *Pylon* a recent experience in New Orleans is shaped by the biographical subtext of Faulkner's life there in 1925–1926, on the cusp of his turn from poetry to fiction. Quentin's centrality to Faulkner's self-presentations is indicated by the closeness of his experience at Harvard in the fictional 1910 to Faulkner's at Yale in 1918, and it is reinforced by Faulkner's return to that intimate fictional time in *Absalom, Absalom!*.

If crises of the moment were distanced somewhat in what he simultaneously was writing, the fiction nonetheless retains a strong sense of the confusion and chaos inherent in things, moments, events coming into being in his life. For just that reason, there is a dimension of inverse causality to Faulkner's work. His characters typically are retrospective, contemplative, consumed to know the antecedent causes of events still in process and speculating on their consequent effects. As Player and then stage manager, he consistently sought means for the controlled expression of disruption, which he later defined as arresting the motion of life so that it might move again for the reader.[38] Self-presentation was such a means, and as he drew on previous work in the late 1930s and early 1940s he reprised modes of performance he had created in his work for a decade and more. What had worked he retained and developed; what did not work well the first time, he typically tinkered with before discarding.

The increased self-consciousness of this can be gauged in his return to

the sermon as a mode of performance in *Light in August*. The Rev. Shegog's theatrics in *The Sound and the Fury* are set in the collective consciousness of his audience, whose experience of faith is brought about by
their witnessing his transfiguration from monkey to circus performer to
the communal voice of the Word of God speaking in their hearts. The
Reverend Whitfield preaches his funeral sermon in *As I Lay Dying* only
to the women and family in the house. His text is not transcribed as is
Shegog's, but Tull makes the same distinction between Whitfield the man
and Whitfield as Word, here to suggest the frailty of the flesh and, by implication, the adulterer-minister's hypocrisy. "His voice is bigger than
him," Tull says. "It's like they are not the same. It's like he is one, and his
voice is one, swimming on two horses side by side across the ford and
coming into the house, the mud-splashed one and the one that never even
got wet, triumphant and sad" (AILD, 91). Whitfield himself says that God
"will accept the will for the deed, Who knew that when I framed the
words of my confession it was to Anse I spoke them, even though he was
not there" (AILD, 179). Unlike Shegog, whom Faulkner displays for the
congregation to hear and see, and Whitfield, who stands apart and secretly
outrages the Word he preaches, Hightower is represented as retrospectively recreating the scene of his heresy for his own contemplation. Looking back on that scene, he envisions himself in the pulpit self-consciously
watching himself in the moral mirror of his outraged auditors. The performative dimension of the sermon is explicit in the language of the central passage.

> He seems to watch himself among faces, always among, enclosed and
> surrounded by, faces, as though he watched himself in his own pulpit, from
> the rear of the church, or as though he were a fish in a bowl. And more than
> that: the faces seem to be mirrors in which he watches himself. He knows
> them all; he can read his doings in them. He seems to see reflected in them
> a figure antic as a showman, a little wild: a charlatan preaching worse than
> heresy, in utter disregard of that whose very stage he preempted, offering in-
> stead of the crucified shape of pity and love, a swaggering and unchastened
> bravo killed with a shotgun in a peaceful henhouse, in a temporary hiatus
> of his own avocation of killing. (LIA, 488)

Hightower's dreaming, his reverence for his grandfather, and details of
the grandfather's life as he knows it all connect the exiled minister to the
life circumstance of his creator, William Faulkner, the self-presenting

performer whose medium, like Hightower's, Shegog's, and Whitfield's, is words.

Still, Faulkner's and Hightower's words and visions are not God's but Faulkner's own. Like his defrocked character who leaves church with a hymn book before his face, Faulkner hid his own actual face in his books for his own contemplation. And revealed it there. Bound on his "wheel of thinking" (LIA, 488), Hightower presents himself to himself simultaneously as actor and audience of his performance, as both performer and judge. His self-recognitions are analytic. As he judges the charlatan showman he sees in the faces of the congregation, so is he judged damned by those people and by the ultimate Judge he now imagines the people seeing "behind him and looking down upon him, in his turn unaware, the final and supreme Face Itself, cold, terrible because of Its omniscient detachment" (LIA, 488–489). Moved to self-inquisition by his presentation of himself as heretic-performer, he confesses himself the usurper of both the pulpit and purposes of the Creator. Literally, now, the "*Gail Hightower D.D.*" of the little sign in his yard is "Done Damned in Jefferson" (LIA, 60, 61). And more. Faulkner extends his character's performance to an equally reflexive confrontation with his nature and his natural end as an isolated man of words. "[F]ramed by the study window like a stage" (LIA, 466) in the fading copper light of Chapter 20, Hightower comes to see his life as profoundly unlived, an imaginary "single instant of darkness in which a horse galloped and a gun crashed" (LIA, 491). The wheel of thought "turns with the slow implacability of a mediaeval torture instrument, beneath the wrenched and broken sockets of his spirit, his life" (LIA, 490–491), and Hightower confronts the fate of dreamer and writer alike: "I have not even been clay" (LIA, 491).[39]

Rosa Coldfield reaches a similar conclusion for the same reasons. The "poetess laureate" of Yoknapatawpha County, as Mr. Compson calls her in *Absalom, Absalom!* (AA!, 6), is specifically a writer whose diminutive size, infamous virginity, seclusion in her father's house, and one thousand or more odes to Southern soldiers recall Emily Dickinson's life and art. The passage in which she describes clinging to her dream as a patient clings to "the last thin unbearable ecstatic instant of agony in order to sharpen the savor of the pain's surcease" (AA!, 113) both quotes and very nearly summarizes Dickinson's Poem 125, which begins "For each ecstatic instant / We must an anguish pay."[40] And like Dickinson's, Rosa Coldfield's is a vicarious life, her watching a surrogate for living. She says of Sutpen and herself, "I had had all my life to watch him in, since apparently and for what reason Heaven has not seen fit to divulge, my life was destined to end on an afternoon in April forty-three years ago, since anyone who even had as little to call living as I had had up to that time would not call what I have had since, living" (AA!, 12). In one sense Faulkner appraised his own imaginative performances by figuratively watching aspects of himself as a man of words in characters such as Hightower and Rosa, distancing his own self-judgments by exaggerating theirs, and controlling their confusions by other, more abstract self-presentations—the Player in *Light in August* and the stage manager in *Absalom, Absalom!*.

This is not to say that writing was for him a lesser or diminished form of living as dreaming and watching are for them. Writing was a physical as well as an imaginative act, and language, in a definition Faulkner ascribed to General Compson, was a mode of communion, a "meagre and fragile thread . . . by which the little surface corners and edges of men's secret and solitary lives may be joined for an instant now and then" (AA!, 202). In Faulkner's art and life, the word and the flesh exist together in a mutually sustaining, though often tragically unbalanced relation, at once tormenting and ecstatic. In Hightower and Rosa, the predominant imagination may be gauged against the dissolution of their physical bodies, his large and foul and "shapeless, almost monstrous, with a soft and sedentary obesity" (LIA, 89), hers childlike with "the rank smell of female old flesh long embattled in virginity" (AA!, 4). Still, the flesh that fails them inspires their most human visions. Seeing himself as his grandfather, Hightower knows himself the "debaucher and murderer of my grandson's wife, since I could neither let my grandson live or die" (LIA, 491). Rosa says of herself that she knows neither leaf nor bloom of womanhood, "But root and urge I do insist and claim" (AA!, 115).

The unlived life of the watcher-dreamer-voyeur is as old in Faulkner as the self-tormenting marionette Pierrot on his stage and the stone-bound Marble Faun in his garden. The productive tensions between life and art for the artist who is fully a man are portrayed in *Mosquitoes* in the sculptor Gordon. Temporarily diverted by Pat Robyn's likeness to the torso he sculpts, he cries to himself,

fool fool you have work to do o cursed of god cursed and forgotten form shapes cunningly sweated cunning to simplicity shapes out of chaos more satisfactory than bread to the belly form by a madmans dream gat on the body of chaos le garçon vierge of the soul horned by utility o cuckold of derision. (MOS, 47)

The passage has a hard to phrase emotional logic of its own. As a man susceptible to the temptations of the world, the artist is "cursed of god." But Gordon's art is unique, in the world and the novel: he has a vision of the divine perfection that preceded the fall, and he struggles to recreate by the sweat of his brow that "cursed and forgotten form" visible to him now in the cunning perfection of the modern Eve, Pat Robyn. Beautiful objects like the bust in his studio are "shapes out of chaos," more gratifying to the exiled idealist ("le garçon vierge of the soul") than the bread he must earn by his labor. The bust is simpler, and safer because armless and legless, yet insufficiently alive: despite his vision of ideality, he is possessed like Adam of the carnal knowledge that makes him the "cuckold of his [own] derision."[41]

In the voluble mixed company of would-be artists, critics, and hangers-on who populate *Mosquitoes*, Gordon is the brooding, silent sovereign of his studio, only temporarily dispossessed of his domain by Mrs. Maurier. Despite, or because of, the contradictory impulses in him as a man and an artist, he *does* sculpt—as Robyn's brother with his mechanical pipe, for example, cannot; and in the end he *is* a lover—as Mr. Talliaferro is not. But if productive contradiction is his distinction it is also his curse. The paradox is affirmed at the end of *Mosquitoes* in an impressionistic scene where he offers his whore to the heavens as the body of love. Fairchild and the Semitic man watch him "(. . . lift a woman from the shadow and raise her against the mad stars, smothering her squeal against his tall kiss.) *Then voices and sounds, shadows and echoes change form swirling, becoming the headless, armless, legless torso of a girl, motionless and virginal and passionately eternal before the shadows and echoes whirl away*" (MOS, 339). In combination the gesture of human self-assertion and defiance and the ideal it evokes emphasize both the achievement of Gordon's art and his own splendid failure. The torso he shapes, after all, is form alone, an incomplete woman, headless, armless, legless, and radically not alive. Pat Robyn is its living but shallow image.

Talliaferro's failure, conversely, is a failure to live *or* to create; it lies in his inability to speak his love into being in *any* form. Jilted by voluptuous Jenny, he says of himself, "Surely a man would not be endowed with an impulse and yet be denied the ability to slake it. . . . But must I become an old man before I discover what it is? Old, old, an old man before I have lived at all" (MOS, 347). If Talliaferro is Prufrock, Fairchild is like the women of Eliot's poem who "come and go / Talking of Michelangelo."[42] He only talks about art, and despite the ironically "lusty pride of his Ohio valley masculinity," the one story he has published is in the *Dial*, "a home for old young ladies of either sex" (MOS, 209). That Anderson's *Dial* story was about Faulkner makes Fairchild all the more the direct forerunner of the Anderson figure in Faulkner's "Artist at Home" who only copies life. Fairchild only talks about art, and when he turns from Gordon to the tragicomic Talliaferro in *Mosquitoes*, he cries, "O Thou above the thunder and above the excursions and alarms, regard Your masterpiece! Balzac, chew thy bitter thumbs! And here I am, wasting my damn life trying to invent people by means of the written word!" (MOS, 345).

No one aboard the *Nausikaa* or in the night city of New Orleans has heard of the "little kind of black man" named Faulkner, an appreciative suitor unable to dance who describes himself to Jenny Steinbauer as "a liar by profession" (MOS, 144, 145). But Faulkner is present in his novel in his characters' performances as he was actually present on the boat trip Sherwood Anderson financed in March 1925—idealized in the self-sufficient Gordon, self-criticizing in Fairchild and Talliaferro, self-parodying in the "Faulkner" Jenny describes. She in turn takes her name from Gertrude Stegbauer, a woman Faulkner unsuccessfully courted in Charleston in 1925.[43] If the aesthetic theorizing in the novel disables artists like Fairchild and the poet Mark Frost, Faulkner himself put much of the theory into practice in his self-presentations. *They* are the true lies he tells. Fairchild's sense of the artist as double man is an especially pervasive motif in Faulkner's work where, as here, he regularly presents himself as both actor and audience, twinned as Fairchild also says, in a dimension where "fact and fallacy gain verisimilitude by being in cold print" (MOS, 251). It is a realm very like that Quentin and Shreve will create orally in *Absalom, Absalom!* when they "overpass to love" (AA!, 253). There is "a kind of voraciousness," Fairchild also says, "that makes an artist stand beside himself with a notebook in hand always, putting down all the charming things that ever happen to him, killing them for the sake of some problematical something he might or he might not ever use" (MOS, 320). In fact it is not Faulkner but Fairchild himself, and characters isolated from living like him, who "kill" life for the sake of a problematic something. Hightower recognizes this in himself at the end, and Mr. Compson ironically says of Rosa that by dying she has *"gained that place or bourne where the objects of the outrage and of the commiseration also are no longer ghosts but are actual people to be actual recipients of the hatred and the pity"* (AA!, 301–302).

iii. If I Forget Thee

However tenuous the balance, Gordon's wholeness is unique in *Mosquitoes* and in much of the fiction that follows. But the troubling incompleteness of characters there, and in *Soldiers' Pay* before it, shaped more complex character pairings in subsequent novels—Horace and Bayard in *Flags*, Quentin and Dalton Ames in *The Sound and the Fury*, Horace and Lee Goodwin in *Sanctuary*, Darl and Cash in *As I Lay Dying*. Representing the divisions between sensitivity and sensuality, isolation and community, words and deeds, each pair is constituted of aspects of a whole self. Clearly, by the time of *Mosquitoes*, Faulkner had recognized the tenuous balance of his own contradictory wholeness as a man of genius. He came to understand the definitive paradox of his simultaneous involvement in and estrangement from the cultural norms of his home place, and he presented his multiple sense of himself in such doubled and paired characters and their dilemmas. "I aint so sho that ere a man has the right to say what is crazy and what aint," Cash Bundren says late in *As I Lay Dying*. "It's like there's a fellow in every man that's done a-past the sanity or the insanity, that watches the sane and the insane doings of that man with the same horror and the same astonishment" (AILD, 238). The conception is close enough to Fairchild's sense of the artist as double man to have come from *Mosquitoes*, perhaps even from Anderson himself when Faulkner knew him in New Orleans in 1925. But the language of the passage is closer still to another book which it seems almost to quote.

In the chapter of *Walden* titled "Solitude," Henry David Thoreau conceives of himself alone at the pond as a divided entity in a nonetheless "wholesome" state of being. "With thinking," he says, "we may be beside ourselves in a sane sense," and in the extended theatrical metaphor that follows, he depicts himself as simultaneously participant in and spectator of his life, both actor and audience.

I only know myself as a human entity; the scene, so to speak, of thoughts and affections; and am sensible of a certain doubleness by which I can stand as remote from myself as from another. However intense my experience, I am conscious of the presence and criticism of a part of me, which, as it were, is not a part of me, but spectator, sharing no experience, but taking note of it; and that is no more I than it is you. When the play, it may be the tragedy, of life is over, the spectator goes his way. It was a kind of fiction, a

work of the imagination only, so far as he was concerned. This doubleness
may easily make us poor neighbors and friends sometimes.

   I find it wholesome to be alone a greater part of the time.[44]

Solitude, like self-consciousness, is the necessary condition of the artist,
be he sculptor or writer, and in Thoreau's case it leads to self-discovery
and underlies the essential "first person" narrative that he characterizes
as a writer's "simple and sincere account of his own life, and not merely
what he has heard of other men's lives."[45] Thoreau is himself a canny "ac-
countant": his demanding motto is "Explore thyself," wherein "are demanded the eye and the nerve."[46] For Faulkner's characters the domain of
the self is a more dangerous and often a more tragic scene of life than for
Thoreau. The destructively un-*whole*-some example in *As I Lay Dying*
is Darl Bundren's splitting into two entities, "our brother Darl" and a
spectator-Darl called "I" who records his insane doings and his eventual
end "in a cage in Jackson where, his grimed hands lying light in the quiet
interstices, looking out he foams" (AILD, 254). Cash says of him, "This
world is not his world; this life his life" (AILD, 261).

   Faulkner mentioned Thoreau only once, and in passing, in the class
conferences at Virginia in 1957–1958 and not at all in published interviews and letters. The copy of *Walden* in his personal library is dated
1946, but he could easily have known and used the book much earlier,[47]
perhaps even as early as *Mosquitoes* where Fairchild's writer standing beside himself with a notebook echoes Thoreau's figuratively note-taking
spectator. Heavily allusive to begin with—*The Odyssey* supplies the
title; Addie, Whitfield, and Jewel are modeled on Hawthorne's Hester
Prynne, Arthur Dimmesdale, and Pearl—*As I Lay Dying* appears to draw
on *Walden* in other ways, as well. Cash Bundren is aptly described at the
point in Chapter 1, "Economy," where Thoreau writes that "'carpenter'
is but another name for 'coffin-maker'";[48] the coffin Cash builds and Var-
daman bores with auger holes recalls a related passage from "Economy"
where a railroad toolbox "six feet long by three wide" suggests to Thoreau
"that every man who was hard pushed might get such a one for a dollar,
and, having bored a few auger holes in it, to admit the air at least, get into
it when it rained and at night, and hook down the lid, and so have freedom in his love, and in his soul be free."[49] To this complex of allusions in
As I Lay Dying there might be added the "$28 12 1/2" cents Thoreau says
he spent on his house.[50] By Cash's account he fell from the church
"twenty-eight foot, four and a half inches, about" (AILD, 90), the "about"

explaining the inch/cent difference: twenty-eight feet twelve and a half *inches* would make *twenty-nine* feet one half inch. If the parallel seems extravagant, it is no less so—and no less functional—than the many such parallels that develop in *Walden* from Thoreau's allusions to his own wide reading. Walden Pond, like Yoknapatawpha County, is a place and a way to tell stories, and in the matter of self-presentation Thoreau concludes, "I fear chiefly lest my expression may not be *extravagant* enough, may not wander far enough beyond the narrow limits of my daily experience, so as to be adequate to the truth of which I have been convinced. *Extra vagance*! It depends on how you are yarded."[51]

Other echoes of Thoreau are in the Edenic interlude in *If I Forget Thee, Jerusalem*, where Harry Wilbourne and Charlotte Rittenmeyer retreat from Chicago to a temporary life in the woods. The loon that comes to the pond in the fall with "his wild laughter" in Thoreau's Chapter 12, "Brute Neighbors,"[52] is a probable source of the loon in the Wisconsin lake in Faulkner's Chapter 5, where Harry knows from its "raucous idiot voice" exactly what it is and will look like, not by natural observation, like Thoreau, but because he is a modern man who "believes only what [he] reads" (*Jerusalem*, 90). Like the unnamed "first person" of "Economy,"[53] Harry too is an Adam (*Jerusalem*, 93) and he too keeps meticulous accounts of his food stores and money. As Thoreau says in "Economy," "It would be some advantage to live a primitive and frontier life, though in the midst of an outward civilization, if only to learn what are the gross necessaries of life and what methods have been taken to obtain them."[54] Harry would agree. Reading *Walden* himself, as Harry may have, Faulkner would also have been drawn to Thoreau's own allusiveness, which ranges widely across his reading, and to strategies of self-presentation and performance that reveal while concealing him as the unnamed I-Eye of the book and pond called Walden. As Thoreau puts it, and as Faulkner well knew, "We commonly do not remember that it is, after all, always the first person that is speaking. I should not talk so much about myself if there were anybody else whom I knew as well."[55]

However well he knew *Walden*, and he seems to have known the book well, Faulkner certainly knew the nineteenth-century American literary conventions of the doubled artist and of veiled self-expression that Thoreau adapts to his own uses. Chief among the writers he read regularly and admired was Melville, who was struggling with similar problems of revelation and concealment in *Moby-Dick* in 1850 when he wrote, in his review of Hawthorne's *Mosses from an Old Manse*, that the artist is always and inevitably in his work.

No man can read a fine author, and relish him to his very bones, while he reads, without subsequently fancying to himself some ideal image of the man and his mind. And if you rightly look for it, you will almost always find that the author himself has somewhere furnished you with his own picture.—For poets (whether in prose or verse), being painters of Nature, are like their brethren of the pencil, the true portrait-painters, who, in the multitude of likenesses to be sketched, do not invariably omit their own; and in all high instances, they paint them without any vanity, though, at times, with a lurking something, that would take several pages to properly define.[56]

Hawthorne was himself much concerned not to reveal that "lurking something" in *The Scarlet Letter*, which novel Melville also knew as he knew Hawthorne, too, that summer of 1850. In "The Custom House," Hawthorne had written that some authors "indulge themselves in such confidential depths of revelation as could fittingly be addressed, only and exclusively, to the one heart and mind of perfect sympathy; as if the printed book, thrown at large on the wide world, were certain to find out the divided segment of the writer's own nature, and complete his circle of existence by bringing him into communion with it." Asserting that "It is scarcely decorous . . . to speak all, even where we speak impersonally," Hawthorne concluded that the writer must "keep the inmost Me behind its veil. To this extent and within these limits, an author, methinks, may be autobiographical, without violating either the reader's rights or his own."[57]

With the passage from *Walden*, Hawthorne's essay and Melville's review theorize the core of a convention of self-presentation that Faulkner would have found realized in much imaginative writing of the nineteenth century, not least in *Walden* itself. And in Whitman, who in "Song of Myself" declared himself participant and spectator, "Both in and out of the game."[58] Writing, as so often, from immediate circumstances, Faulkner often was less concerned than Hawthorne with others' rights and sensibilities—notably Anderson's and the others he parodied in *Mosquitoes* and Estelle's in the marriage novels—than he was with concealing as he drew upon and performed the "inmost Me." A case in point is *If I Forget Thee, Jerusalem* which was written, as he later would tell yet another lover, to overcome the heartbreak of his affair with Meta Carpenter (SLWF, 338). As personal as the Ur-*Sanctuary*, the immediacy of *If I Forget Thee, Jerusalem* is retrospective and reflective rather than anticipatory. Like *Pylon*, the book is palimpsestic in the way that it portrays immediate imperatives with one lover from prior personal experiences with another in the New Orleans of 1925, in this case Helen Baird. Balancing all of this in his most contrapuntal novel, the stage manager-novelist turned in his self-presentations to still more open and self-conscious modes of expression. Like Whitman in one late poem, he might almost be said there to advance "From behind the screen where I hid" to declare, "Camerado, this is no book / Who touches this touches a man."[59]

The scriptural title *If I Forget Thee, Jerusalem*, restored in the 1995 Corrected Edition, asserts immediately what the editor's substitute title *The Wild Palms* does not—that the book is founded in and on memory. Faulkner's love affair with Meta Carpenter, on which the novel is largely based, began in Hollywood in December–January 1935–1936 and extended into April 1937 when Meta married Wolfgang Rebner.[60] When Faulkner was periodically away in the winter and spring of 1936, he wrote Meta regularly, and he saw her regularly in Hollywood, even when Estelle and Jill were with him there from July 1936 through May 1937. In August 1936, he arranged for Ben Wasson to bring Meta to dinner at his and Estelle's home as his date.[61] When Meta accepted Rebner's marriage proposal in December, Faulkner continued to write her. A letter dated February 27, 1937, six weeks before her marriage, was written from Beverley Hills to Meta at her cottage on Sunset Strip. It contains a two-page cartoon strip of Meta and Faulkner spending their day together and ending in bed.[62] Sometime that spring or summer, Faulkner wrote a six-page holograph story entitled "Wild Palms" about a doctor on the Gulf Coast of Mississippi who rents his guest house to an unmarried couple. He typed the manuscript, then apparently decided to expand the story, which he began doing in a holograph manuscript dated September 15, 1937.[63]

That fall he set aside his "Wild Palms" manuscript and sometime after mid-October, as his Memphis pilot's log shows,[64] he went to New York to settle with Random House about *The Unvanquished*. Three things occurred there of special significance to *If I Forget Thee, Jerusalem*: he met Sherwood Anderson for the first time in over a decade and began to renew his friendship with him; he saw Meta and Wolfgang Rebner, just back from Europe, and confessed his grief to her in words he would give Harry Wilbourne in the novel, "Between grief and nothing I will take grief"; and he drank so excessively that he badly burned his back.[65] By November 16 he was flying his plane again in Memphis, and he returned to his novel. Chapter 4 of the holograph manuscript is dated February 13, 1938. Random House received the complete typescript in June.

Richard Gray traces Faulkner's dilemma while writing *If I Forget Thee, Jerusalem* to his situation at this time as both husband to Estelle and grieving lover to Meta Carpenter, and characterizes the conflicts in the book as being between love and responsibility, erotic experience and suffering, the isolation of the lover and the larger world. Gray speaks of Faulkner's "writing out, and out of, his agony." [66] For the novelist who had characterized himself as Player and stage manager, the opening chapter that developed from the original short story provided a means of both standing beside himself and presenting what he saw. In Chapter 1, the first "Wild Palms," Faulkner drew on memories of the Gulf Coast from the times he was there with Helen Baird in 1925 and with Estelle on their honeymoon in 1929; he cast the situation and events of the chapter in a symbolic setting that represented his own doubleness; and he created characters through which he could present his loss of Meta from the perspective of his present married life with Estelle. The unnamed doctor is the center of consciousness in Chapter 1, the "Complete Householder" that Harry says later in the novel he fears to become (Jerusalem, 113); from the doctor's perspective, Harry has proved himself *"on the body of love and of passion and of life"* (Jerusalem, 15) as the doctor never has and never will do. The two are paired by the ironic similarities between them: their paired houses with the veil-like oleander hedge between them "house" contradictory modes of living, the respectable in the doctor's tight tongue-and-groove house where he lives with his "gorgonlike" wife Martha (Jerusalem, 13), and the illicit in the ship-lap "shack" (Jerusalem, 15) where Charlotte hemorrhages and dies. The doctor owns both, as William Faulkner at this time had "owned" both lifestyles. Writing in this opening chapter from the house of respectability—literally Rowan Oak in late 1937 and 1938—the novelist was writing of love and loss from behind a Hawthornian veil of his own, concealing as he simultaneously sought to express his inmost grief. Like the envious, unhappy doctor he was "groping just without the veil and even touching but not quite, almost seeing but not quite, the shape of truth" (Jerusalem, 11). By answering Harry's midnight knocking and entering the house of love, the doctor expects to come "nearer the veil at the instant when it would part and reveal in inviolable isolation that truth which he almost touched" (Jerusalem, 12). For Faulkner, that intimate truth was lodged in immediate and past experience that lurked nearer the surface of this novel than any other.

Faulkner wrote the first chapter of the "Wild Palms" narrative as the doctor's story of discovery and moral outrage, and the last as the story of

Harry's choosing bereavement over death. Childless and unmanned by his wife, the doctor is a secret voyeur watching Charlotte from a "fattish unshaven mask" that veils the shrewd, analytic "doctor within the Doctor" (Jerusalem, 9); Harry is a doctor who aborted his child for love and lost all but memory in the bargain. The counterpointed first and last chapters of "The Wild Palms" narrative bring together a tangle of issues in Faulkner's life from a decade and more. Manhood is at issue with fatherhood here, as it is in the pairing of Horace and Lee Goodwin in *Sanctuary* and the Reporter and Roger Shumann in *Pylon*, the other New Orleans novel of the 1930s. In their reactions to Charlotte's death by abortion, the doctor and Harry represent the two sides of Faulkner's response to his broken relationship with Meta. Faulkner told Meta that he and Estelle had had no sexual relationship since Jill's birth and she believed he had refound his manhood with her; but he also told her that what he most feared about leaving Estelle was losing his only child.[67] Almost certainly memories of marriage matters entered this mix. The pain of Estelle's marrying Cornell Franklin in 1918 and Helen Baird's marrying Guy Lyman in 1926 was repeated now in Meta's marrying Rebner as one love affair evoked another.[68] Charlotte Rittenmeyer is exactly described in an undated letter to Helen where Faulkner remembered her as "a sullen-jawed yellow-eyed belligerant humorless gal in a linen dress and sunburned bare legs sitting on Spratling's balcony,"[69] and Harry, like the Reporter in *Pylon*, is just twenty-seven, the age Faulkner was when he courted Helen in New Orleans and at her family's summer home at Pascagoula. If Faulkner, like Harry, no longer had his lover in 1938, he found himself as bereft in his barren home as the doctor, with a wife who, if no Gorgon, had turned him figuratively to stone. The child Harry aborts in Chapter 7, and the fatherless child born in Chapter 8 on an island in Old Man River likewise raise the question in *If I Forget Thee, Jerusalem* that moves *Pylon*, "Who's your old man?"

The contrasting lives of the doctor and Harry are handled with considerable skill in the first and final chapters of the "Wild Palms" narrative, yet it is questionable whether Faulkner felt himself the authorial sovereign of his fictional cosmos at this time. As late as July 1938, when he and Robert Haas were debating some of the language and the title of the manuscript, he expressed doubts about the quality of the book. Writing it he was again a prisoner—of grief for his lost love, and of social proprieties he had characterized in *Absalom, Absalom!* as "devious intricate channels of decorous ordering" (AA!, 112). Still, and however ironic, there was a modicum of safety in imprisoning conventions, as the tall convict knows. Once Faulkner could say with Melville's Captain Ahab, "Who's over me?"; now he lived in a world that demanded to be governed by appearances. The shape of truth that the doctor senses behind the veil in *If I Forget Thee, Jerusalem* is rooted in as it seems phrased from Ahab's sense of the universal masking behind which "some unknown but still reasoning thing puts forth the mouldings of its features from behind the unreasoning mask."[70]

Faulkner's love affair with Meta had put forth such mouldings in his marriage during the months Estelle and Jill were with him in Hollywood, and it does the same in the novel he based on that affair. The dinner party to which Faulkner invited Ben Wasson and Meta is an example. Meta came to see it as a "punitive act against his wife" which Faulkner had staged to compare his two women.[71] It was equally a brazen performance, one that he reproduced in *If I Forget Thee, Jerusalem* where Charlotte stages a dinner for Harry with her husband, displaying her new lover to Rittenmeyer in the nominally veiling confines of their "modest though comfortable apartment in an irreproachable neighborhood near Audobon Park" (Jerusalem, 36). The transparency of Faulkner's similar performance in Hollywood, indicated by Estelle's so easily seeing through it, is evidence of his similar need to reveal his other life to his wife while outwardly subscribing to the conventions of marriage. That Faulkner's life and art then occupied the same stage and seemed to him nearly interchangeable is suggested in a scene where Harry tries to read and discovers that his and Charlotte's life together is *exactly backward. It should be the books, the people in the books inventing and reading about us—the Does and Roes and Wilbournes and Smiths—males and females but without the pricks or cunts"* (Jerusalem, 44–45). The language of *If I Forget Thee, Jerusalem* in this circumstance does just that, reinventing and "reading" Faulkner and Meta in the same language he used in erotic letters to her, where he described her as "my April and May cunt."[72]

As in past performances, Faulkner also showed forth features of his life in *If I Forget Thee, Jerusalem* by masking allusions. He had drawn on Shakespeare in *Absalom, Absalom!* to portray Rosa's literary sensibility, giving her both Miranda's wonder at the brave new world that has such people in it as Charles Bon[73] and Caliban's despair at losing the world he glimpses in Trinculo and Stephano. Caliban's "I cried to dream again"[74] is echoed in Rosa's *"Why did I wake, since waking I shall never sleep again!"* (AA!, 115). As the Prospero-like stage manager and sovereign of the novel, Faulkner extended her knowledge of Shakespeare to the equally famous stabbing scene from *Hamlet,* having her describe living as *"one constant and perpetual instant when the arras-veil before what-is-to-be hangs docile and even glad to the lightest naked thrust if we had dared, were brave enough (not wise enough: no wisdom needed here) to make the rending gash"* (AA!, 114). Ahab's long speech in *Moby-Dick* about the masked universe is recalled here, as well, and the two in combination carried from *Absalom, Absalom!* into Chapter 1 of *If I Forget Thee, Jerusalem.* Ahab's determination to "strike through the mask!"[75] and Hamlet's stabbing "a rat" through the arras curtain in his mother's closet[76] are the dual sources of Faulkner's portrayal of the doctor's midnight resolution to rend the veil behind which the truth of Charlotte's trouble lies. Harry, too, of course, has made a "naked thrust," in Rosa's metaphor, through the arras veil that guards Charlotte's womb, and with tragic results. His knocking at the beginning of Chapter 1 and Charlotte's "Oh damn bloody bloody" at the end (Jerusalem, 18) summon *Macbeth,*[77] another tale of knives and a slain baby and the Shakespearean play Faulkner most often quoted in his fiction. The final words of Chapter 1, Harry's "You can come in now" (Jerusalem, 19), invite doctor and reader alike behind the "screen" (Jerusalem, 5), *"barricade"* (Jerusalem, 14), and "veil" (Jerusalem, 6, 10, 11, 12, 14) of marital (and medical) impropriety, where *Hamlet* is again recalled in the overheard fantasy conversation Charlotte carries on with her husband, Rat Rittenmeyer—"it was 'rat,' the noun, which the doctor believed he heard" (Jerusalem, 17).

In Faulkner as in Shakespeare and Melville, reaching through illusion toward "truth" brings tragic knowledge and tragic results. Faulkner may have foreseen such an outcome for himself in the fall of 1937 when he began and then stopped work on *If I Forget Thee, Jerusalem,* for like the Ur-*Sanctuary,* the book he was setting on the Gulf Coast was very close to home. Eighteen months earlier, before returning to Hollywood and Meta in February 1936, he had visited Helen Baird Lyman and her husband Guy at Picayune, Mississippi,[78] his memories of her then providing him both the immediate setting of his "Wild Palms" story and, in the novel, a model for Charlotte and her husband. Now his reunion with Sherwood Anderson in New York prompted more memories of New Orleans in 1925–1926,[79] and his meeting Meta and Wolfgang Rebner there intensified the distress of his most recent loss. There too, and in conjunction with these two events and his heavy drinking, he scarred his back badly on a hotel radiator. Helen Baird had a similar burn scar, as does Charlotte in the novel. Faulkner's injury related him in yet another way, and now after the fact, both to Sutpen, who looks "like a man who had been through some solitary furnace experience" (AA!, 24), and to the source of that conception in fire-scarred Ahab, who looks "like a man cut away from the stake, when the fire has overrunningly wasted all the limbs without consuming them."[80] Scarred literally now like Melville's sovereign hero and his own fictional one, the authorial sovereign who had declared with his character, "*Be Sutpen's Hundred* like the oldentime *Be Light*" (AA!, 4), bent himself to reprising his love and loss in his memory novel *If I Forget Thee, Jerusalem*.

From New Orleans memories, in addition to Helen, he drew on his University of Mississippi fraternity brother Dr. Russell Pigford, a medical intern there in 1925–1926, who had gone to Tulane Medical School and on to an internship at Touro Infirmary.[81] From his California experience he took the Gulf Coast hospital with its "vaguely Spanish (or Los Angeles)" stucco (Jerusalem, 248) and Harry's impression of "the little lost towns" of the West with their "broad strong Western girls got up out of Hollywood magazines . . . to resemble Joan Crawford" (Jerusalem, 176). Joan Crawford played the female lead that Faulkner wrote into *Today We Live*, the film Howard Hawks made from the story "Turn About." In addition to extensive and well-documented borrowings in the novel from Anderson and Hemingway,[82] the subject matter and even the language of Harry's pulp magazine stories may have been inspired by another Hollywood writer, Nathaniel West, whom Faulkner met there in the spring of 1936, and by the confessional letters in his 1933 novel *Miss Lonelyhearts*.[83] What Harry says of his Chicago stories—"after I started writing them I learned that I had no idea of the depths of depravity of which the human invention is capable" (Jerusalem, 112)—Miss Lonelyhearts learns from his New York correspondents. Faulkner also may have drawn on West's book for the idyll in Wisconsin, from the chapter titled "Miss Lonelyhearts in the Country." Miss Lonelyhearts and Betty's several days away from the city on a Connecticut farm are a postlapsarian version of Harry and Charlotte's stay at McCord's camp: the farm has a pond with a loon, Betty like Charlotte wears no clothes, and she loses her virginity there as Harry says he does figuratively. In Wisconsin, as he later tells McCord, he begins to understand that since meeting Charlotte in New Orleans he has been "in eclipse," outside of "the current of time that runs through remembering" (Jerusalem, 116). He blames his condition on "solitude" (Jerusalem, 116), the title of the chapter in *Walden* from which some material of the Wisconsin episode is taken, but in Harry's sense of himself, unlike Thoreau's, the six weeks stay by the lake is a time of one constant ejaculation. The loss of virginity that "would have been two seconds at fourteen or fifteen," he explains to McCord, "was eight months at twenty-seven" (Jerusalem, 118). Immediately behind the multiple literary sources of this self-presentation is Faulkner's 1936 idyll with Meta in March, April, and May before Estelle and Jill joined him in California. The description of Charlotte as "a little solider than the Hollywood magazine cod liver oil advertisements" (Jerusalem, 93) evokes that time and place, and details such as Harry's kissing Charlotte's "sun-impacted flank as she stopped beside the cot, tasting the impacted sun" (Jerusalem, 94) seem to derive more from memories of weekends at the Miramar Hotel on the beach at Santa Monica than from an imagined late fall in Wisconsin.

Chicago, the Wisconsin lake hideaway, and the Utah mines in *If I Forget Thee, Jerusalem* necessarily were invented places. Faulkner had been to none of the three, although he might have seen them on stage sets on the Universal Studio lot or read of them. He had used Utah in the 1930 story "Idyll in the Desert," but there are no identifying place names or geographical details for that setting in the story or for Utah or Chicago or Wisconsin in the novel. There are for New Orleans and for the river journey. The "Old Man" chapters include the names Vicksburg, Baton Rouge, Atchafalaya, Carnarvon, and Carrollton, and the convict's voyage to New Orleans follows the course of the flooded river through the Sunflower-Yazoo delta, maps of which, drawn in his hand, Faulkner stored in a box with his typescript.[84] The several scenes in the novel where art interrupts love-making, conversely, are self-presentations of more immediate and personal experience. Meta notes that "His own work was my rival" and describes Faulkner's leaving her earlier at night when he was writing, sometimes going straight from her bed to his work table.[85] Just so, in Chicago, Charlotte works far into the night on her puppet figures while Harry sleeps; later she sleeps during the day while he writes. There is special point to the fact that neither produces what Faulkner would have called art. Neither is a Gordon, with whom they temporarily share the New Orleans milieu from which all three derive.

What Harry discovers at the end of the "Wild Palms" narrative Faulkner may be said to have discovered in writing the book, that "there was just memory, forever and inescapable, so long as there was flesh to titillate. And now he was about to get it, think it into words" (Jerusalem, 272). What Harry is about to get is what Meta remembered Faulkner putting into words to her in New York, the understanding that "*if memory exists outside of the flesh it wont be memory because it wont know what it*

remembers so when she became not then half of memory became not
and if I become not then all of remembering will cease to be.—Yes he
thought *Between grief and nothing I will take grief"* (Jerusalem, 273).
This was the climax of his theorizing in *Light in August*, where "Memory believes before knowing remembers" (LIA, 119) and in *Absalom, Absalom!*, where Rosa declares, "That is the substance of remembering—
sense, sight, smell: the muscles with which we see and hear and feel"
(AA!, 115). And it was deeply, intimately personal. Faulkner called it "the
theme of the whole book" (SLWF, 106). That Harry is masturbating while
he thinks this seems clear from Faulkner's emphasis on the clashing
palms (Jerusalem, 264–265) and the repeated statement that his emerging
idea will "stand still to his hand" (Jerusalem, 266, 272). Venus here is not
the soiled man Harry earlier imagined, masturbating "in a subway lava-
tory with a palm full of French post-cards" (Jerusalem, 115), but instead
the "bright star" in the west that stands over Harry at the end of the novel
and guides his memory of Charlotte. That Faulkner should phrase his and
Harry's commitment to memory of a beloved in these terms is consistent
with his and Meta's relationship from the beginning. Meta describes his
letters as affecting her "almost physically. . . . I would go to bed early,
sometimes without food, and think on Bill happily, as a novitiate on her
lord." He was similarly affected, describing a wet dream in one letter and
telling her he found it difficult to sleep at night: Meta writes that "Bowen
[their name for his phallus] was trying to take him over completely."[86]

Following his return from New York, the intimate memories on which
the novel is based stood to his own hand and he wrote steadily if not with
his accustomed swiftness through that winter and spring. In effect, memory freed him as it does the psalmist from whom the title of the novel is
taken.

> How shall we sing the Lord's song in a strange land?
> If I forget thee, O Jerusalem, let my right hand forget her cunning.
> If I do not remember thee, let my tongue cleave to the roof of my mouth;
> if I prefer not Jerusalem above my chief joy. (Psalm 137: 4–6)

If his own hand and tongue were freed then, they freed him to present
himself in Harry, at least, more directly and personally than he perhaps
ever had. Michael Grimwood rightly finds that the book is "as close as
any novel he ever published to being autobiographical," and that the
contrapuntal structure he devised permitted him to project onto Harry
"his desire to escape toward meaningful (artistic) leisure with a beautiful

young woman" and onto the convict "not only his misogyny but *his* capacity for endurance, *his* flirtation with anonymity."[87]

Working with Maurice Coindreau on the French translation of *The Sound and the Fury* in Hollywood the previous summer, Faulkner had read Coindreau the self-parody "Afternoon of a Cow," in which he portrayed himself as a Mississippi rube, the source of the material his alter-ego Ernest V. Trueblood records in the novels that bear the name Faulkner. Grimwood finds that the story "expresses as directly as anything else Faulkner ever wrote his own perception of his situation as a writer," including he says, his doubleness and his "chronic sense of degradation."[88] It may equally well be a self-parody, like the *Sanctuary* introduction, in which Ernest V. Trueblood represents those critics who portrayed him as knowing nothing of what he was doing.[89] Unlike his secretary Mr. Trueblood, the Mr. Faulkner of "Afternoon of a Cow" is nearly inarticulate, not a writer but a farmer subjected by his cow to what Trueblood delicately describes as "the full discharge of the poor creature's afternoon of anguish and despair." Whatever Faulkner's collapsing home life at this time and Meta's forthcoming marriage to another man contributed to the story, Mr. Trueblood attributes the degradation not to Faulkner but to the cow, "the lone female among three men." He calls it "one of those invasions of female privacy where, helpless victim of her own physical body, she seems to see herself as object of some malignant power for irony and outrage" (USWF, 430).

If I Forget Thee, Jerusalem, in a sense, is equally an invasion of privacy by a novelist with the same malignant power of irony, and one that ends, moreover, with a judgment consistent with Mr. Faulkner's experience in "Afternoon of a Cow." "'Women, shit,' the tall convict said" (Jerusalem, 287). The veil before what Hawthorne called "the inmost Me" slips in the tale as it does in the novel that followed where, like Hawthorne's, Faulkner's own "native reserve . . . thawed" after Meta's marriage to the extent of his openly restaging in his book situations and events of the love affair. Like the convict telling his story when he returns to Parchman prison, Faulkner's own "innate and inherited reluctance" for speaking of himself "dissolved and he found himself, listened to himself, telling it quietly, the words coming not fast but easily to the tongue as he required them" (Jerusalem, 280). The distinction between the deed and the word, and between Faulkner-as-source and Faulkner-as-writer dissolved with it, as well.

When he had finished the novel, he found himself hardly able to judge it. Beset, as he told Robert Haas, by family difficulties attendant on materials of his life that he had written into his book, and by problems with his burned back, he was reluctant to say that the book was a success. "I have lived for the last six months in such a peculiar state of family complications and back complications," he wrote Haas, "that I still am not able to tell if the novel is all right or absolute drivel. To me, it was written just as if I had sat on the one side of a wall and the paper was on the other and my hand with the pen thrust through the wall and writing not only on invisible paper but in pitch darkness too, so that I could not even know if the pen still wrote on paper or not" (SLWF, 106). His elaborate metaphor derives, perhaps, from another memory of Melville, in the speech in which Ahab declares the white whale the wall of the masked universe shoved near to him and insists he will "strike through the mask." Ahab poses a question there that Faulkner poses for the various prisoners of *If I Forget Thee, Jerusalem* and for himself: "How can the prisoner reach outside except by thrusting through the wall?"[90] The unnamed doctor in the novel thrusts literally through the wall of appearances when he enters Charlotte's bedroom, discovering there, beyond the realm of his imagining, that there are no limits to *"love and passion and tragedy"* and that lovers in fact can *"become as God Who has suffered likewise all that Satan can have known"* (Jerusalem, 235). Harry becomes as God with Charlotte and discovers suffering when he thrusts himself figuratively through a wall of convention, leaving his unlived life in New Orleans for the love he tells McCord is "freedom" (Jerusalem, 111). Faulkner did so by striking off his own mask and, like the God the doctor describes, writing the chaos of his immediate love and suffering into his novel. Were he to have judged the novel from another Melvillean perspective, he might have said with the "grand, ungodly, god-like" Captain of the *Pequod*, "Oh, now I feel my topmost greatness lies in my topmost grief."[91] He was not far from that self-judgment when he said of *The Hamlet* the next year, "I am the best in America, by God" (SLWF, 113).

VI. Old Moster

Old Moster jest punishes; He dont play jokes.

— The Mansion

---

i. The Snopes Legacy

Psalm 137 did more than provide Faulkner the original title of the memory book he wrote to stave off heartbreak: he found in it an expression of his relationship to the imaginative Jerusalem that is Yoknapatawpha County. If he privately felt himself still an exile in his Oxford home in 1938, he might yet, in the words of the psalmist, "sing the Lord's song" as the sole owner and proprietor of his fictional cosmos. Here was his great imaginative resource, and he returned to it now with a characteristic burst of creative energy that began with his turning again to the Snopeses. He was at work on that saga two months before *If I Forget Thee, Jerusalem* was published in January 1939 as *The Wild Palms*, and that work released still more in kind.

Faulkner conceived the story of the Snopes clan and began to write it in the mid-1920s in "Father Abraham." The "Father Abraham" Snopeses originated with Yoknapatawpha County itself, in conjunction with and, perhaps, in conscious counterpoint to the aristocratic Sartoris family of *Flags in the Dust*. In the summer of 1933, after the publication of *Sanctuary* and *Light in August*, he began again on his Snopes book, this time calling it "The Peasants";[1] in October he began another Yoknapatawpha project "about a nigger woman" that he called "Requiem for a Nun" (SLWF, 75). During the 1930s he worked on the Snopes material intermittently: by late 1938 five Snopes stories were separately in print— "Spotted Horses" (1931), "Centaur in Brass" (1932), "Lizards in Jamshyd's Courtyard" (1932), "Mule in the Yard" (1935), and "Fool About a Horse" (1936). In the novels he had written then, Snopeses were linked directly to the Sartorises in *Flags in the Dust* and episodes of *The Unvanquished* (1938); a Snopes was a cotton speculator in *The Sound and the Fury*; Jewel Bundren in *As I Lay Dying* (1930) owned one of the wild Texas ponies from "Father Abraham"; and Clarence and Virgil Snopes were characters in *Sanctuary*. So deeply imbedded were Snopeses in Faulkner's conception of Yoknapatawpha County, indeed, that he referenced events from Snopes stories yet to be written in *The Hamlet* (1940) on the 1936 map of the county, identifying "Varner's store, where Flem Snopes got his start" and the "Old Frenchman place, which Flem Snopes unloaded on Henry Armstid and Suratt, and where Popeye killed Tommy."[2] By December 1938 Faulkner could outline for Robert Haas the course of Flem Snopes's rise through "The Peasants" and two novels he named "Rus in Urbe" and "Ilium Falling" (SLWF, 107–109). Within the year the Snopes novels were renamed *The Hamlet*, *The Town*, and *The Mansion* (SLWF, 115). *The Hamlet* was published April 1, 1940.

Firmly in the grip of his fictional county again, he was writing steadily and well. His imaginative identification with this material was such that he began work on two new Yoknapatawpha projects before he finished *The Hamlet* and conceived and described still others. In May 1939 he wrote "Hand Upon the Waters," a Gavin Stevens mystery story included in *Knight's Gambit* (1949), and between October and March 1940 he wrote five of the stories about the McCaslins and their heirs that became *Go Down, Moses* (1942). He told Haas in late April about two other Yoknapatawpha novels, a "blood-and-thunder mystery novel" that became *Intruder in the Dust* (1948) and "a sort of Huck Finn" one (SLWF, 122, 123) that became *The Reivers* (1961). With the notable exception of *A Fable*, the Yoknapatawpha County fiction begun or conceived during the eighteen-month period from November 1938 to April 1940 constitutes virtually all of the new fiction he would write in the last twenty-four years of his life. This is the more surprising in that his return from California in 1938 marked the beginning of a period of the most serious difficulties in his life, financial and personal.

In one sense Faulkner's return to Yoknapatawpha County fiction constituted his reclaiming a legacy, an artistic recommitment to a decade-old vision of himself adumbrated in the self-styled figure of "the Player and the game He plays" in the closing pages of *Flags in the Dust* (Flags, 369). It was also, and importantly, a practical measure that permitted him to write quickly from a store of familiar material in order to sell stories and novels. Always a source of serious concern to him, Faulkner's finances now became as convoluted and difficult to sort out as Ratliff's goat-trade with Flem Snopes, to which they no doubt contributed. Since his purchase of Rowan Oak in April 1930, he had been steadily fashioning a public identity in Oxford as a landowner and serious citizen. He went to Hollywood in 1935 for purely financial reasons; returned from there in 1938, he materially extended his image at home by new property acquisitions. A good part of the nineteen thousand dollars he received for film rights to *The Unvanquished* went to buy Bailey's Woods and Greenfield Farm early in 1938,[3] making Faulkner something of a landed gentleman if not exactly what Moon Mullin later would call a "plantation man."[4] For more than a decade thereafter, money was a pervasive and intricately detailed motif in letters to agents and Random House editors. "I have a big family to support, and a fair investment in property to protect" (SLWF, 110), he wrote Haas in March 1939. And there was more. He had Haas send Meta Carpenter $150 that month, to be charged against his royalties on *The Hamlet*,[5] and when Phil Stone was threatened with foreclosure on a $7,000 note from his father's estate, Faulkner borrowed another $1,200 against royalties and cashed in a $4,800 life insurance policy to help pay his friend's debt.[6] His own inheritance was his theme in the May 1940 letter where he spoke of his "raging and impotent exasperation" at inheriting nothing except "my father's debts and his dependents, white and black without inheriting yet from anyone one inch of land or one stick of furniture or one cent of money" (SLWF, 122). In stating this, he was restating what had long been a theme of his fiction.

Here Faulkner represented in himself essentially the same frustration he had publicly attributed to Murry Falkner in the 1932 introduction to *Sanctuary*, where he says that his father "supplied me with bread at need despite the outrage to his principles at having been of a bum progenitive"

(ESPL, 176). Juxtaposition of his statements in the private letter and the published essay highlights the theatrical nature of the patriarch's relationship to his dependents: when the son became the father, the angle of presentation changed accordingly. Such changes produced changes in fictional self-presentations, as well. Mink Snopes might live in the assurance that "*Old Moster jest punishes; He dont play jokes*" (Mansion, 398), but Faulkner was fully the masterful Old Moster of his art now, if not of his life, and he knew better. He could and did move his characters around "like God" (Lion, 255), joking and punishing as he went. Inheritances of several kinds furnished material for both.

Genealogy in Faulkner is narrative. The line of inheritance from father to son manifests itself in his fiction in the repetitions that are keys to the past, the source and subject of the legendary families and regional histories undergirding the great novels of the 1920s and 1930s. The legendary John Sartoris is only the first of Faulkner's characters to set the matter in perspective.

> "In the nineteenth century," John Sartoris had said, "chortling over genealogy anywhere is poppycock. But particularly so in America, where only what a man takes and keeps has any significance, and where all of us have a common ancestry and the only house from which we can claim descent with any assurance, is the Old Bailey. Yet the man who professes to care nothing about his forebears is only a little less vain than he who bases all his actions on blood precedent. And a Sartoris is entitled to a little vanity and poppycock, if he wants it." (Flags, 82)

The ironies attendant upon genealogical legacies in *Flags in the Dust* prompt the speculation at the end of the novel that "perhaps Sartoris is the name of the game itself—a game outmoded and played with pawns shaped too late and to an old dead pattern, and of which the Player Himself is a little wearied" (Flags, 369–370). Faulkner fashioned himself as the Player but he never wearied of the game. Inheritances in the decade from *Flags in the Dust* to *If I Forget Thee, Jerusalem* include characters' names and stories as well as material things: the mortally dangerous Sartoris name, Quentin Compson's grandfather's watch and Harry Wilbourne's medical school tuition, Addie Bundren's and Joanna Burden's fathers' words, the legend of Hightower's grandfather, and the terrible absence of a paternal surname in Joe Christmas, Charles Bon, and Jackie Shumann. Little wonder, from this perspective, that Faulkner's own complex pride of ancestry should occasionally slip. At home in Mississippi, where Falkner family ancestors were for him a powerfully felt presence, his often problematic sense of his Mississippi legacy crossed readily from his life into his fiction.

In this regard Louis Rubin's long-held belief in a "faraway country" of Southern writing is interestingly germane. Rubin argues that the fictional South of the Southern Literary Renascence is a product of its writers' drastically altered perspectives on their Southern home. The breakup of the traditional South in the early twentieth century called into question both the traditional values of a supportive and largely homogenous community and the implicit assurances of identity once lodged there. Writers who left the South then, as Faulkner did for periods from 1918 to 1926 and again in the 1930s and 1940s when he was in Hollywood, acquired a spiritual detachment unavailable in, and even to, the home place. They brought that potentially destructive freedom to bear on representations of home. Characterized from a modernist perspective by ironic distance, myth-ordered experience, and the reflexivity that turns the work in upon itself, the new writing reconstituted the lost cultural experience in the way that Rubin argues for the "faraway country." Fashioned from the writer's "desire to effect an order greater than the one everyday life can provide for his experience,"[7] the faraway country as Faulkner conceived and employed it in his Yoknapatawpha County fiction is both a place and a way to tell stories. Rubin's formulation also anticipates Richard Poirier's sense of the writer's dynamic, exploratory relationship to the scene of his writing and supports, from a regional perspective, the sense of Faulkner's writing as a self-disruptive but self-affirming act that reconstitutes the World in the Word. In his version of the faraway country, the actual is paired with legend and myth, the lost home with the remembered sanctuary, new experience with innocence. *The Hamlet* is a clear example.

As early as 1918 he had begun to see that the Oxford of his childhood and the old South itself were irretrievable: the spiritual detachment that began with his residence in New Haven and Canada then exhibits itself in letters that celebrate a past he knew was already behind him. Nostalgic, funny, sometimes elegiac, the letters from the RAF camp in Toronto are filled with names of Oxford boys, living and recently dead, whose mention gives a sense of the lost childhood he would reshape in his fiction. There are Rodney and Ed Lewis, Ed Beanland, who died in the war, Edison Avent, who was rejected for service, and a Mississippian in Toronto who, he said, knew all the boys from Meridian. Thinking of home in Toronto, he might reimagine the actual past, but he found there were limits even to that. "Is David Carter still doing business at the old stand?" he asked Maud. "And 'Toc' Whitehead? I cant imagine his place without Jack and Van Hiler and Roselle and Mal and eleven niggers of various size and condition back there entertaining David, while Red Frazier gets cigarettes out of the tobacco case" (TofH, 126). In another letter the invented experience of "flying in Canada" supplants the lost innocence of times "only ten years ago. . . . Ed and Vic and Helen and . . . Sallie and us, running over the streets all night and living in the present." Things could be the same again, he assured himself and Maud, through a deeper imaginative identification with the childhood home: "when its all over and Jack and I are back again and we are sitting around the table at night, we'll go back about ten years and start living there, for even though we are both objective kids now, I can—and Jackie too—realize that home is greater that [sic] war, or lightening [sic] or marriage or any other unavoidable thing" (TofH, 117–118). At his most extreme distance from such sentimentality, he described himself in 1947 as an unacknowledged genius "crouching in a Mississippi hole trying to shape into some form of art his summation and conception of the human heart and spirit in terms of the cerebral, the simple imagination" (SLWF, 261). The faraway country in the major new fiction Faulkner planned and wrote after 1938 derived from a combination of such love of home and such disaffection.

Faulkner reveled in Jill, and as she grew up in Oxford in these years her childhood may have reminded him of his own. Certainly the distance he felt then between the Oxford of the present and the past is manifest in his fiction, where such places as Frenchman's Bend and the big woods of the Delta became the scenes of further self-presentations and performances. *The Hamlet* mythologizes Faulkner's childhood in the self-contained South at the turn of the century; *Go Down, Moses* makes a legend of his mixed experience of ancestry and its legacies. In both books, the world seems larger, its people more heroic, events more portentous than the actual. Mr. Compson despairingly contemplates a version of such a lost, heroic world in *Absalom, Absalom!*, and Quentin and Shreve tenuously recreate it out of "old tales and talking" (AA!, 243). V. K. Ratliff lives it in *The Hamlet* as does Ike McCaslin in "The Old People" and "The Bear." Early in *The Hamlet*, in a reflexive faraway country of his own, Ratliff sets the tone of the book when he makes a tall tale of a childhood adventure with Ab Snopes, before Ab was soured, when he confronted Pat Stamper with "twenty-four dollars and sixty-eight cents in his pocket and the entire honor and pride of the science and pastime of horse-trading in Yoknapatawpha County depending on him to vindicate it" (Hamlet, 38). In the same manner, Faulkner projected heroic stature on his own childhood companions and their courtships and attempted seductions. A group of boys and girls like those he named in his letters attends Eula at "singings and baptisings and picnics" (Hamlet, 142), where "the youths of fifteen and sixteen and seventeen who had been in school with her and others who had not, swarmed like wasps about the ripe peach which her full damp mouth resembled" (Hamlet, 141). A picnic photograph of Faulkner in 1911 with another boy and three girls is emblematic of that idyllic time. Both boys are in coats and ties, the girls in hats and summer dresses. Faulkner, in knickers, holds a guitar.[8]

Labove's position at the University of Mississippi likewise is a projection and a performance of Faulkner's brief, problematic career there, not as a football player like Labove, or like Faulkner's Oxford classmate Possum McDaniel, on whom Labove may be modeled,[9] but as a poet who lived as "fiercely free" in imagination as Labove does on the field and who shared Labove's "sardonic not-quite belief" (Hamlet, 121) in the unreality of the university and its systems of values. Labove's playing a game in which he carries "a trivial contemptible obloid across fleeing and meaningless white lines" (Hamlet, 121) prompts Faulkner's linguistic game-playing in such passages.[10] His frustrated love of Eula grotesquely exaggerates Faulkner's continuing obsession with Estelle in the 1920s and calls into question cultural values Faulkner both shared and parodied in him and other characters, female virginity primary among them. Houston has an "inherited southern-provincial-protestant fanaticism regarding marriage and female purity" (Hamlet, 235); Mink Snopes has been "bred by generations to believe invincibly that to every man, whatever his past actions, whatever depths he might have reached, there was reserved one virgin, at least for him to marry; one maidenhead, if only for him to deflower and destroy" (Hamlet, 263). Sharing their beliefs, Labove is the more horrified to find himself "drawn back into the radius and impact of an eleven-year-old girl who . . . postulated that ungirdled quality of the very goddesses in his Homer and Thucydides: of being at once corrupt and immaculate, at once virgins and the mothers of warriors and of grown men" (Hamlet, 125). That familiar formulation was generated by Faulkner's own reading and by personal experience that challenged his sense of the classical ideal. In *The Hamlet* he seems consciously to have recalled the years when Estelle was in Oxford with her children and he made her both love poems and the gift book *Royal Street: New Orleans* with the misogynistic tailpiece "Hong Li."[11] Drawing on such resources now as then, he reified the reshaped image of his past in the present.

Like Labove's Frenchman's Bend school and the university, the Old Frenchman place is again the scene of theatrical performances in *The Hamlet*, and as in *Sanctuary* the antebellum past is most strongly felt there. Horace Benbow's sense of the old house being haunted by wraiths in nineteenth-century costume recurs in Ratliff's imagining a barouche in the lane, "the women swaying and pliant in hooped crinoline beneath parasols, the men in broadcloth riding the good horses at the wheels" (Hamlet, 373). The *Sanctuary* scenes of voyeurism and sexual display become communal theatre of the grotesque in *The Hamlet*: backed by the columned house, mad Henry Armstid digs for gold in a garden like the peristyle-backed garden of *The Marionettes*; like theatre-goers the audience comes to the old house as if "entering another world, traversing another land, moving in another time, another afternoon without time or name"; they watch Armstid "with the rapt interest of a crowd watching a magician at a fair" (Hamlet, 403, 404). Even so detached a commentator on Snopes performances as V. K. Ratliff is not immune to the lure of the Old Frenchman place. Lump Snopes's peep show with Ike and the cow and Flem's horse show address respectively the salacious male imagination and masculine identity, neither of which appeals to a self-confident bachelor with "that hearty celibacy as of a lay brother in a twelfth-century monastery" (Hamlet, 47). Morally offended by the former, Ratliff declares, "This here engagement is completed" (Hamlet, 217). He distances himself from the "Snopes circus" from fear of the dangers of theatric illusion: "I'd just as soon buy a tiger or a rattlesnake. And if Flem Snopes offered me either one of them, I would be afraid to touch it for fear it would turn out to be a painted dog or a piece of garden hose when I went up to take possession of it" (Hamlet, 309, 308). Flem's midnight digging in the garden of the Old Frenchman place, however, is a performance imbedded in Frenchman's Bend culture, scripted in the Frenchman legend with which the novel opens and "the stubborn tale of the money he buried somewhere about the place when Grant over-ran the country on his way to Vicksburg" (Hamlet, 4). Will Varner's longtime ownership of the house, and Flem's digging there, reactivate that tale and with it Ratliff's addiction to trading and "the science and pastime of skullduggery" (Hamlet, 91). Literally, Eula's dowry is a playhouse and the shameful concluding spectacle of Armstid "spading himself into the waxing twilight" is a Flem Snopes production: "Couldn't no other man have done it," one watcher says. "Anybody might have fooled Henry Armstid. But couldn't nobody but Flem Snopes have fooled Ratliff" (Hamlet, 405).

If Frenchman's Bend is the faraway country of Faulkner's childhood, such episodes of madness owe some of their force to his life in 1940 as an internationally recognized artist in a parochial Mississippi town. His lifelong presentation of himself there as an artist, if not a madman, declared his manifest sense of difference from his townspeople as did his sizable property acquisitions in the last years of the Depression, for all of the financial trouble they caused him. Despite such performances, Faulkner regularly complained of invasions of his privacy and property. Madly digging for gold before an audience on the lawn of his antebellum mansion, Armstid is made in the image of his creator's sometimes outraged image of himself at work at Rowan Oak.[12] Malcolm Cowley would argue in 1945 that Faulkner's primary achievement was to make of his home place a "mythical kingdom . . . complete and living in all its details," but the apocryphal county really never stood, as Cowley insisted, "as a parable or legend of all the Deep South."[13] Faulkner told Cowley just that early in their correspondence, albeit disingenuously. "I'm inclined to think that my material, the South, is not very important to me," he wrote. "I just happen to know it." But he also explained, "I am telling the same story over and over, which is myself and the world" (SLWF, 185).

Very possibly he was thinking of himself and the world of Oxford and the great unacknowledged gift of his art when he described Eula Varner as a product of the "little lost village, nameless, without grace, forsaken, yet which wombed once by chance and accident one blind seed of the spendthrift Olympian ejaculation and did not even know it, without tumescence conceived and bore" (Hamlet, 164).[14] Olympian imagery of this sort pervades the novel, the language heightened especially in scenes of sexual desire. Eula's appearance is Dionysian, "honey in sunlight and bursting grapes, the writhen bleeding of the crushed fecundated vine beneath the hard rapacious trampling goat-hoof"; Jody Varner sees himself as a pandering stage-Apollo, "transporting not only across the village's horizon but across the embracing proscenium of the entire inhabited world like the sun itself, a kaleidoscopic convolution of mammaliam ellipses" (Hamlet, 105, 111). Flem is a figure of financial rather than sexual power on display to the communal gaze at Varner's store as on a stage, "the men, the women, the children—the infants who had never before crossed the doorsteps beyond which they had been born, the sick and the aged who otherwise might never have crossed them but once more—coming on horses and mules and by wagonsful" (Hamlet, 58).

Ike's idyll with the cow provides an extended example of the same performative impulse: the heightened language of the idyll that distinguishes

Ike from Flem relates him in extended ironic counterpoint to Eula and the other lovers of "The Long Summer."[15] And to Faulkner. A passage in which the abiding Southern earth gives birth to dawn has its roots in the self-presentations of *Mississippi Poems* (1924) and extends into *The Mansion* (1959). Dawn is the withheld subject of the long poetic sentence that begins, "Roofed by the woven canopy of blind annealing grass-roots and the roots of trees, dark in the blind dark of time's silt and rich refuse—the constant and unslumbering anonymous worm-glut and the inextricable known bones—Troy's Helen and the nymphs and the snoring mitred bishops, the saviors and the victims and the kings—*it* wakes, up-seeping, attritive in uncountable creeping channels" (Hamlet, 200; emphasis added). Conceptually the passage is related to the early poem "Mississippi Hills: My Epitaph," in which the poet imagines a life-after-death for himself in the living Mississippi earth:

> Where is there the death
> While in these blue hills slumbrous overhead
> I'm rooted like a tree? Though I be dead,
> This soil that holds me fast will find me breath.
>
> (MP, 156)

Expanded from *The Hamlet*, Mink Snopes's dying vision in *The Mansion* establishes this as a recurring motto for the secret self, a declaration in the appropriately mixed language of achievement and failure, fallen innocence and resurrected imagination that Mink—and certainly William Faulkner with him—is "equal to any, good as any, brave as any, being inextricable from, anonymous with all of them: the beautiful, the splendid, the proud and the brave, right on up to the very top itself among the shining phantoms and dreams which are the milestones of the long human recording—Helen and the bishops, the kings and the unhomed angels, the scornful and graceless seraphim" (Mansion, 435–436).

Often such language spectacles display Faulkner's regional affinities as well as his more universal, classical sensibility.[16] Ratliff is at the center of this mode of expression as he is of the conscious game-playing and self-presentation in the vernacular storytelling of the novel. Faulkner represented the community's loss of Eula through him at the end of Book 2 in the mixed idiom of a rural tale-teller whose sense of the "spendthrift Olympian ejaculation" is balanced by the understanding that "it was just meat, just galmeat" (Hamlet, 166). In Book 3 he turned from Ratliff to the very personal patterns of marriage matters made familiar by earlier novels. In 1918, like Labove, Faulkner fled his beloved; like Jack Houston, he was drawn back years later into marriage with his school sweetheart. Like Mink Snopes with his wife, and Houston with the woman he steals from a brothel, he was plagued by the memory of Estelle's former suitors and her husband. He represented that in Horace's thoughts of Belle's first husband in *Sanctuary* and Quentin's of Caddy's suitors in *The Sound and the Fury*, and he reprised his torment and theirs in Mink, who imagines his wife as "the confident lord of a harem" (Hamlet, 263) and his marriage bed "surrounded by the loud soundless invisible shades of the nameless and numberless men" (Hamlet, 245). He joined Mink's blighting vision to Houston's hope for a child by his prostitute lover, but in language so self-righteously judgmental as to blight that hope in its turn. Houston thinks,

> Perhaps they would have a child after a while. He thought of waiting for that, letting that be the sign. At first that eventuality had never occurred to him—here again was the old mystical fanatic protestant; the hand of God lying upon the sinner even after the regeneration: the Babylonian interdict by heaven forever against reproduction. He did not know just how much time, just what span of chastity, would constitute purgatorium and absolution, but he would imagine it—some instant, mystical still, when the blight of those nameless and faceless men, the scorched scars of merchandised lust, would be effaced and healed from the organs which she had prostituted. (Hamlet, 236).

This is a very personal matter, indeed. If Houston's common-law wife is the whore of Babylon, the withheld hand of God is Faulkner's own.

In combination with a passage involving Eula's pregnancy and marriage to Flem Snopes, Houston's doomed hope for a child recalls in the novel the birth and death of Faulkner's and Estelle's infant daughter Alabama in 1931. Faulkner wrote of that event almost immediately in the story "The Brooch," and consciously alludes to it in *The Hamlet* in the scene where Flem leaves with Eula for Texas holding "the straw suitcase on his knees like the coffin of a baby's funeral" (Hamlet, 161). As Noel Polk points out, "This is hardly an image Faulkner could have used without knowing exactly where it came from, since he himself carried Alabama's coffin on his knees to the cemetery."[17] Reactivated in 1938 by his return to a loveless home from a failed love affair in Hollywood, the pain of that memory carried into other self-mocking performances. To describe

Labove's sexual temptation Faulkner drew again on the frustrated desire of the marble faun, representing Labove as "the virile anchorite of old time. . . . his teeth clenched in his scholar's face and his legs haired-over like those of a faun" (Hamlet, 131). Labove imagines Eula's husband in classical terms as "the crippled Vulcan to that Venus" and as a figure from fairy-tale legend, "a dwarf, a gnome, without glands or desire, who would be no more a physical factor in her life than the owner's name on the fly-leaf of a book" (Hamlet, 131). Two elements of the vision directly relate to Faulkner and Estelle then—the association of the wife with books, like his own into which he steadily had been writing her and himself, and especially the difference in their physical size. Faulkner described himself in Mink as "small, almost a head shorter" than his wife, a man who knows "the immitigable discrepancy between will and capability due to that handicap of physical size" (Hamlet, 245, 246) and whose deepest impulse is to self-presentation and written display: "What he would have liked to do would be to leave a printed placard on the breast itself: *This is what happens to the men who impound Mink Snopes' cattle*" (Hamlet, 242). A third element is crippling impotence, with which Faulkner afflicted Popeye in the months before his own marriage and subsequently employed as a metaphor for the frustrating family and financial responsibilities that interrupted his writing.

Polk properly links Alabama's death to Faulkner's sense in the early 1930s of "the destructive nature of his marriage," and concludes, "In the works of this period, these elements and many related others from the external world of Faulkner's life in Oxford appear in an astonishing variety of combinations and permutations. . . . if it was not conscious use at first, over the course of the several novels and the dozen stories, he became very conscious indeed of how he, the quintessentially private person, had worked his own life into his fiction. This increasing awareness in its turn created its own problems that he, as usual, began to deal with in the fiction."[18] He capitalized on that legacy in 1938–1940 for the mythic self-presentations of *The Hamlet* and for new but equally personal performances of the fiction that immediately followed.

ii. Father's Will

In late March 1940, several days before the publication of *The Hamlet*, Faulkner executed a Last Will and Testament that revised and extended an earlier will made in June 1934. He had larger assets now and more fiscal responsibilities, and he distributed his bequests in more explicit detail to Estelle and her children, their daughter Jill, his mother, his niece Dean, and other family members and dependents. He named Jill his primary beneficiary; the executors were Phil Stone and his brother M. C. (Jack) Falkner, to each of whom he bequeathed a complete manuscript and, to Jack, first editions of his books. His brother John was to have free use of Greenfield Farm and an option to purchase it until Jill came of age, at which point ownership reverted to her. His tenant and later house servant Ned Barnett was to have a rent-free house at the farm, the right "to cultivate a five-acre piece of ground," and the use of "such livestock and tools as are on said farm and necessary to cultivate the land left to him." He also distributed specific personal items: a silver cigarette case to Jack, and Zeiss binoculars, a Leica camera, and guns to Jill with rights to their "proper use" to Malcolm Franklin and John's sons James and Murray.[19] His preoccupation with inheritances also extended to the enabling imaginative energy generated from book to book by his and his family's life in the South, the gathering whole constituting his own artistic legacy to the future. He was engaged in that connection with others' artistic legacies, as well, especially those of Hawthorne and Melville, in whose work he increasingly found authorization for his own. Each of these legacies contributed to the self-presentations and performances of *Go Down, Moses*.

Turning in 1941 to revisions of the McCaslin and Beauchamp stories he had based on the "relationship between white and negro races here" (SLWF, 139), he drew some details of the fiction from his recent will. In Part 4 of "The Bear," the last new writing in *Go Down, Moses*, he endowed Lucas Beauchamp with land rights similar to those he had granted Ned Barnett, and he used the charged word "selfprogenitive" (GDM, 269) to describe Lucas's consciously distinguishing himself from his grandfather Lucius Quintus Carothers McCaslin, in whose will, like Faulkner's dependents in his own will, Lucas and his brother and sister and their father are named heirs. Part 4 is a text about texts, a chronicle like the McCaslin ledgers themselves of "the tamed land which was to have been [Ike's] heritage. . . . to hold and bequeath" (GDM, 243–244). The ledgers bring together the book's themes of miscegenation, incest, and the search for a father in the larger context of what it means, as David Minter says, "to be a descendant and an inheritor."[20] They contain the genealogical record of the black and white characters of the novel and they document the legacies bequeathed to them in and by *"Father's will"* (GDM, 257).

Faulkner had for years exerted his self-fashioning will on his own genealogical inheritance before creating Lucas and Ike—by changing the spelling of his surname, as Lucas does his given name, and by reimagining the generations of his family in fictions where given names advance across generations, as do John and Bayard in the Sartoris family, and where sons reconceive and figuratively beget their own fathers, as does the *"philoprogenitive"* Quentin Compson (TSATF, 122). He would do so again in *Go Down, Moses*, extending his past practice to still more personal family material. In its representation of inheritances as well as in chronology of composition, *The Hamlet* is the immediate precursor of *Go Down, Moses*, surprisingly so since by and large the Snopeses' lack of antecedents distinguishes them from aristocratic Sartorises and large-land-owning McCaslins. Yet genealogy and inheritance clearly were at issue in the Snopes texts from the start, as the title "Father Abraham" suggests. Parts of the two novels were written simultaneously in 1939, and a link between them is established in the opening pages of *The Hamlet* when Ab Snopes is reported to have wintered the previous year "in a old cotton house on Ike McCaslin's place" (Hamlet, 10). Faulkner sustained the story of the biblical founder in *The Hamlet* by naming—Ab's name recalls Abraham as Ike Snopes's is short for Isaac—and by allusion through a number of typically ironic turns on inheritance. In *The Hamlet* the father's will is embodied in old Will Varner. The son of Varner's great old age is not Jody, however, but Flem Snopes, the son-in-law-elect whose rise from clerk to estate manager is described as "the usurpation of an heirship" (Hamlet, 98). The Abrahamic motif touches even Ratliff, who declares himself saved from bankruptcy by an act of God: "Him or somebody had done sent me a sheep just like He done to save Isaac in the Book. He sent me a goat-rancher" (Hamlet, 87). The actual Isaac of *The Hamlet* is sent a cow, which his Snopes cousins sacrifice on the altar of public opinion and replace with a carved wooden icon. As I. O. Snopes explains it, "The Snopes name has done held its head up too long in this country to have no such reproaches against it like stock-diddling" (Hamlet, 222).

The theme of withheld inheritance represented in Ike Snopes carried into the succeeding novel, as well, and into retrospective assessments of other fictional aristocratic families in the 1940s. As old in Faulkner as *Soldiers' Pay*, where the Rector's line ends with the death of his son, family decline generated the deeply autobiographical performances in *The Sound and the Fury* and *Absalom, Absalom!*. On his twenty-first birthday Isaac McCaslin declares himself chosen to reverse such declines, "an Isaac born into a later life than Abraham's and repudiating immolation:

fatherless and therefore safe declining the altar because maybe this time the exasperated Hand might not supply the kid" (GDM, 270–271). Ike Snopes effectively repudiates the Snopes name by his inability to pronounce it when he tells Ratliff he is "Ike H-mope" (Hamlet, 95). By relinquishing his inheritance, Ike McCaslin also relinquishes the McCaslin surname. Despite, or because of, his unfulfilled promise to his wife to reclaim the farm, she bears him no son: the last McCaslin in Go Down, Moses is a Beauchamp baby fathered out of wedlock by an Edmonds.[21]

In 1945, during his longest dry spell as a writer, Faulkner extended the Compson genealogy backward into the seventeenth century, detailing the family decline in terms of dispossession, misuse, and doom and leaving as the last Compson another childless bachelor. Ikkemotubbe is described as a "dispossessed American king" who sells his land to "the grandson of a Scottish refugee who had lost his own birthright by casting his lot with a king who himself had been dispossessed" (Appendix, 704). As in Go Down, Moses, the sale of the land incurs a family doom that falls on Jason Lycurgus Compson II, who mortgages and sells parts of his Mississippi birthright; on Jason Lycurgus III, who sells the pasture for Caddy's wedding and Quentin's year at Harvard; and on Jason Lycurgus IV, who assumes "the entire burden of the rotting family in the rotting house" (Appendix, 717) then sells his birthright for a boardinghouse, leaving no sons. The connection between the 1942 novel and the 1945 "Appendix" is important to Faulkner's self-presentations at this period, not least because Ike McCaslin's forebear in the Yoknapatawpha fiction is Faulkner's own early fictional persona, Quentin Compson III, of whom he wrote in the "Appendix" that he "loved and lived in a deliberate and almost perverted anticipation of death, as a lover loves and deliberately refrains from the waiting willing friendly tender incredible body of his beloved, until he can no longer bear not the refraining but the restraint, and so flings, hurls himself, relinquishing, drowning" (Appendix, 710). The language of temptation and relinquishment identifies Quentin with Ike; the association of sex with death describes Ike's seduction by his wife at the end of Part 4 of "The Bear," where he submits himself to her as to the sea: "it was like nothing he had ever dreamed, let alone heard in mere man-talking until after a no-time he returned and lay spent on the insatiate immemorial beach" (GDM, 300).

In addition, Quentin's struggle with his legacy as a Compson and a Southerner in his fragmented chapter of The Sound and the Fury and in Absalom, Absalom! reflects Ike's struggle to understand and act on the

McCaslin past he finds chronicled in the fragmental ledgers. Both characters *"Tell about the South"* (AA!, 142) in attempts to explain themselves
to themselves, Quentin with Shreve and Ike with Cass Edmonds; both
take as their texts their father's writing; and both are inextricably bound
to the region and the past that writing portrays and makes tangible to
them. At the center of Ike's talk with Cass, the ledgers represent "a
whole land in miniature, which multiplied and compounded was the entire South, twenty-three years after surrender and twenty-four from eman-
cipation" (GDM, 280). Like Mr. Compson's letter to Quentin in New England, the ledgers also are a "pandora's box" (AA!, 208) of miscegenation
and incest that Ike opens at his peril.[22] Ike does not leave the South as
Quentin does—his stage is the plantation commissary rather than a Massachusetts college room—but his version of God's plan for the South is as
much a faraway country as is Quentin and Shreve's recreation of Sutpen's
Hundred in 1910. Both accounts are mythically ordered, distanced by
irony, and in the end reflect their tellers' spiritual disillusionment. Quentin's closing perspective is that of a man "older at twenty than a lot of
people who have died" (AA!, 301): he cannot refute Shreve's prophecy
"that in time the Jim Bonds are going to conquer the western hemisphere"
nor really deny the charge that he hates the South (AA!, 302, 303). In his
actual old age, Ike's response to the charge that he has forgotten love is his
vision of a modern South like Shreve's *"where white men rent farms and
live like niggers and niggers crop on shares and live like animals, where
cotton is planted and grows man-tall in the very cracks of the sidewalks,
and usury and mortgage and bankruptcy and measureless wealth, Chinese and African and Aryan and Jew, all breed and spawn together until
no man has time to say which one is which nor cares"* (GDM, 347). Quentin's and Ike's disillusionment reflects the novelist's distanced perspective
on the racial culture of his native region, shaped in the case of *Go Down,
Moses* by the added frustrations attendant on Faulkner's financial difficulties. Representations of race and miscegenation in the two novels,
however, appear to have significantly different sources in the novelist's
experience.

Where the male partner is white, miscegenation is represented in *Absalom, Absalom!* as a tacitly accepted historical fact of antebellum Southern plantation life. Clytemnestra lives at Sutpen's Hundred as her father's
daughter born of a slave woman who is neither portrayed nor identified in
the novel; excepting only Rosa, her antecedents are never represented as
an issue for her or her white family. Charles Bon's racial identity is acci-

dental, his purported mixed blood deriving not from a Southern master–
slave union but from Sutpen's legal marriage to a West Indian planter's
daughter. Mixed race is the cause of Bon's abandonment by his father
and his subsequent quest for paternal acknowledgment. But in neither
Clytie's nor Bon's case is Sutpen's act of miscegenation attributed to large
cultural wrongs, as is Old Carothers McCaslin's in *Go Down, Moses,* or
to a representative history of old family sin and shame to be purged, erad-
icated, and cured by repudiations and relinquishments. Indeed, the major
characters of *Absalom, Absalom!* treat race almost as a cultural abstraction.[23] According to Quentin and Shreve, Sutpen reveals Bon's mixed race
to Henry to preserve his design, and Henry murders his brother because
he is *"the nigger that's going to sleep with your sister"* (AA!, 286). The in-
validated result of accident and misunderstanding, Bon's blackness, like
Joe Christmas's in *Light in August,* is left purposely ambiguous. Certainly
both characters suffer from their own and the white community's assumption of their blackness, but their mixed blood, whatever it contributes to sexual conflicts in the novels, does not result from the sexual
exploitation of one race by another. Nor is that historical reality either investigated in the novels or condemned.[24] *Go Down, Moses* is quite another case.

The difference may be illustrated by two trips from Mississippi to
New Orleans, the nineteenth-century seat of the Southern slave trade.
Mr. Compson theorizes that Thomas Sutpen travels there in 1860 to confirm his suspicion that Henry's college friend is his son by his abandoned
first wife, finding, as Henry does later, that Bon is married to his octoroon
mistress and has a son of his own. According to Mr. Compson, who does
not suspect Bon may be black, it is the marriage rather than the inter-
racial sex that appals the plantation-bred "Henry Sutpen of Sutpen's Hundred in Mississippi" (AA!, 94)—not the fact of miscegenation but the ceremony recognizing and formalizing racial intermixture. In *Go Down,
Moses* Old Carothers McCaslin makes the three-hundred mile journey to
New Orleans in 1807 to purchase a black mistress. Two years later he
marries her to his slave Thucydus, and a year after that she bears him the
daughter who will bear him the son he remembers in his will. Initially Ike
assumes the $1,000 legacy is payment for miscegenation: *"So I reckon
that was cheaper than saying My son to a nigger* he thought. *Even if My
son wasn't but just two words. But there must have been love* he thought.
*Some sort of love. Even what he would have called love: not just an af-
ternoon or a night's spittoon"* (GDM, 258). The insistence on love in all

forms of sexual relation is common among Faulkner's young idealists as
it was also to Faulkner in his several extramarital relationships.[25] Quentin Compson seeks the same assurance in *The Sound and the Fury* when
he demands, *"did you love them Caddy did you love them"* (TSATF, 149),
and in *Absalom, Absalom!* he and Shreve insist upon Bon's love for Judith
because "there are some things that just have to be whether they are or
not" (AA!, 258). What distinguishes *Go Down, Moses* from the Compson
novels is the incestuous miscegenation between father and daughter that
Ike subsequently discovers in the ledgers, thinking, *"His own daughter
His own daughter. No No Not even him"* (GDM, 259). Father-daughter incest is a different and, for Faulkner, a more personal matter than Quentin's idealizing desire for his sister or the "pure and perfect incest"
(AA!, 77) Mr. Compson imagines for Henry Sutpen in his half-brother
Bon's marrying Judith.[26] In the Ur-*Sanctuary*, on the verge of his marriage
to Estelle in 1929, Faulkner had projected his own anxiety about having a
stepdaughter on Horace Benbow, who feels a guilty attraction to Little
Belle. The addition of incest to miscegenation in *Go Down, Moses* com-
bines the recurrent theme of incest with a heretofore unaccessed area of
Faulkner family racial experience, at once compounding Ike's shameful
inheritance and giving personal historical validity to the Southern slaver's
heritage of human ownership and exploitation.

When he turned to the McCaslin stories after the publication of *The
Hamlet*, Faulkner faced a problem analogous to that he claimed he had
faced when he revised the Ur-*Sanctuary*. He said in the 1932 introduction
to *Sanctuary* that the book was written for money and that he had to
make of the original "cheap idea" something that would not shame *The
Sound and the Fury* and *As I Lay Dying* (ESPL, 176, 178). In fact, the revisions make the book less personally revealing. The problem now was to
make the stories he had called "trash" (SLWF, 122) when he wrote them
for magazines into something that would not shame the rest of his work.[27]
His answer was Part 4 of "The Bear." In the mid-1930s he had extended
the apocryphal history of the Falkner family set forth first in *Flags in the
Dust* into the past in the stories of *The Unvanquished*, where he modeled
John Sartoris's Civil War heroics on his great-grandfather's experience as
captain and then colonel in the Magnolia Rifles; now for the first time he
took as a resource for fiction the Old Colonel's mulatto shadow family.
Joel Williamson has assembled evidence that William Clark Falkner was
the father of his mulatto slave Emeline's daughters Fannie Forrest Falkner
(1864–1866) and Lena Falkner (b. 1867) and that the Old Colonel's great-

grandson the novelist knew their story.[28] In opening this material to fictional adaptation, Faulkner risked opening a pandora's box of his own. He had written about miscegenation as a historical reality in *Absalom, Absalom!*, and he recently had written his own adulterous love affair with Meta into *If I Forget Thee, Jerusalem*. The Old Colonel's relationship with Emeline combined the two illicit loves. Distanced by historical time, the Old Colonel "became" Old Carothers in the novel, Emeline and Fannie "became" Eunice and Tomy, and Faulkner's knowledge of his revered ancestor's relationship with his slave "became" Ike McCaslin's discovery in the ledgers. In the same way, in *The Sound and the Fury*, Faulkner had given Quentin his own grief over the loss of Estelle, and even his own written words, imaginatively heightening the loneliness and disaffection he felt in New Haven in 1918 in ways that lead Quentin to suicide. Faulkner's knowledge of his great-grandfather's life is likewise transformed and intensified in *Go Down, Moses* by the addition of Old Carothers's incest with his slave daughter. That revelation propels Isaac to relinquish his inheritance, which Faulkner pointedly did not do. Instead of committing suicide when Estelle married in 1918, he had written a book; instead of self-sacrificial repudiation of his forebear now, he did the same again.

His adaptation of this family history has much to say about Faulkner's creative processes and his ongoing fictional performances. He had projected his image of himself as war hero and artist on Bayard Sartoris and Horace Benbow in *Flags in the Dust*, imagined himself as child, lover, and father in *The Sound and the Fury*, and portrayed Estelle in both Temple and Belle in *Sanctuary*. Now he historicized William Clark Falkner in the same way, distancing fiction from fact by dividing and rewriting family history, using the same historical sources to create several different fictional characters and events. The Old Colonel's legacy to Fannie Forrest Falkner was not children of an incestuous coupling, like Tomy's in the novel, but an education at Rust College in Holly Springs, where she met and then married Matthew Dogan, who in 1889 became professor of mathematics at Central Tennessee College and then president of Wiley College in Marshall, Texas.[29] If the historical Fannie Falkner was Tomy, Fannie and her husband Matthew also were cast as Tomy's granddaughter Fonsiba Beauchamp and her educated husband, whom Ike finds on a barren Arkansas farm "in the same ministerial clothing in which he had entered the commissary five months ago and a pair of gold-framed spectacles which, when he looked up and then rose to his feet, the boy saw did not even contain lenses, reading a book in the midst of that desolation" (GDM,

266). Born in 1869 Fonsiba is close in age to Fannie, and as the "chief of her family" (GDM, 263) Cass Edmonds is concerned for her and her welfare in the way that the Old Colonel was for his mulatto daughter.[30]

The reconstituted history included peripheral family, as well. Mammy Callie Barr, to whom the novel is dedicated, is the recognizable model for Molly Beauchamp, and Faulkner's real fondness for Callie is reflected in Roth's for Molly.[31] Likewise, Faulkner's Greenfield Farm contributed to his depiction of the McCaslin farm, with the difference that Uncle Buck and Uncle Buddy McCaslin are named for Phil Stone's great-uncles Theophilus and Amodeus Potts, whose father acquired one hundred square miles of land along the Tallahatchie River in the nineteenth century. The Potts brothers, also called Buck and Buddy, farmed the land and Stone's father General Stone acquired it as the hunting camp Faulkner visited often and wrote into "The Old People" and "Delta Autumn."[32] He had used Stone before, first in the self-presentations he projected on the lawyer Horace Benbow and later as Benbow's fictional successor Gavin Stevens, whose love of Linda Snopes in *The Town* reinscribes Faulkner's Prufrockian relationship in the early 1950s with young Joan Williams.

In *Go Down, Moses* he portrayed himself as the biblical Ishmael as well as Isaac, giving his materialism to the ironically dispossessed but wealthy Lucas Beauchamp and his high idealism to Isaac; to Lucas his love of the land and farming and to Isaac his love of the hunt and the "tremendous, primeval, looming, musing" wilderness (GDM, 337) that inspired the finest poetic performances of the book. Like Lucas, Faulkner had a daughter, and his stepdaughter was recently and secretly married as is Lucas's Nat; like Isaac, he had no son. A decade later, in the essay-story "Mississippi," he would rewrite his life through his fiction yet again, modifying Ike's fictional experience as his own in the way that he earlier had made his own and others' into Ike's in the novel. Among other fictions he reprised there, the ending of the essay modifies and perhaps glosses Quentin's agonized expression of his troubled relationship to the South. Quentin's repeated "I dont hate it" at the end of *Absalom, Absalom!* is echoed in Faulkner's admission of "Loving all of it even while he had to hate some of it because he knows now that you dont love because: you love despite; not for the virtues, but despite the faults" (ESPL, 42–43). Writing to Saxe Commins in 1954, Estelle described that interfusion of actual and fictional realities when she wrote, "Bill's article, 'Mississippi,' in next month's Holiday explains the two Bills—He is so definitely dual I think—Perhaps artists must needs be."[33] His distrust of facts; his daring, multifaceted constructions; his insistence on imaginative license to create characters from diverse sources and move them around in his role as Player, stage manager, God—all of these speak to the willed artistic reality of the work he fathered, the outcome, again, of very personal performances of *his* knowing and imagining, of *his* mind and experience.

Ike's repudiation of his heritage in the long, clarifying section of "The Bear" about ancestors and inheritances has been read as evidence of a turn in Faulkner's language toward a declamatory rhetoric that continued to the end of his career.[34] In fact there is a multilayered literary performance in the fragmented and typographically differentiated one long sentence of the chapter: in the varied epistolary forms of the ledgers that substitute for "oral intercourse" (GDM, 252) between Buck and Buddy; in the quotations of the titles *The Sound and the Fury* and *Sanctuary* (GDM, 271–272) that proclaim and valorize Faulkner's previous work as part of the long Southern record; in the sometimes oratorical language of God's plan for the South that fueled his subsequent public pronouncements on race; and in an apocalyptic passage about God's leaving the South a "worthless tideless rock cooling in the last crimson evening" (GDM, 272) that carried into the 1950 Nobel Prize Address. Part 4 has a literary genealogy, as well, and is scripted according to American literary custom.

Noting Faulkner's report that he was reading *Moby-Dick* to Jill in 1940, Eric Sundquist suggests that he responded increasingly then to Melville's "brooding meditations on the revealed and unrevealed powers of paternity" and that, in "The Bear" as in *Absalom, Absalom!*, he was "moving further away from his own early 'modernism' and placing himself, deliberately or not, more clearly in the tradition of classic nineteenth-century American fiction."[35] On such themes, Faulkner superimposed the figure familiar from Melville and Hawthorne of the American artist as disinherited outcast. A predecessor and likely model of that self-presentation in *Go Down, Moses* is Hawthorne, who presented and resolved the issue for himself in "The Custom House," the 1849 essay he published as the self-authorizing introduction to *The Scarlet Letter*. In the early 1940s Faulkner would have found there and in the novel a profoundly personal resource for sustaining his own threatened sense of himself as an artist and man.

On the question of fathers, few American novelists have had more to say in their work than Hawthorne and Faulkner. About their literary progenitors, neither said very much at all. Asked about his reading, Faulkner customarily named the pantheon of nineteenth-century New England writers he had found in his grandfather's library. At the University of Virginia in 1957, he said that good materials had always been scarce in the literary economy, and he admitted taking "tricks" and "plots" from *The Scarlet Letter*, adding only that "we don't know just who Hawthorne took his from. Which he probably did because there are so few plots to write about" (FU, 115).[36] Yet *The Scarlet Letter* is one novel about whose sources Hawthorne did publicly write, and what he said and the forms in which he cast it are direct points of contact to Faulkner. In "The Custom House" Hawthorne wrote of his debt to the Salem witch trials conducted by his Puritan ancestors, and to the manuscript record of adultery in Colonial Boston he claimed was written by a Salem customs officer a century before him and stored in the custom house attic. Dispossessed of his ancestry by the ghost of John Hathorne, who would think him a "worthless, if not positively disgraceful . . . writer of story-books,"[37] he finds an "official ancestor" in Mr. Surveyor Pue, insisting in both the introductory essay and the novel that the story of Hester Prynne is "authorized and authenticated" by Pue's manuscript.[38] In fact the manuscript and the scarlet letter it enfolds are fictions in a fiction, useful tricks Hawthorne employed to bridge the distance between an American past absent of literary models and an American present lacking a literary tradition.

If Hawthorne felt compelled to authorize his story-book writing by inventing literary progenitors, Faulkner adopted his, prominent among them Hawthorne and Hawthorne's inventions. There are many points of similarity between the two writers in their respective centuries, biographical as well as textual. As a novelist in his own richly historic time and place, Faulkner like Hawthorne was heir to and prisoner of the house of custom that threatened to dull while it demanded to be served by the artist's imagination, and the theme of inheritance in Hawthorne's work as in his own is a recurrent expression of that condition. Faulkner might look to his great-grandfather as a writer of books, but he found in his slaveholding a system still more inhumane than John Hathorne's witch trials and Indian wars. Each shared with the other both a two-sided duty to family and alienation, as artists, from mainstream America. Unable to turn fiction into financial custom, Hawthorne went to make his living as Surveyor in the Salem custom house, sending his name abroad, as he says, on bales of imported goods; in the mid-1930s and again during World War II, Faulkner indentured himself to Hollywood. By 1945 much of his work was out of print, and his name went abroad in scattered screen credits on films. Feeling himself orphaned for his idle ways from heroic ancestors, seeing himself as an outcast in America, at the same time knowing himself heir to literal ancestral houses and customs, each novelist came to see that, as an American artist, he would have to seek his artistic identity through his art and by reconstituting history live in and with it.

At the center of *Go Down, Moses* is a literal custom house, the McCaslin plantation commissary, and Nathaniel Hawthorne haunts it as a literary forefather, the shade of an "official ancestor" on whose imaginative work Faulkner drew for artistic authorization and authentication in the manner of Hawthorne on Mr. Surveyor Pue. The conjunction of the situations in which each man saw himself writing is matched by significant conjunctions of their two texts, each of which is concerned with ancestry. Hawthorne's Salem custom house is a house of history representative of his own and Salem's mercantile past; Faulkner's McCaslin commissary is similarly representative. Both the ledgers in the fiction and the fictional manuscript in the essay are enigmatic, incomplete, inconclusive; each documents a story of hidden sin in which an unwedded mother is the sexual and political prisoner of the patriarchy.[39] In "The Custom House" Hawthorne emulates Pue and frees himself as an artist by rewriting Pue's story of Hester Prynne. In the parallel situation of Faulkner's novel, Isaac McCaslin finds actual ancestresses in Eunice and Tomy and adopts the values of an unofficial ancestor to repudiate his great-grandfather's crimes against them. As he tells Cass, "Sam Fathers set me free" (GDM, 286). As its title affirms, *Go Down, Moses*, like Hawthorne's essay and novel, is a captivity narrative: steeped in nineteenth-century referents, shaped to Southern customs and historical realities, it reflects something of Faulkner's own disillusioned sense of financial bondage in the late 1930s and early 1940s. It also represents the artistic freedom he exercised early and late to use such materials as he chose.

The women captives of the two books are empowered only ironically, Mistress Prynne as keeper of the secret of Pearl's paternity, Eunice as mistress of her own life and death. Hawthorne might find assurance of his own identity in his leaving the custom house to write his novel, but he returned Hester to anonymity in Colonial Boston, tracing on her grave the sign of the unwedded mother: "ON A FIELD, SABLE, THE LETTER A, GULES."[40] Faulkner's brief treatment of Eunice is closer to Hawthorne's representation of Hester in the cryptic Pue manuscript, and she, too, is hieroglyphic: black therefore slave, female therefore vulnerable to sexual exploitation by her white master. She is stigmatized, too, by the way her life and death are transcribed: literally, she is marginalized by the white male writers of the ledgers who inscribe her with ungrammatical crudity in a few scattered entries.

> *Eunice Bought by Father in New Orleans 1807 $650. dolars. Marrid to Thucydus 1809 Drownd in Crick Cristmas Day 1832*
>
> . . . .
>
> *June 21th 1833 Drownd herself*
>
> . . . .
>
> *23 June 1833 Who in hell ever heard of a niger drownding him self*
>
> . . . .
>
> *Aug 13th 1833 Drownd herself*
>
> . . . .
>
> *Tomasina called Tomy Daughter of Thucydus @ Eunice Born 1810 dide in Child bed June 1833 and Burd. Yr stars fell*
>
> . . . .
>
> *Turl Son of Thucydus @ Eunice Tomy born June 1833 yr stars fell Fathers will* (GDM, 255–257)

The brothers' collaborative text is hardly declamatory: rather, they appear to adopt Faulkner's own strategy of at once revealing and concealing the personal past as Hawthorne did the secrets of his "inmost Me."[41]

The words *"Fathers will"* echo in *The Scarlet Letter* as in *Go Down, Moses* and across a century in Hawthorne's and Faulkner's lives and art. Arthur Dimmesdale speaks for the patriarchal laws of his time and place when he says of his heavenly Father at the end of the novel, "He hath proven his mercy, most of all, in my afflictions. . . . His will be done!"[42] Hester accepts and suffers those laws; in giving up her love and her life, Eunice entirely repudiates them, albeit in vain. No one except the sixteen-year-old Ike demands to know the identity of her daughter's father, or of her daughter's son, and she is never empowered by Tomy's birth as Hester is by Pearl's. In a place and time where miscegenation has secret sanction, Tomy's paternity is an open secret. Tomy's Turl's paternity is a secret betrayal that drives Eunice to drown herself. Her only appearance outside the ledgers is in Ike's grieving, empathetic vision of her, "walking into the icy creek on that Christmas day six months before her daughter's and her lover's (*Her first lover's* he thought. *Her first*) child was born, solitary, inflexible, griefless, ceremonial, in formal and succinct repudiation of grief and despair who had already had to repudiate belief and hope" (GDM, 259).

Having implicated himself in the McCaslin lives he reconstructs, Ike makes an analogous gesture of repudiation. Faulkner makes it clear that Eunice, like Hester, was bound—and still more significantly, betrayed—by love. It remains for Eunice's great-great-great-granddaughter to speak for her and thereby expose the futility of Ike's self-sacrificial gesture on her part. Like Eunice and Tomy before her, The Girl in "Delta Autumn" bears a child out of wedlock by a white man who, if not a McCaslin, is of McCaslin descent. Empowered by the secret of her own and her child's paternity, she charges Ike with willfully living down his ancestor's sin at the expense of living. She is speaking for Eunice and Tomy and even Ike's lost wife when she demands of him, in words that Hester might justifiably have addressed to Chillingworth, "Old man, . . . have you lived so long and forgotten so much that you dont remember anything you ever knew or felt or even heard about love?" (GDM, 346).

Faulkner was equally implicated in the ancestral past, both of his family and of his artistic forebear. He must have found in Hawthorne's great story of love and bondage both a model and a mode of artistic self-presentation for his own story of historical wrongs. Hawthorne described the realm of imagination in "The Custom House" as "a neutral territory, somewhere between the real world and fairy-land, where the Actual and the Imaginary may meet and each imbue itself with the nature of the other," a nineteenth-century New Englander's version of the twentieth-century Southerner's faraway country where "Ghosts might enter . . . without affrighting us."[43] Faulkner described Yoknapatawpha County as such a place, compounded of the actual and apocryphal, where he could move his people around "like God" (Lion, 255). Like Ike in the McCaslin commissary he modeled on that at his Greenwood Farm, he was himself "juxtaposed not against the wilderness but against the tamed land which was to have been his heritage" (GDM, 243) early in 1941, when he took up the McCaslin stories: he knew his genius then and his artistic mastery of his world. Like Ike he knew himself "Chosen" (GDM, 286).

But no more than Hawthorne was he declaiming against the culture of his region when he took Southern history as a legacy to his art. When the appropriately named Will Legate prompts Ike to speak about God's will in "Delta Autumn," Ike names not only the corrupted legacy of "the woods and fields [man] ravages and the game he devastates" (GDM, 332) and the old "wrong and shame" of slavery (GDM, 334). God's will includes love, which Ike forfeited by repudiating "the wrong and shame, at least in principle, and at least the land itself in fact, for his son at least" (334). Like

Quentin and Shreve near the end of their story of incestuous miscegenation in *Absalom, Absalom!*, Ike finds himself in a neutral territory like theirs, inside history, "where there might be paradox and inconsistency but nothing fault nor false" (AA!, 253). His tone is appropriately elegiac, encompassing all lost and wasted loves of the novel, including especially his own, and deriving, as elsewhere in the fiction, from loves and losses of the novelist's own, reprised here and performed again, like the wilderness in their own way, "being myriad, one" (GDM, 313). Ike speaks both as and for the God he describes, when he tells Legate, "I think that every man and woman, at the instant when it dont even matter whether they marry or not, I think that whether they marry then or afterward or dont never, at that instant the two of them together were God" (GDM, 332).

iii. Cuiser Tools dan Dat

When Faulkner answered Joan Williams's first letter in August 1949, he told her that "Something charming came out of it, like something remembered out of youth: smell, scent, a flower, not in a garden but in the woods maybe, stumbled on by chance, with no past and no particular odor and already doomed for the first frost: until 30 years later a soiled battered bloke aged 50 years smells or remembers it, and at once he is 21 again and brave and clean and durable."[44] In its way this first letter, like many that followed it, was for Faulkner what Dilsey calls one of the Lord's "cuiser tools" (TSATF, 293). It was heavily edited: several lines in the initial version of this passage were crossed out in thick red pencil and the self-expressive business about doom and the "soiled and battered bloke" added to it. Perhaps Faulkner already knew then that he had found a young woman not only to write to but for, as Joan later said.[45] He had told Malcolm Cowley of his need for "a new young woman" in 1946.[46] Among those he had found and written into his fiction over the years are Estelle, Gertrude Stegbauer, Helen Baird, Meta Carpenter Wilde, and Dean Faulkner's friend Ruth Ford.[47] He was a week shy of his fifty-second birthday when he wrote first to Joan; she was twenty. He invited her to write him her questions. "Cuiser" than the first, his second letter two weeks later constructed a veiled erotic scene and included a sexual proposal. Joan had asked about writing. "A woman must ask these of a man while they are lying in bed together," he told her, "when they are lying at peace or at least quiet or maybe on the edge of sleep so you'll have to wait, even to ask them."[48] They met again in December, when Estelle made a picnic lunch and joined them; a week later he wrote Joan, "as soon as I look at the blank sheet of paper, I want to write you a love letter on it," and he introduced the idea of their "writing together to get the good stuff out of Joan Williams."[49]

Soon Estelle was opening and reading Joan's letters and drinking heavily. The drama of his home life generated melodramatic responses in Faulkner's correspondence with Joan: in one heavily edited letter the following July, he asked her to write him in care of Quentin Compson, then canceled that and substituted in pencil the name A. E. Holston, a fictional founder of his Jefferson, Mississippi, whom he by then was writing into the prose prefaces of *Requiem for a Nun*.[50] Joan returned to Bard College after Christmas, and Faulkner met her in New York in February. He wrote her from the train home with a draft of the first act of the novel that was now also a play, describing Temple's servant Nancy Mannigoe as a "'nigger' woman, a known drunkard and dope user, a whore with a jail record in the little town, always in trouble. Some time back she seemed to have reformed, got a job as nurse to a child in the home of a prominent young couple. Then one day suddenly and for no reason, she murdered the child. And now she doesn't even seem sorry." He told Joan, "You can begin work here."[51] The next month he assured her he needed a collaborator.[52] "After you read the enclosed section," he wrote then, "maybe we can decide what is wrong with Temple."[53]

He could hardly have expected her to know anything substantive about the Nancy he described let alone about Temple. What was "wrong" with Joan was the issue. She was a twenty-year-old Memphis college girl with the middle-class values of her place and time, and she wanted to write. From the start, Faulkner's letters linked his encouragement of her art with his hopes as her would-be lover. She was as frightened by that as she was flattered. The more she resisted his declarations of love, the more he saw himself as a Pygmalion, "creating not a cold and beautiful statue, in order to fall in love with it, but Pygmalion taking his love and creating a poet out of her."[54] She reminded him of the young Temple Drake of *Sanctuary*, and to that extent, at least, she inspired his return to Temple in the *Requiem* material he had conceived twenty years before. In offering her a part in writing what also now was a play, he asked in effect that she write herself into being for him there as the Mississippi college girl he had conceived and modeled on Estelle in 1929. He wanted what Temple characterizes in *Requiem for a Nun* as the "good letters" (RN, 573) into which he now imagined her having written herself and her desire for her lover Red from a Memphis brothel. Those letters are new to *Requiem*—Temple writes no letters in *Sanctuary*—and they were inspired both by Meta Carpenter Wilde's letters to Faulkner in the 1930s and 1940s and by those he now encouraged Joan to write him.[55]

He presented his early letters to Joan as if they were literary manuscripts, canceling passages with the red pencil and revising his self-presentations for effect, performing for her in the role of professional writer on the sheets of blank paper he said invited him to write of love. Alternately pleading and grieving, he wrote her love letters for nearly three years before they became lovers, spoke often of the doomed and fading scent of April she had brought him, and sent her a sadly resigned love poem about a lost April love titled "From an Old Man to Himself."[56] When Joan did become his lover in the summer of 1952, he wrote her a letter cast as a dialogue in which his phallus insists it belongs to her now, and he quoted—imperfectly, from memory, and without attribution—the opening lines of Ezra Pound's sonnet "A Virginal," which read:

> No, no! Go from me. I have left her lately.
> I will not spoil my sheath with lesser brightness,
> For my surrounding air hath a new lightness;
> Slight are her arms, yet they have bound me straightly
> And left me cloaked as with a gauze of æther;
> As with sweet leaves; as with subtle clearness.
> Oh, I have picked up magic in her nearness
> To sheathe me half in half the things that sheathe her.[57]

"Anguish" and "grief" were terms he used for the artist and the lover interchangeably, and not even his most serious self-presentations were exempt from an amorous subtext. "And now I realise for the first time what an amazing gift I had," he wrote Joan in April 1953; "uneducated in every formal sense, without even very literate, let alone literary, companions, yet to have made the things I made. I dont know where it came from. I dont know why God or gods or whoever it was, selected me to be the vessel" (SLWF, 348). Into this moving self-presentation of his double sense of himself as man and artist, he inserted an explicit erotic proposition reclaimed nearly word for word from a love letter he had written Meta Carpenter Wilde in July 1936.[58] Quoting Harry in *If I Forget Thee, Jerusalem*, he would tell Joan, as he had Meta, "between grief and nothing I will take grief."[59] Meta remembered that "The idealization of me as a girl far too young for him was to last for a number of years and to appear in some of his letters to me. I never protested and my acceptance of his vision of me as a maiden nourished his fantasy."[60] When Joan considered the difference in their ages, to which he regularly alluded in his letters to her, she wished that she could have been born earlier, or he later; he replied, "Earlier I was too busy writing to have had time for you."[61] When she failed to submit to his seductions, however, Old Moster punished her by blaming the failure on Joan's finding him a physically distasteful old man.[62] At the end of their love affair in December 1953 he characterized himself as the loving father she never had and their love as incest;[63] two weeks later he wrote her about nineteen-year-old Jean Stein's infatuation with him, characterizing it to Joan as to Saxe Commins two months later as a "repetition."[64] "Who wouldn't like to read the letters Faulkner wrote to the woman he loves and desires," he had written Joan in an erotic letter of January 1953. "I think some of them are pretty good literature."[65]

From all such writing as this and its long history in the novels, and doubtless, too, from his script writing in Hollywood, Faulkner's literary self-presentations and performances took the overtly dramatic form in *Requiem for a Nun* of a three-act play with long prose prefaces to each act. He had not considered his story a play when he mentioned it first in 1933; this was the first time he had written drama since *The Marionettes* in 1920. But there was a certain amount of melodrama in his writing about the book now in addition to the drama in it. In a statement he often repeated, Faulkner told Joan in March 1950, "the play is yours too. If you refuse to accept it, I will throw it away too. I would not have thought of writing one if I hadn't known you."[66] He conceived of it, he told her, not only as a play but as "some kind of novel, can be printed as such, rewritten into a play. Of course, we'll make no commitment until after we decide together, we'll just finish it and hold until we get together on it."[67] He told Robert Haas it was "an interesting experiment in form" (SLWF, 305). And in seduction. What he told Joan about his need for a collaborator addressed a personal desire for a young woman correspondent and lover, but he was most deeply interested, as always, in the literary quality of the book. Unsure of himself as a dramatist, he wrote Haas about having the dramatic sections rewritten by Robert Sherwood (SLWF, 302–303, 311).

If the play was a tool of seduction, it became a focal point for seductions of more women than Joan. Faulkner also was sexually interested at

this time in Ruth Ford, whom he also cast as Temple, insisting to the producer Lemuel Ayres that she have the part in the stage production. He
told his agent Harold Ober, "I have known Miss Ford a long time, admire
her rather terrifying determination to be an actress, and wrote this play
for her to abet it" (SLWF, 324). While the historical prefaces of *Requiem*
went steadily forward, the dramatic sections about alcoholism, adultery,
abandonment, and a dead child on which Joan was working reflected his
increasingly tangled love life. Faulkner told Meta about the play in March
1950 when he asked her to write him pseudonymously as he asked Joan
that July;[68] when Joan refused to go to Hollywood with him in January
1951, he wrote immediately to Meta.[69] They became lovers again that
winter in Hollywood, where Faulkner continued to write Joan, asking her
in one letter to write that she loved him.[70] When he returned from California he immediately began writing Meta again. He was in Paris in April
1951, at the invitation of the Gallimards, and resumed a love affair with
the Swedish widow Else Jonsson begun at the Nobel Prize ceremony in
1950. Saxe Commins collaborated by arranging their rooms at the Hotel
Leutitia then.[71]

His life and his art were closely aligned that summer and fall. Temple
Drake, of course, was very much on his mind as he brought the novel toward publication and worked at adapting the dramatic chapters for the
stage. So, too, were the three real young women whom Temple recalled to
him. *Requiem for a Nun* was published September 27, 1951. That month,
a week before leaving to work on the play in Cambridge, he wrote Else
about it (SLWF, 322), and in one three-day period there he wrote about it
to both Meta and Joan.[72] Financing for the American production did not
materialize that fall, nor for a proposed French production in Paris the
next spring. In January 1952, with production of the play in doubt, Faulkner proposed assignations to Meta and Joan in letters written the same
day.[73] In his attempts to seduce Joan in 1950, he had boasted of his sexual
vigor with Else in a December letter from London, after the Nobel Prize
ceremony; when he arranged to be with Else in Paris in May 1952, at the
conference where his play was to have been performed, he wrote Joan re-
gretfully that it was her face he would see in Else's bed.[74] In July he sent
Joan a message of love in Swedish that he doubtless had learned from Else,
warning her to choose a translator with care.[75] Joan became his lover in
August, a month after his return from Europe; thereafter his letters to her
became frankly erotic.

Together these women and his portrayals of them in the letters he

wrote them, sometimes simultaneously, came to comprise a living, contemporary composite of the doomed girl-figure he had modeled on Estelle
in the early poetry and *The Marionettes* and introduced into *The Sound
and the Fury* and *Sanctuary*. He described her at the University of Virginia in 1957 as "my heart's darling." Writing *The Sound and the Fury*, he
said at Virginia, "I used the tools which seemed to me the proper tools to
try to tell, try to draw the picture of Caddy" (FU, 6). So increasingly fine
was the line between the actual and imagined by 1950, that matters from
his fiction crossed as readily into his life as did his life into fiction. Marriage matters based on the death of his and Estelle's first child, their alcoholism, and his adulteries went into the three acts of the novel-play with
characters in whom he had represented such things in previous work.
He offered drafts of the play to Joan now as he had his first letters, as manuscripts for her to respond to and revise as his new beloved. His erotic
Swedish love note, conversely, was a gambit borrowed from fiction. In the
story "Knight's Gambit" (1949), Gavin's sixteen-year-old American correspondent receives an erotic letter in German intended for his Heidelberg
mistress, and he wonders "how whoever translated the German for her,
translated the English too" (KG, 236).

Compounded of actual and written women he had known and imagined in the interim, the Temple of *Requiem* is a fallen if outwardly reformed version of the Temple he created from Estelle in *Sanctuary* twenty
years earlier. But that girl did not disappear: she recurs in the last years of
his career in Linda Snopes in *The Town* (1957), and then in *The Mansion*
(1959), where she is educated as a lady at the Jefferson Seminary, a girl's
college analogous to Estelle's Mary Baldwin College, Cho-Cho's Mississippi Synodical College in Holly Springs, Joan's junior colleges in Memphis and Baltimore and Bard College, and Jill's Pine Manor Junior College.
Derived from Horace Benbow in *Sanctuary*, the Gavin Stevens who judges
Temple in *Requiem* and courts Linda in *The Town* is another Pygmalian,
who performs with all of the dedication and painful disappointment that
Faulkner expended on Joan. Although she comes to maturity as a widowed
war veteran in *The Mansion* (1959), her virginity is figuratively reconstituted for Gavin by her deafness, and he pursues her as Faulkner pursued
his own young women, in writing. "Immured" by her deafness, "inviolate
in silence, invulnerable, serene" (Mansion, 203), it is Linda now who
shocks Gavin into silence by offering what Faulkner asked of both Meta
and Joan in his letters and in the same language: "'But you can [fuck] me,'
she said" (Mansion, 238). After Joan's divorce a year later, Faulkner used

the same "explicit . . . hard brutal gutteral" word for love (Mansion, 238) in a letter to her, adding that he knew it was a word she didn't like.[76]

Reasons for such recurrences can be found in passages of the fiction where Faulkner implicitly worked out and justified his aesthetic. Far from declamatory, they commonly are phrased in the rich poetic language with which he also performed his most intimate self-presentations. When Quentin speaks to his father of Caddy's lost virginity and his own suicide in *The Sound and the Fury*, Mr. Compson tells his son, "you cannot bear to think that someday it will no longer hurt you like this" (TSATF, 177). As novel followed novel into the 1950s, Faulkner's repeated return to the girl-figure and to similarly significant figures and situations of his imagination accommodated his analogous impulse for self-torment by preserving the pain of the moment in print. Joan's letter in 1949 brought back to him his feeling for Caddy, "something remembered out of youth," as he put it to Joan then, and the connection of that fictional girl with the actual Joan he immediately began fictionalizing made "a soiled battered bloke aged 50 years" seem to himself once again "brave and clean and durable." The manifest reality of that kind of association for Faulkner, together with the numbers of real and fictional models it involved and the unexpected connections between them, is lodged in something else Mr. Compson tells Quentin: that "it is hard believing to think that a love or a sorrow is a bond purchased without design and which matures willy-nilly and is recalled without warning to be replaced by whatever issue the gods happen to be floating at the time" (TSATF, 178). There were a number of such figurative bonds in his own life, purchased with and without design, and he floated them along with new issues he invented in the lives of his characters, not least in the life of Quentin Compson. They include the interlinked delights and pains of innocence and unrequited love, marriage matters, child births and abandoned children, heroism and cowardice, self-sacrifice and achievement and defeat. Mr. Compson describes suicide, in the same passage of *The Sound and the Fury*, as "an apotheosis in which a temporary state of mind will become symmetrical above the flesh and aware both of itself and of the flesh it will not quite discard" (TSATF, 177). To make an earlier point yet again, the figure is a reflexive description of that novel, which preserves its creator's state of mind of the moment in the self-aware writing that likewise, and so often tormentingly, remembers the flesh.

In a way that he could not have considered in 1928–1929, *Absalom, Absalom!* revalidated Quentin's (and Faulkner's) anguish seven years later in terms of Mr. Compson's (and Faulkner's) thesis, by extending the pain of his own and Quentin's lost love beyond *The Sound and the Fury* into a fictional history that reproduces it in still another character, Henry Sutpen. *Requiem for a Nun* may be said to reprise *Sanctuary* in this way, in a still deeper historical, even archaeological context and with a cast of characters that has grown and changed with the author, some of them the same and some replacements for those who dropped away over the years. Alabama Red's sexual potency in *Sanctuary* and Temple Drake's desire for him are preserved in *Requiem* in the erotic letters Faulkner invented there for Temple from his own. Revived in Temple by Pete's reading of the letters, desire and loss are *re*-presented in a fictional present extended and enlarged by new issues floated by the god-like novelist, including that of a new young lover to, for, and with whom he could write. Attendant on the negotiations between life and art, art and life, such transfigurations and mutations informed as they manifestly enriched the work that the self-presenting novelist performed in the four decades of his writing life.

At the end, in *The Reivers* (1961), he looked back in time to the heroes and adventures of his childhood in which so many of the young idealists of his fiction are sourced. Lucius Priest's journey in that novel to a Memphis brothel with Boon Hogganbeck and Ned William McCaslin in grandfather's automobile echoes Ike McCaslin's trip to Memphis for whiskey with Boon at a later time in an earlier book. Lucius Priest's, at least, may have come about from events as simple as one Faulkner described in his earliest extant letter, where he wrote his mother on August 16, 1912, "We went to Davidsons bottom in the auto yesterday and what Ches calls 'ar dam' ole leech' got on my foot. He had his head under the skin and Ches cut him out with a butcher knife" (TofH, 40). Ches Carothers was the black driver for Faulkner's grandfather, J. W. T. Falkner, and the model, with Faulkner's servant Ned Barnett and his character Lucas Quintus Carothers McCaslin Beauchamp, for Ned in *The Reivers*. Like a latterday Huck Finn, the hero of another very serious "boy's" book that he invoked when he described *The Reivers* to his editor years later, the twelve-year-old Faulkner signed himself in his letter, "Yure erfexxionnite sun" (TofH, p. 40).

A Fable presents a different case of Faulkner's writing from life. There he invented a chapter of war missing from his own experience that he had not—perhaps could not have—invented for Donald Mahon in 1925. Faulkner knew the actions of World War I from stories he heard in Toronto and from books such as R. H. Mottram's *The Spanish Farm*, but he visited the battlefields of France in 1925 only after he had written *Sol-diers' Pay*, then again in 1951 while he was working on *A Fable*.[77] For all the substantial differences between the two books, there are elements enough alike to see them as related in more than the World War I subject matter. In the much altered atmosphere of the post–World War II 1950s, the now Nobel laureate played variations in *A Fable*, as he repeatedly had done in previous work, upon the earlier novel, its characters, and its self-presentations. The books share the familiar figure of the innocent young man, for example: Faulkner wrote himself into and out of *Soldiers' Pay* in Julian Lowe, the noncombatant cadet who disappears from the novel to write letters from his mother's home, and he reimagined Lowe and him-self in the pilot Levine, who writes letters to his mother and commits sui-cide. The situation of the heroes, too, is both familiar and different. Faulk-ner longed for but despaired of Donald Mahon's combat experience, as does Lowe, and for years after the war he feigned a wound like Mahon's and still occasionally wrote of it.[78] Rector Mahon's son is replaced, in *A Fable*, by the principled corporal who repudiates combat and is sacrificed by the old general, according to the self-conscious Christian symbolism of the novel, as a son of god.[79] The similarities and differences in Faulkner himself between the two novels may be seen in the distance between his 1918 photograph in the uniform of an R.A.F. cadet and his late-1950s pho-tograph dressed for the Farmington Hunt Club.[80] (Fig. 20) Cadet Faulk-ner's ill-fitting tunic and military breeches, his walking stick, and espe-cially his white-banded cap recur in the greatly modified context of the professionally posed portrait in which the Nobelist performs for the cam-era in a crimson hunting coat, white riding jodhpurs, and top hat, a riding crop held in gloved hands across his bent knee. The boy of 1918, who loved uniforms and longed to be a flying officer, was the Faulkner who imagined himself flying on a buckskin pony in "Carcassonne" in the mid-1920s and wrote, "*I want to perform something bold and tragical and austere*" (CSWF, 899). The man he became, who rode the actual horses in the uniform of celebrity, fulfilled and performed that aspiration.

"The weaver-god, he weaves; and by that weaving is he deafened, that he hears no mortal voice; and by that humming, we, too, who look on the loom are deafened; and only when we escape it shall we hear the thousand voices that speak through it."[81] Herman Melville affirmed the weaver-god in himself in the Bower of the Arsacides near the end of *Moby-Dick*. At home in Oxford, Mississippi, William Faulkner affirmed himself such a one. His fiction, like Melville's novel and the white whale itself, is hiero-glyphical, deriving its multiform surfaces and its deepest soundings from his sorrows and joys. In it, as in his life, he interwove the actual and imag-inary, and what he imagined to be actual and imaginary, including espe-cially what another poet laureate, his own Rosa Coldfield, calls *"a might-have-been which is more true than truth, from which the dreamer, waking, says not 'Did I but dream?' but rather says, indicts high heaven's very self with: 'Why did I wake since waking I shall never sleep again?'"* (AA!, 115).

For the performance of this work he required a figurative Bower in the Arsacides of his own. He needed solitude to write. Publication, as Lewis J. Budd reminds us, is a public act: the fiction validated the private self and forestalled Faulkner's thinly veiled dread of oblivion, but it threatened the protean writer with public exposure in a world he had not imagina-tively created and could not control by a stroke of his pen.[82] He accord-ingly invented public selves from the private, at first to proclaim himself an artist in materials he made and privately published for friends and la-ter to hide himself in the variety of personae that he assumed separately and together. In this regard, the letter to Joan Williams distinguishing be-tween "the work and the country man whom you know as Bill Faulkner" (SLWF, 348) is a several-fold fabrication, a composite portrait for a former lover that presents him as a still vital artist and man—and one chosen by the gods, at that. In retrospect, there never *was* a significant distance be-tween the man and the work, and they became closer the older he grew. With the Reverend Shegog of his first masterwork, he had fleshed his po-etic voice "succubus like" (TSATF, 294) in his own body and life. What he wrote transformed and consumed him; he came to speak in his fiction, like Shegog in his sermon, in a voice that was likewise transformed and transforming, "sinking into their hearts and speaking there again when it had ceased in fading and cumulative echoes" (TSATF, 294).

Henry James wrote of another Southerner, in *The Bostonians*, that "He had a passionate tenderness for his own country, and a sense of in-timate connection with it which would have made it as impossible for him to take a roomful of Northern fanatics into his confidence as to read aloud his mother's or his mistress's letters."[83] That was not the case with William Faulkner. The same sort of intimate subtext in the 1954 letter to Joan Williams underlies even his most famous interview, with Jean Stein in 1956, about the creation of Yoknapatawpha County.[84] There he de-scribed himself as the Old Moster of his fictional world, sublimating the

Fig. 20 "Tally-ho, William Faulkner," Farmington Hunt Club, Late 1950s
(Courtesy of Jill Faulkner Summers)

actual "little postage stamp of native soil" into his apocryphal "cosmos,"
creating a "keystone in the Universe; that, as small as that keystone is, if
it were ever taken away, the universe itself would collapse." He could
move his characters around, he told Jean, "like God" (Lion, 225). That Jean
was his young lover then only intensifies the inherently private nature of
the statements Faulkner made for her to publish, as she did later that year
in *The Paris Review*. The text of the interview, like the texts of his novels and stories, is a retrospective scene of mixed fiction and fact that
Faulkner coolly controlled, his answers—and even the questions he perhaps proposed that she ask—constituting yet another of the artist's grand
self-presentations and performances. To Jean Stein then, the work he described must have seemed made in the God-like image he invoked, the
man and the artist inextricably one in the written word.

Notes

Chapter I. Self-Presentation and Performance

1. Cf. Faulkner's memory in 1925 that "At the age of sixteen, I discovered Swinburne. Or rather, Swinburne discovered me, springing from some tortured undergrowth of my adolescence, like a highwayman, making me his slave. My mental life at that period was so completely and smoothly veneered with surface insincerity—obviously necessary to me at that time, to support intact my personal integrity—that I can not tell to this day exactly to what depth he stirred me, just how deeply the footprints of his passage are left in my mind. It seems to me now that I found him nothing but a flexible vessel into which I might put my own vague emotional shapes without breaking them." "Verse Old and Nascent: A Pilgrimage," p. 114.

2. See Eliot, "Tradition and the Individual Talent," pp. 7, 9.

3. Poirier, *Performing Self*, p. 98.

4. Poirier puts this position into the context of nineteenth-century American literature in his "Prologue: The Deed of Writing," *Renewal of Literature*, pp. 3–66.

5. Minter, *William Faulkner: His Life and Work*, pp. 87–88.

6. Poirier, *Performing Self*, pp. xiii, xiv.

7. Poirier, *Performing Self*, p. xiii.

8. Poirier gives Faulkner passing mention in his "Preface," where he says, "If Faulkner, for example, really meant to summarize himself in the tedious, and loud, ironies of his Christian symbolisms in *The Sound and the Fury* or *Light in August*, he would be a writer not worth the trouble. In the act of reading him, however, anyone responsive to the local power of his writing soon recognizes that Faulkner needed his structurings the way a child might need a jungle gym: as a support for exuberant, beautiful, and testing flights." *Performing Self*, p. xv.

9. Bleikasten, *The Most Splendid Failure*, p. 201.

10. Matthews, *The Play of Faulkner's Language*, p. 108.

11. Bleikasten, *Most Splendid Failure*, p. 200.

12. Gresset, *Fascination*, pp. xv, xvi.

13. Gresset notes this conjunction in a different context in his "Faulkner, Home and the Ocean," p. 45.

14. Cohen and Fowler, "Faulkner's Introduction to *The Sound and the Fury*," pp. 262–283. Cohen and Fowler transcribe seven manuscript fragments of varying length (MSS A–F), arranged in order of composition, and the one distinctive typescript (TS H) of four which preceded the typescripts of the two published introductions. They argue that writing the introduction "triggered a profound self-analysis about [Faulkner's] own development as a writer" and find in the manuscripts "an astonishing frankness as he explores the autobiographical origins of the novel" (268). The two complete typescripts of the introduction have been published. The shorter is James B. Meriwether, ed., "An Introduction to *The Sound and the Fury*," *Southern Review*, 8 (1972), 705–710, cited here as SoR. The longer, a ten-page typescript, is James B. Meriwether, ed., "An Introduction to *The Sound and the Fury*," *Mississippi Quarterly*, 26 (1973), 410–415. Repr. James B. Meriwether, ed., *A Faulkner Miscellany* (Jackson: University Press of Mississippi, 1973), pp. 156–161, cited here as Miscellany. Quotations from the manuscripts and typescripts in *American Literature* are cited as AL.

15. Cohen and Fowler, "Faulkner's Introduction to *The Sound and the Fury*," p. 263.

16. Compare the far less dynamic descriptions of the "loony" in the 1925 sketch "The Kingdon of God," who has several of the attributes Faulkner ascribes to Benjy in the novel and the introduction. "He screamed, a hoarse, inarticulate bellow. . . . The idiot's voice rose and fell on waves of unbeliveable sound. . . ." *New Orleans Sketches*, pp. 57–58.

17. See especially Meriwether and Millgate, *Lion in the Garden*, p. 245; Gwynn and Blotner, *Faulkner in the University*, p. 1.

18. See Polk, "Introduction," *The Marionettes*, pp. ix–xxxii, rev. from "William Faulkner's *Marionettes*," *Mississippi Quarterly* 26 (Summer 1973), 247–280; Sensibar, *The Origins of Faulkner's Art*, where she argues that "Faulkner celebrates not so much the child as the sex act itself, the 'eternal gesture,' of which Cho-Cho is the 'flower'" (25); and Watson, *William Faulkner, Letters and Fictions*, p. 51.

Chapter II. Photographs, Letters, and Fictions

1. Shloss, *In Visible Light*, p. 14.

2. Barthes, *Camera Lucida*, pp. 79, 31.

3. Cofield, "Many Faces, Many Moods," p. 109.

4. Berger, *About Looking*, p. 35.

5. Sontag, *On Photography*, p. 161.

6. Minter, "Faulkner, Childhood and the Making of *The Sound and the Fury*," p. 392. Blotner says that "the line between reality and imagination was not as compelling for him as it was for others." *Biography* (1984), pp. 66–67. Sensibar sees in his impostures "ways of imposing a fictional screen over his private life." *Origins of Faulkner's Art*, p. 9. She finds in "the relation between creativity and sexuality" evidence that his man-

hood was at issue in his role-playing. "'Drowsing Maidenhead Symbol's Self,'" p. 133. See also Minter, *Life and Work*; Watson, *William Faulkner, Letters and Fictions*; and Wittenberg, *William Faulkner: The Transfiguration of Biography.*

7. James Dahl quotes Maud Falkner as saying that her painting of Faulkner standing in front of a plane was done from such a photograph. "A Faulkner Reminiscence: Conversations with Mrs. Maud Falkner," p. 1027.

8. Sontag, *On Photography*, p. 22.

9. Minter, "Faulkner, Childhood and the Making of *The Sound and the Fury*," p. 392.

10. Gresset, "Faulkner's Self-Portraits," p. 3.

11. Gresset, "Faulkner's Self-Portraits," p. 2.

12. Gresset takes up the issue of letters in his essay "A Public Man's Private Voice: Faulkner's Letters to Else Jonsson."

13. Berger, *About Looking*, pp. 55–56.

14. References here are to Sontag's definitions in *On Photography*. Epistolary conventions and Faulkner's knowledge and use of them in his own correspondence and fiction are described in Watson, *William Faulkner, Letters and Fictions.*

15. Sontag, *On Photography*, p. 3.

16. Sontag, *On Photography*, p. 6.

17. Sontag, *On Photography*, p. 16.

18. Sontag, *On Photography*, p. 22.

19. Sontag, *On Photography*, p. 23.

20. Faulkner had used the same image a month earlier, in a letter of August 3, 1918, where he said that the pine trees at night "look like poured ink." TofH, p. 88. The image recurs in *Soldiers' Pay* where Gilligan walks at night "between dark trees like spilled ink upon the pale clear page of the sky" (312).

21. The story apparently dates from the mid-1920s, shortly after Faulkner's return from Europe. See Blotner, *Biography* (1974) p. 692, and Skei, *Short Story Career*, p. 38.

22. Shloss, *In Visible Light*, p. 254.

23. Howard, *William Faulkner: The Carl Petersen Collection*, pp. 15, 16.

24. Cofield, "Many Faces, Many Moods," p. 109.

25. Cofield, "Many Faces, Many Moods," pp. 109, 110.

26. A copy of the photograph with the notes transcribed by Carvel Collins is in the Carvel Collins Collection at the Harry Ransom Humanities Research Center (Photos by Faulkner).

27. Grimwood speaks of characters with such afflictions as constituting part of "Faulkner's secret history of his body." *Heart in Conflict*, p. 57.

28. Gresset, "Faulkner's Self-Portraits," p. 13.

29. The 1930 story is based on Judge Oldham and his son Edward, who died when he was nine. Faulkner used the same epigraph for Howard Allison, "*Auf Wiedersehn, Little Boy*" (CSWF, 796), as the Oldhams did for Edward. Blotner, *Biography* (1984), p. 259.

30. The story was written in 1930 before the death of Faulkner and Estelle's daughter Alabama and revised and submitted for publication in 1931, a week after that event. Polk, *Children of the Dark House*, p. 156.

31. The German may be modeled on Nicholas Llewellyn, a law student Faulkner knew at Yale in 1918 who had studied in Germany and served for a time in the German army before deserting. Bland in "Ad Astra" is named for a shell-shocked British officer stationed in New Haven that spring, and Faulkner's description of the subadar in the story is drawn from two Hindu co-workers at the Winchester Arms Co. in New Haven and a cadet in Toronto named Durla Bushell. See Watson, *Thinking of Home*, pp. 28–29; Collins, "'Ad Astra' through New Haven," pp. 108–127.

32. Blotner speculates that "The Leg" is the "queer short story, about a case of reincarnation" Faulkner described in a letter on October 15, 1925. SLWF, p. 31. Skei points out that its earliest known date is late 1928. *Short Story Career*, pp. 41–42.

33. Sensibar, *Origins of Faulkner's Art*, p. 24; Blotner, *Biography* (1984), pp. 72–73. With Blotner, Sensibar notes that Borden was an invented stationing. Sensibar speculates that Faulkner's copy of Hodgson's *Poems* may have contained a similar inscription to Estelle. Faulkner asked Maud to send him the Hodgson book in Toronto in August 1918 (TofH, 90). He never was a member of the Royal Flying Corps.

34. Sensibar reads the drawings in *The Marionettes* as precursors of fictional photographs, including that in "The Leg," through which, she argues, Faulkner questioned phallocentric ways of speaking and acting out desire. "Faulkner's Fictional Photographs," pp. 295–302.

35. Collins points out that Faulkner used this idea elsewhere in *Helen* and quarried lines from Poem X to express it in poems he later included in *A Green Bough*. HAC, pp. 71–72.

36. Blotner says Estelle was "Torn and anguished" by Faulkner's charge that "her fickle heart" had betrayed them: "she told him that she did not prefer Cornell to him, but she did not know what she should do or, at this point, what she could do." *Biography* (1984), p. 56.

37. See Polk, "'Hong Li' and *Royal Street*," pp. 143–144; Watson, *William Faulkner, Letters and Fictions*, pp. 48–52.

38. Sensibar, *Origins of Faulkner's Art*, p. 114.

39. Sensibar, *Origins of Faulkner's Art*, pp. 160–163.

40. Sensibar, "Faulkner's Fictional Photographs," p. 296.

41. For obvious reasons, the phrase "the dungeon was Mother herself" has elicited Oedipal psychological readings. See especially Polk, "'The Dungeon Was Mother Herself,'" pp. 61–64, and his *Children of the Dark House*.

42. In *As I Lay Dying*, at a parallel moment, Addie Bundren will refer to "The shape of my body where I used to be a virgin" as nameless emptiness represented by a literally blank space of text (AILD, 173).

43. These range from the indispensable, such as Blotner's *Faulkner: A Biography*, to the very good and helpful, among which are Adams's "The Apprenticeship of William Faulkner," Millgate's *Achievement*, Minter's *Life and Work*, Sensibar's *Origins of Faulkner's Art*, and Wittenberg, *Transfiguration of Biography*. Gray's *The Life of William Faulkner* seems to me sometimes to present such issues as too smoothly and logically sequential. See also Meriwether, ed., *Essays, Speeches and Public Letters by William Faulkner*, and Meriwether and Michael Millgate, eds., *Lion in the Garden: Interviews with William Faulkner, 1926–1962*.

44. Information to the author from Thomas L. McHaney. In April 1918 Benet was elected chairman of the *Yale Literary Magazine* and wrote for the magazine prodigiously. Badger was a student at Yale then and one of Benet's close friends, whom he nominated for his Wolf's Head Club and encouraged to join in a letter of July 1918. They remained friends and correspondents during Benet's lifetime. See Fenton, ed., *Selected Letters of Stephen Vincent Benet*, pp. 13, 16–18.

45. Watson, "Two Letters about William Faulkner, 1918," p. 18.

46. A great deal has been written about the Faulkner-Stone and Faulkner-Anderson relationships. For appraisals in the present context, see especially Snell, *Phil Stone of Oxford*, pp. 90–110; and Watson, "Faulkner in New Orleans: The 1925 Letters," pp. 196–206.

47. Faulkner mentions Chaplin and the Keystone Kops in connection with the silent screen actor Ben Turpin in a letter from Toronto, October 10, 1918. TofH, pp. 112–113.

48. A similar, more detailed epistolary performance, in a 1925 letter from France, describes his arrest for loitering at Dieppe. Paraded through the town by the gendarme and interrogated in French, he is released when the commanding officer realizes he is a poet. TofH, pp. 219–222.

49. Gaston Bachelard argues that "the house shelters daydreaming" and that it is "one of the greatest powers of integration for the thoughts, memories and dreams of mankind. The binding principle in this integration is the daydream. Past, present and future give the house different dynamisms, which often interfere, at times opposing, at others stimulating one another. In the life of a man, the house thrusts aside contingencies, its councils of continuity are unceasing. Without it, man would be a dispersed being." *Poetics of Space*, pp. 6–7.

50. Phil Stone to Carvel Collins, August 16, 1954. Brodsky and Hamblin, *Faulkner: A Comprehensive Guide to the Brodsky Collection*, Vol. 2, *The Letters*, p. 154.

51. Howard, *William Faulkner: The Carl Petersen Collection*, p. 15.

52. Howard, *William Faulkner: The Carl Petersen Collection*, p. 16.

53. See Watson, *William Faulkner, Letters and Fictions*, pp. 79–83.

54. Faulkner may have borrowed the word "philoprogenitive" from T. S. Eliot's "Polyphiloprogenitive" in "Mr. Eliot's Sunday Morning Service." In the December 1928 story "Miss Zilphia Gant," Zilphia's virgin daughter conceives an imaginary child by masturbating, "violat[ing] her ineradicable virginity again and again with something evoked out of the darkness immemorial and philoprogenitive." USWF, p. 379.

55. See especially Blotner, *Biography* (1984), pp. 10, 207; Murry C. Falkner, *The Falkners of Mississippi*, p. 12; Minter, *Life and Work*, pp. 16, 23; and Jay Martin, "'The Whole Burden of Man's History and His Impossible Heart's Desires': The Early Life of William Faulkner," p. 623.

56. Murry Falkner, *The Falkners of Mississippi*, p. 90.

57. Bleikasten, "Fathers in Faulkner," pp. 115, 117. Bleikasten argues, "There would be little point . . . in looking for some father archetype, for what seems to be at issue in Faulkner's intricate family chronicles is not the father as a person (a character), nor even the father as genitor, as the actual begetter of sons and daughters, but rather the haunting question of fatherhood, in its psychoethical as well as in its wider cultural implications" (115).

58. In fact, a series of complications with Liveright's advance on *Soldiers' Pay* kept Faulkner in Europe longer. He sailed December 9 aboard the S. S. *Republic*, arriving in New York December 19. See TofH, pp. 226–230.

59. Such "crossings" are treated in some detail in Watson, *William Faulkner, Letters and Fictions*. See especially chapters 1, "The Two Canons," and 2, "Crossings."

60. Blotner, *Biography* (1984), p. 73.

61. Sensibar argues that "Faulkner became an artist in a culture that defined art as a feminine occupation." See "Faulkner's Fictional Photographs," p. 293.

Chapter III. Marriage Matters

1. Polk, "Afterword," p. 298.

2. See especially Polk, "The Space Between *Sanctuary*," "Afterword," and *Children of the Dark House*; Wittenberg, *Transfiguration of Biography*; Minter, *His Life and Work*; and Martin, "'The Whole Burden of Man's History and His Impossible Heart's Desire.'" On Estelle's importance to Faulkner's writing, see also Moser, "Faulkner's Muse: Speculations on the Genesis of *The Sound and the Fury*"; and Rollyson, "'Counterpull': Estelle and William Faulkner."

3. Coindreau, "Preface to *The Sound and the Fury*," p. 49. See also Blotner, *Biography* (1984), p. 212; Watson, *William Faulkner, Letters and Fictions*, p. 55.

4. Polk, "Afterword," pp. 298–299. Polk lists a number of specific similarities between the two characters and concludes that "Horace is, in effect, a forty-three-year-old and completely jaded Quentin, surely what Quentin would have become had he lived another quarter-century." "Afterword," p. 299. See also Wittenberg, *Transfiguration of Biography*, p. 98.

5. Blotner gives her birth date as February 19, 1896. *Biography* (1984), "Genealogy," p. 752. Williamson, citing Mississippi census records, gives her birth date as February 19, 1897. *William Faulkner and Southern History*, p. 146. I have followed Williamson.

6. Blotner, *Biography* (1974), pp. 174–175. Most of the following chronology is reconstructed from the two-volume (1974) and one-volume (1984) *Biography*. Documentation of specific points is provided.

7. Blotner, *Biography* (1974), p. 179.

8. Blotner, *Biography* (1974), pp. 192–193.

9. Blotner, *Biography* (1984), pp. 58–59.

10. Blotner, *Biography* (1974) p. 243.

11. Blotner, *Biography* (1974), pp. 282–283.

12. Blotner, *Biography* (1974), p. 315.

13. Blotner, *Biography* (1974), pp. 306, 310–311. See also Sensibar, Introduction to *Vision in Spring* and *Origins of Faulkner's Art*.

14. Blotner, *Biography* (1974), p. 315; TofH, pp. 154–155, 160–161.

15. Blotner, *Biography* (1974), pp. 376, 483.

16. Wasson, *Count No 'Count*, pp. 79–80.

17. Blotner, *Biography* (1974), p. 399; Watson, "Faulkner's 'What Is the Matter with Marriage,'" p. 71.

18. TofH, p. 184.

19. Collins, "Biographical Background for Faulkner's *Helen*," p. 18.

20. Blotner, *Biography* (1974), p. 483.

21. Blotner, *Biography* (1974), pp. 504, 506, 523–524.

22..On "Hong Li" see Polk, "'Hong Li' and *Royal Street*." *Royal Street: New Orleans* is part of the Dean Faulkner Mallard Collection of Faulkner materials purchased in 1966 by the Harry Ransom Humanities Research Center. The 1966 purchase included, in addition to *Royal Street*, an unsigned copy of *The Marionettes* and 148 letters from Faulkner to his mother and father, 1912–1925. Had Faulkner given *Royal Street* to Estelle, presumably, it would not have been available for sale in 1966.

23. Blotner, *Biography* (1984), pp. 188–189.

24. See Williamson, *William Faulkner and Southern History*, p. 218. Information based on Williamson's reading of the Blotner papers, now part of the Louis Daniel Brodsky Collection at Southeast Missouri State College.

25. Blotner, *Biography* (1974), pp. 523–524.

26. Blotner, *Biography* (1974), pp. 541–543.

27. Brodsky and Hamblin, *A Comprehensive Guide to the Brodsky Collection*, Vol. 2: *The Letters*, p. 8.

28. Blotner, *Biography* (1984), pp. 213–219. Blotner cites specific similarities and differences between Faulkner and Quentin, between Estelle, Sallie Murry Wilkins, and Caddy, and between Murry Falkner and Jason.

29. The book was turned down by Harcourt, Brace and published by the new firm of Jonathan Cape and Harrison Smith, formed when Smith left Harcourt in 1929.

30. Blotner, *Biography* (1974), p. 604.

31. Blotner, *Biography* (1984), p. 240. Given his offer to repay the loan with ten percent interest by March 1, 1930, this dating would constitute a standard loan period of one year.

32. Blotner, *Biography* (1984), p. 240.

33. Sensibar finds the letter "a shorthand version of some of the most redundant and powerful images of desire" in Faulkner's fiction. "'Drowsing Maidenhead Symbol's Self,'" p. 138.

34. Smith did not reject the novel out of hand as Faulkner later claimed. Polk shows that galleys 2, 3, and 4 were set May 16, 1930, the remainder in November. Publication was postponed to allow for the setting and publication of *As I Lay Dying*. See *Sanctuary: The Holograph Manuscript and Miscellaneous Pages*, Vol. 1, p. viii.

35. Blotner, *Biography* (1974), pp. 619–624.

36. Blotner, *Biography* (1974), pp. 624–625, 629.

37. Blotner, *Biography* (1974), p. 630.

38. Blotner, *Biography* (1984), p. 245.

39. Blotner, *Biography* (1974), p. 633.

40. Victoria Fielden Johnson in an interview with L. D. Brodsky. Brodsky, *Life Glimpses*,

pp. 133, 136, 138, 145. Blotner says nothing of Malcolm's living with the Oldhams, nor does Malcolm Franklin in his memoir, *Bitterweeds: Life with William Faulkner at Rowan Oak.*

41. Poirier, *Performing Self*, p. xiii.

42. Collins points out that several of the poems in the gift book predate Faulkner's acquaintance with Helen Baird and cites an untitled typescript version of Sonnet XV dated March 1925 in the Berg Collection at the New York Public Library. The "courtship" in *Helen* is organized chronologically and by location, beginning in "Pascagoula—June—1925 and ending with Sonnet XV in "Paris—September—1925." See Collins, "Biographical Background for Faulkner's *Helen*," p. 78; Sensibar, *Faulkner's Poetry*, p. 32.

43. Watson, "Faulkner's 'What Is the Matter with Marriage,'" p. 71.

44. See Watson, *William Faulkner, Letters and Fictions*, pp. 43–48.

45. Elmer Hodge, like Faulkner, has been in the Canadian armed forces and, as a prospective artist, tours the art galleries of New York following his service as Faulkner did when he went there in 1921, in part to learn to draw and paint. Among the verbal echoes from that period is Elmer's comment that men are like lice (Elmer, 413); in a 1921 letter to his mother, Faulkner said of his first subway ride, "The experience showed me that we are not descended from monkeys, as some say, but from lice." TofH, p. 157.

46. Collins considers and rejects the latter possibility in his introduction to *Mayday*, pp. 24–25.

47. McHaney, "The Elmer Papers: Faulkner's Comic Portraits of the Artist," p. 281; Watson, "Literary Self-Criticism: Faulkner in Fiction on Fiction," pp. 58–60.

48. In Wasson's account, when Estelle turned from the piano to kiss him, as Belle does Horace, they were interrupted by Cho-Cho, as Belle and Horace are by Little Belle. Wasson reports being surprised to find the scene in *Flags* when he edited the manuscript in 1928, but he retained it in *Sartoris* nonetheless. *Count No 'Count*, pp. 80–81, 84.

49. Wittenberg, *Transfiguration of Biography*, p. 89.

50. Except to distinguish between the two, I draw freely on both the original and the first published versions of the novel, which are cited here as SO (*"Sanctuary": The Original Text*) and SR (*Sanctuary*, the revised version).

51. In combination with the name Old Frenchman place, and Popeye's association with marriage and adultery in Flaubert's novel, Popeye may be said to be exercising his right of *droit de seigneur*, a term Faulkner used to describe Manfred de Spain's cuckolding of the impotent Flem in *The Town* (273). As titular owner of the Old Frenchman place, Goodwin also propositions Temple, on Sunday through Tommy, who paws at her himself.

52. Wittenberg was among the first to make this point about Temple's appearance at the trial and the trip to France. See *Transfiguration of Biography*, p. 101.

53. "False entry" describes Popeye's crime against Temple in the barn the Goodwins use as an outhouse. See Watson, *William Faulkner, Letters and Fictions*, pp. 108–109.

54. Wittenberg makes a similar point from a different perspective in *Transfiguration of Biography*, p. 98.

55. In his discussion of the sequence of Faulkner's writing in this period, Polk speculates that some of *Sanctuary*, in some form, preceded *Flags in the Dust*, perhaps as early as 1925. He finds that "The holograph manuscript of *Sanctuary*—recording Faulkner's

thousands of revisions, his constant shifting of passage after passage, page after page—and the revised galleys, characterized by the same restless shifting of large blocks of material, demonstrate how very difficult *Sanctuary* was to write." *Children of the Dark House*, p. 42.

56. Brodsky and Hamblin, *A Comprehensive Guide to the Brodsky Collection*. Vol. 2: *The Letters*, p. 8; emphasis added. Falling, as it does, in the period following the rejection of *Flags in the Dust*, when Faulkner was struggling without success to revise the novel, the letter has implications for that book, as well. See Watson, *William Faulkner, Letters and Fictions*, pp. 66–67.

57. Collins, "A Note on *Sanctuary*," p. 16. The following discussion is based upon materials in the Carvel Collins Collection at the Harry Ransom Humanities Research Center. Cf. Watson, "Carvel Collins's Faulkner: A Newly Opened Archive"; and Blotner, *Biography* (1974), pp. 604–609, and (1984), pp. 234–235.

58. "Notes on an Interview with Dorothy Ware, 8–24–51." Carvel Collins Collection, file "Dorothy Ware."

59. Blotner, *Biography* (1974), pp. 608–609.

60. Blotner, *Biography* (1974), pp. 341–343.

61. Information about the McNamara trial is based on notes and transcriptions from the Memphis *Commercial-Appeal*, October 1919, August 1920, in the Carvel Collins Collection, file "*Sanctuary*—novel." See Watson, "Carvel Collins's Faulkner: A Newly Opened Archive," pp. 268–270.

62. Polk, *Children of the Dark House*, p. 42.

63. See Wasson, on his experience with Estelle and his editing *Flags* with Faulkner in New York. *Count No 'Count*, pp. 80–81, 83–91. His homosexuality is a possible source of Horace's squeamishness about women. Wasson also was associated with theatre, having helped to found the dramatic club at the University of Mississippi with Faulkner and others, and it was he who arranged for the sale of copies of *The Marionettes* in 1920. His claim that he edited *Flags* alone has been called into question by some commentators, but his account accords with Faulkner's own in the preface to *Sartoris*. See Putzel, "Text of the Yale Preface," pp. 295–298.

64. For a discussion of Horace's letters in *Flags* and the relation of fictional letters to problems of authorship in the novel, see Watson, *William Faulkner, Letters and Fictions*, pp. 64–76.

65. Polk, *Children of the Dark House*, p. 45. Polk writes, "After Smith postponed publication of *Sanctuary*, Faulkner was left holding not just an unpublished novel, but a nightmarish world which he could not exorcise, a myriad of images, doubtless from his own psychological preoccupations that he returned to obsessively in the months that followed. By the fall of 1930, he had worked his way through many of those preoccupations, or at least brought them under some artistic control. Looking at those galleys, he must have felt himself looking at a self he thought he had long since abandoned—or escaped." *Children of the Dark House*, p. 44. Polk also deals with these issues in "The Space Between *Sanctuary*" and "Afterword."

66. Polk notes among the consequences of Faulkner's reordering scenes that "The [revised] narrative is almost completely straightforward, moving from its beginning to its conclusion with economy and precision. More important, the revised novel establishes new relationships among Horace, Temple, and Popeye." "Afterword," p. 302.

67. Although dates in *Sanctuary* are specified only occasionally, unlike *The Sound and the Fury* where they are used as chapter titles, the chronology of the novel is internally clear and consistent.

68. Faulkner compared New Haven to Memphis in terms of play houses and movie theatres in his first letter to Maud, April 5, 1918. TofH, p. 44. The Oxford movie theatre was managed in 1925 by Robert X. Williams, husband of Faulkner's cousin, Sally Murry Wilkins.

69. Blotner describes Estelle wearing "gorgeous silk dresses" on her honeymoon and "an exotic Chinese robe" in 1930–1931. *Biography* (1984), pp. 245, 266. In *The Sound and the Fury* Dalton Ames's shirts of "heavy Chinese silk" associate him with Cornell Franklin, who likewise *"had been in the army"* (TSATF, 92, 148); thinking of Ames' unmanning him, Quentin says of castration, "O that That's Chinese I don't know Chinese" (TSATF, 116).

70. See Matthews, "The Elliptical Nature of *Sanctuary*," pp. 257–258.

71. Quoted from an interview with Jill Faulkner Summers in Sensibar, "'Drowsing Maidenhead Symbol's Self,'" pp. 139–140.

72. See Matthews, "The Elliptical Nature of *Sanctuary*," pp. 246–265.

73. Matthews, "The Rhetoric of Containment," p. 59. See also the companion piece, "Faulkner's Narrative Frames," where Matthews examines Quentin's role as the marginalized frame narrator of three Compson short stories, "That Evening Sun," "A Justice," and "Lion."

74. Matthews, "The Rhetoric of Containment," p. 59. It is worth noting in this connection, as Polk does, that much of the Ur-*Sanctuary* is cast as Horace's stream-of-consciousness, very much in the manner of Quentin's chapter of *The Sound and the Fury*. In the revision, as Polk says, "the early version's stream-of-consciousness [is recast] as direct quotations from Horace as narrator." *Children of the Dark House*, p. 43. The "crevices of contradiction" created by first-person narration in the original manuscript carried into the revision.

75. Matthews finds that "silence, repression and narrative elision" are characteristic of the novel. Ellipsis indicates "the impossibility of representing natural relations that precede language; it disguises and displaces forbidden desires; and it exposes the placelessness of the boundaries thought to discriminate and protect culture from nature." "The Elliptical Nature of *Sanctuary*," p. 248.

76. The phrasing of this scene in the two versions of the novel is slightly different because of the alteration of point of view, but the image of superimposed faces is the same. The revised *Sanctuary* reads, "In the spring the drinking man leaned his face to the broken and myriad reflection of his own drinking. When he rose up he saw among them the shattered reflection of Popeye's straw hat" (SR, 4; cf. SO, 21).

77. Quotations from "Gerontion" are from *T. S. Eliot: The Complete Poems and Plays, 1909–1950*, pp. 21–23. "Gerontion" was first published in Eliot's *Poems* (1920).

78. In his discussion of *The Waste Land* in *Sanctuary*, Polk argues that Horace is a Tiresian figure, and says, "What Horace sees is the substance of *Sanctuary*." *Children of the Dark House*, p. 47.

79. Sensibar discusses Faulkner's use of this and other fictional photographs "to question and critique phallocentric ways of seeing, speaking, and acting out desire." She is right to suggest that in *Sanctuary*, Horace's "forbidden fantasies of lust, incest and

pedophilia" coalesce in the photograph of Little Belle, but she bases her argument on the mistaken assumption that Horace steals it. "Faulkner's Fictional Photographs," pp. 295–296. In fact, neither novel states it is stolen, and in the Ur-*Sanctuary* he plainly takes it from its frame in his own study (SO, 19).

80. Blotner, *Biography* (1984), pp. 58–59.

81. Blotner, *Biography* (1984), p. 241.

82. A copy of the document, filed October 22, 1935, and withdrawn December 3, 1935, is in the Carvel Collins Collection at the Harry Ransom Humanities Research Center. See Watson, "Carvel Collins's Faulkner: A Newly Opened Archive," p. 271. Faulkner's liaison with Meta Carpenter apparently dates from December–January 1935–1936 when he worked with Hawks on *The Road to Glory*.

83. See, for example, Wittenberg, *Transfiguration of Biography*, p. 151.

84. Fitzgerald, *The Great Gatsby*, pp. 77, 78.

85. Howell notes, among other parallels, that the pictured eye of Mottson revokes Fitzgerald's eyes of T. J. Eckleburg. "Hemingway and Fitzgerald in *The Sound and the Fury*," p. 238.

86. Fitzgerald, *The Great Gatsby*, p. 86.

87. Putzel, *Genius of Place*, p. 296. For the date of composition, see Putzel, "Faulkner's Trial Preface to *Sartoris*." Blotner proposes that the preface was written for Faulkner's new agent Morton Goldman in 1930–1931, two years after Ben Wasson's editing of the novel, in September–October 1928. "William Faulkner's Essay on the Composition of *Sartoris*."

88. Putzel, *Genius of Place*, p. 297.

89. Putzel, *Genius of Place*, p. 297.

Chapter IV. Who's Your Old Man?

1. Gray, *Life*, pp. 65–66.

2. Blotner, *Biography* (1974), p. 678.

3. Brodsky and Hamblin, *A Comprehensive Guide to the Brodsky Collection*, Vol. 2, pp. 8, 12.

4. Gresset correctly characterizes Stone's ambiguous stance in the piece as mixed "protection and bitterness with regard to his former protege." *Chronology*, p. 42.

5. For details of this relationship based on Faulkner's 1925 New Orleans correspondence, see Watson, "'My Father's Unfailing Kindness': William Faulkner and the Idea of Home."

6. Faulkner's Al Jackson letters are in *Uncollected Stories*, pp. 474–479; Anderson's one letter, misdated 1927, is in *Letters of Sherwood Anderson*, ed. Jones and Rideout, pp. 162–164. The first letter opens with Faulkner's description of "a boating party across the lake over the week end" (USWF, 474). The Ponchartrain outing was March 21–22, 1925 (TofH, 191–193) and the letters apparently began the following week. William Spratling remembers that the regular tall-tale competition between the two was resumed at Vieux Carre parties. "Chronicle of a Friendship," pp. 12–13.

7. Cohen and Fowler, "Faulkner's Introduction to *The Sound and the Fury*," p. 273.

8. Faulkner, "A Note on Sherwood Anderson," ESPL, p. 8.

9. Meriwether, "Faulkner's Short Story Sending Schedule," pp. 165–180.

10. Faulkner, *These 13: Stories by William Faulkner*. Quotations from the stories are from *Collected Stories*.

11. See Meriwether, "Faulkner's Short Story Sending Schedule," pp. 172–173. The stories in Part II were arranged but not written chronologically. The last story of the section, "Dry September," was submitted to *American Mercury* as "Drouth" February 8, 1930. "A Justice" was first submitted April 11, 1931, to *Woman's Home Companion*.

12. It is significant to the retrospective focus of *These 13* that Faulkner was writing about his immediate present in *Sanctuary* and in stories he chose not to include in the collection, among them "The Brooch," about the death of an infant child and breakup of a marriage.

13. Andre Bleikasten speaks of this impulse, in a related context, as Faulkner's "throwing the power of his writing against the power of the world." "A Private Man's Public Voice," p. 48.

14. It is Fairchild, modeled on Anderson, who publishes in the *Dial*; the retort is made by the Semitic Man, modeled on Julius Weis Friend, who published both Anderson and Faulkner in the *Double-Dealer*, which competed with the *Dial*.

15. Polk treats this situation briefly and concisely in the context of other cuckold fictions, arguing that "the title and what we know of the external circumstances of Faulkner's life invite us to believe that at least at one level the story springs from a conscious recognition of the ways in which he had been exploiting his own psychic life in his fiction." *Children of the Dark House*, p. 155.

16. Joyce, *Dubliners*, pp. 223–224. Faulkner turned to *Dubliners* directly again, and again very personally, in an early draft of the 1953 short story "Mr. Acarius." USWF, pp. 435–448. Originally titled "Weekend Revisited," the story deals with a man institutionalized for alcoholism, as Faulkner was that year in New York. The opening sentence is from Joyce's story "Counterparts" about the destructively alcoholic Farrington: "The barometer of his emotional nature was set for a spell of riot." See Brodsky and Hamblin, *A Comprehensive Guide to the Brodsky Collection*, Vol. 1, p. 193.

17. Anderson, *Memoirs*, p. 28.

18. Cowley, *The Faulkner-Cowley File*, p. 116.

19. In the dedication to his mother in *Winesburg, Ohio*, Anderson says that her "keen observations on the life about her first awoke in me the hunger to see beneath the surface of lives." Faulkner might have said the same of Maud Falkner, who encouraged his artistic development and championed his writing. *Winesburg*, n.p.

20. See Brooks, *Toward Yoknapatawpha and Beyond*, p. 61.

21. Faulkner said in his 1955 interview with Jean Stein, "I prefer silence to sound, and the image produced by words occurs in silence. That is, the thunder and the music of the prose take place in silence" (Lion, 248). Cf. "Carcassonne": "'I would like to perform something,' he said, shaping his lips soundlessly in the darkness, and the galloping horse filled his mind again with soundless thunder" (CSWF, 898).

22. Anderson, *Winesburg*, p. 247.

23. Anderson, *Winesburg*, p. 21.

24. Anderson, *Winesburg*, pp. 24, 22.

25. Anderson, *Winesburg*, p. 22.

26. Putzel, *Genius of Place*, p. 296.

27. Hemingway's Andersonian story "My Old Man" may well constitute another disciple's nod in the same direction.

28. Cho-Cho's daughter Victoria Fielden Johnson was emphatic about this arrangement in her long interviews with Louis Daniel Brodsky in 1985–1987, and I have followed her account on most points. Blotner does not treat this issue. In his 1977 memoir Malcolm implies without directly stating that, except for the period in spring 1930 when the Faulkners were moving to Rowan Oak and a summer when he was ten, he lived continuously with his mother and stepfather. See Brodsky, *Life Glimpses*, pp. 132–180; Franklin, *Bitterweeds: Life with William Faulkner at Rowan Oak*.

29. Cho-Cho married Selby in the fall of 1936 while the Faulkners were in Hollywood. After Selby deserted her, she lived in Shanghai for a time with her father, married Fielden there in 1940, was evacuated when the Japanese invasion began, and returned to Oxford. She and her daughter lived at Rowan Oak, where Fielden joined them until he found work. See Brodsky, *Life Glimpses*, pp. 141–142, 144–147.

30. The four funerals are those of Alabama (1931), Murry (1932), Dean (1935), and Caroline Barr (1940).

31. Dahl, "A Faulkner Reminiscence," p. 1028. Phil Stone believed he recognized his own brother James Jr. in Jason. Snell, *Phil Stone of Oxford*, p. 209.

32. It can be argued that Murry, like Faulkner, was responsible for his own lack of formal education. Murry favored railroading over college and wanted to go to the West; Faulkner favored writing and went to Europe. Murry's brother JWT Jr. and his own three younger sons all were college graduates. Like Murry's father and his brother, his second son Jack Falkner was a lawyer.

33. Jason's impotence on Easter Sunday is suggested by his imagining himself in bed with Lorraine, "only he was just lying beside her, pleading with her to help him" (TSATF, 307). Lorraine's letter and Jason's association of Miss Quentin with her through letters is discussed in Watson, *William Faulkner, Letters and Fictions*, pp. 84–91.

34. Cohen and Fowler, "Faulkner's Introduction to *The Sound and the Fury*," p. 277.

35. The mythic parallel is rooted in Quentin's imagining Dalton Ames's abducting Caddy by reference to "*the swine of Euboleus*" (TSATF, 148) and is supported on April 6, 1928, by Miss Quentin's telling Jason, "I'm bad and I'm going to hell, and I don't care. I'd rather be in hell than anywhere where you are" (TSATF, 189); as Demeter retrieves Persephone from hell, so Miss Quentin twice asks for her mother when confronting Jason (TSATF, 185, 259).

36. Ted Tebbetts, in a letter to Carvel Collins. The Carvel Collins Collection, HRHRC.

37. Jiggs initiates the cruel game, appropriately so since he has abandoned his own two children and their mother in Kansas. Harrington points out that he may be named for the Jiggs of the syndicated comic strip *Bringing Up Father*. *Faulkner's Fables of Creativity*, pp. 45–46.

38. See Brodsky's interviews with Victoria Fielden Johnson. By the time Faulkner and Estelle were married, Ms. Johnson says, Cho-Cho "felt Pappy was her special friend"; Malcolm, conversely, "didn't know where he belonged, which father was really his." Brodsky, *Life Glimpses*, pp. 139, 152.

39. Blotner, *Biography* (1974), p. 624.

40. Blotner, *Biography* (1974), p. 624.

41. Blotner, *Biography* (1984), p. 245.

42. Williamson makes this claim from his reading of the Blotner Papers in the Brodsky Collection at Southeast Missouri State College. *William Faulkner and Southern History*, p. 218.

43. Blotner, *Biography* (1984), p. 329.

44. Faulkner used the same setting and several of the same details for Gordon's studio in *Mosquitoes* (11, 22). See Blotner, *Biography* (1974), p. 515.

45. Faulkner to Anderson, n.d. Carvel Collins Collection, HRHRC. The WWI military context of the occasion is enriched by a holograph postscript that reads, "I read 'The Spanish Farm' yesterday. Miss Elizabeth and I agree it is quite a book."

46. See Blotner, *Biography* (1974), pp. 834–837, 867; Brooks, *Toward Yoknapatawpha and Beyond*, pp. 399–400.

47. Kawin, "Faulkner's Film Career: The Years with Hawks," p. 175.

48. Gresset notes a number of specific references to theatre and argues, in this context, that "*Pylon* is an even more self-conscious work than the preceding ones. The question is whether the novel is not also the most devastatingly self-critical of Faulkner's whole career." *Fascination*, p. 240.

49. Gresset speaks of the Reporter's intoxication, in a wonderful phrase, as an "optical nightmare." *Fascination*, p. 247.

50. See Gresset, *Fascination*, pp. 239–253. Gresset sees fetishism as a primary motif of the novel.

51. Faulkner wrote his own epitaph in the poem "Mississippi Hills—My Epitaph," various versions of which date from *Mississippi Poems* (1924). A two-stanza version concludes *A Green Bough*, published in 1933, the year before he wrote *Pylon*.

52. Gresset assumes "that this scene is perceived, indeed 'written,' by the reporter himself." *Fascination*, p. 252.

53. *Pylon*, p. 82, and *Mosquitoes* p. 296. See Susan P. Johnson, *Annotations to Faulkner's "Pylon,"* "Introduction," n.p.

54. See Zeitlin, "*Pylon*, Joyce and Faulkner's Imagination," pp. 195–199. The parallels he identifies and the circumstances that generated them are extensive and convincing.

55. All three wrote for newspapers at one time in their careers. Lewis was awarded the Nobel Prize in 1930, the first American to be so honored.

56. Brett is singled out as "an image to dance around" by the *riau-riau* dancers and "translated" to wine shops and hotels as the Virgin of San Fermin is translated from church to church. *The Sun Also Rises*, pp. 155–158.

57. "Pyrenæan" is restored in the corrected edition from the editorial revision "Basque" in the original edition. See *Pylon* (New York: Smith and Haas, 1935), p. 63.

58. In a 1935 *Esquire* piece about fishing that recognizes and responds to this usage, Hemingway made his own parodic gesture toward the editorial ellipses used to represent obscenities in the first edition and Faulkner's portmanteau words, writing "Fornicate the illegitimate" in place of vulgarities and saying that his fish behaved with "catfishlike uncatfishivity." He added, "your correspondent has been reading, and admiring,

Pylon by Mr. William Faulkner." *By-Line Ernest Hemingway*, p. 200. Hemingway adopted a similar strategy for obscenities in his 1940 novel *For Whom the Bell Tolls*.

59. Zeitlin makes the intriguing point that Faulkner not only read Joyce but read about his work in Stuart Gilbert's 1931 book *James Joyce's "Ulysses."* "*Pylon*, James Joyce, and Faulkner's Imagination," pp. 188–189.

60. Millgate writes, "*Pylon*, indeed, can be best seen as an experiment in the primarily poetic mode which was soon to produce *Absalom, Absalom!*, and while altogether less ambitious than its great successor, it is not so dissimilar in kind: in both novels tension and meaning are alike sustained by calculated effects of imagery and style." *Achievement*, p. 149. Susan P. Johnson mistakenly says that there are no "overt references" to *Absalom, Absalom!* in *Pylon. Annotations to Faulkner's "Pylon,"* "Introduction," n.p.

61. Kawin speculates plausibly that Faulkner's vision of *Absalom, Absalom!* was affected by his work in Hollywood on *Sutters' Gold*, which "got the first theme out of his system . . . and thereby improved the novel." "Faulkner's Film Career: The Years with Hawks," p. 175.

62. It is worth noting that later in his life Faulkner and Franklin both lived in Charlottesville, Virginia, where they were cordial neighbors if not friends. See Brodsky, *Life Glimpses*, pp. 137–138.

63. Among several advocates of such positions are Sensibar, "'Drowsing Maidenhead Symbol's Self'"; Minter, *Life and Work*; and Moser, "Faulkner's Muse: Speculations on the Genesis of *The Sound and the Fury*."

64. Watson, "Two Letters about William Faulkner, 1918," p. 18.

65. See Snell, *Phil Stone of Oxford*, p. 105; TofH, pp. 64–65.

66. See Reed, *Faulkner's Narrative*, p. 157. Minter notes in the narrators' repetition of each others' stories an element of "play" that accords with the heightened language of performance. *Life and Work*, p. 156.

67. For a discussion of the letters in *Absalom, Absalom!* and their significance as devices of narrative see Watson, *William Faulkner, Letters and Fictions*, pp. 115–126; and Krause, "Reading Bon's Letters and Faulkner's *Absalom, Absalom!*" and "Reading Shreve's Letters and Faulkner's *Absalom, Absalom!*."

68. Sex, death, and race are closely related here. See Polk's argument: "Race is, in *Absalom* and in Faulkner generally, a mask for very serious matters of sexuality and gender" and that the real issue for Henry, as for Quentin in *The Sound and the Fury*, is his sister's virginity. *Children of the Dark House*, pp. 139–141.

69. Both terms, of course, pervade the first eight chapters, where there are well over three hundred instances of *father* and its variants and synonyms and one hundred of *son*.

70. Gray speaks of Quentin and Shreve's immersion in Henry and Charles at such times as "the activity of re-enactment." *Life*, p. 220.

71. Compare Quentin's theatre-based description of "that gaunt tragic dramatic self-hypnotized youthful face like the tragedian in a college play, an academic Hamlet" at the beginning of Chapter 6 (AA!, 142).

72. Kawin, "The Montage Element in Faulkner's Fiction," p. 109.

73. Kawin, "Faulkner's Film Career: The Years with Hawks," pp. 176, 178.

74. Kawin, *Faulkner's MGM Screenplays*, p. 58. The opening event in the film script involves a conflict between a brother and sister and their male companion. *Today We Live*, pp. 129–131. References to the script are from Kawin's reproduction of Faulkner's second draft, pp. 128–255.

75. Kawin, "Faulkner's Film Career: The Years with Hawks," pp. 176; Kawin, *Faulkner's MGM Screenplays*, p. 104.

76. Details of the plot are from Kawin's account in "Faulkner's Film Career: The Years with Hawks," pp. 176–177.

77. Kawin, "Faulkner's Film Career: The Years with Hawks," p. 170.

78. Sundquist, *Faulkner: The House Divided*, p. 123.

79. Putzel, "Text of the Yale Preface," p. 296.

80. Blotner (1974), p. 1204.

81. See Bleikasten's discussion of Faulkner's "romantic dream of autogenesis" and his ironic discovery that "the name with which he signs his work is a kind of imposture." "Fathers in Faulkner," p. 145. Kartiganer makes the intriguing suggestion, in another connection, that Faulkner was "a writer whose life outside writing not only has never truly come clear to us, but in a strange way never existed. It is as if, pace Foucault, it is not the author who disappeared but the man." *Faulkner and the Artist*, p. x.

Chapter V. Stage Manager

1. Fitzgerald, "Absolution," p. 131. For the autobiographical background of the story and its relation to *The Great Gatsby*, see Matthew Bruccoli, *Some Sort of Epic Grandeur*, pp. 191–192.

2. Putzel, "Text of the Yale Preface," p. 297.

3. Melville, "Hawthorne and His Mosses," pp. 247–248.

4. Bleikasten, *The Most Splendid Failure*, p. 50.

5. In a 1955 interview with Cynthia Grenier, for example, Faulkner listed Wolfe, himself, Dos Passos, Caldwell, and Hemingway "according to what they had tried to do and to what measure they had succeeded in their attempt. I put Tom Wolfe first because he tried to do the most. He tried to put the whole universe into his books and failed. His was the most glorious failure. And then myself. I tried the most after Wolfe and failed the most after him." Lion, p. 225. The American predecessor he most admired, he often said, was Melville and the book *Moby-Dick*. See *Lion in the Garden*, pp. 17, 21, 110.

6. Wai-chee Dimock, *Empire for Liberty: Melville and the Poetics of Individualism*, p. 8.

7. Dimock, *Empire for Liberty*, p. 111.

8. Dimock, *Empire for Liberty*, p. 77.

9. Dimock, *Empire for Liberty*, p. 78.

10. Dimock, *Empire for Liberty*, p. 86.

11. See Bleikasten, "Reading Faulkner," pp. 7–8.

12. Melville, *Moby-Dick*, pp. 6, 185–186. Wittenberg notes Faulkner's lifelong admiration for *Moby-Dick* and reports that Faulkner kept a picture of Ahab in his library at

Rowan Oak. *Transfiguration of Biography*, pp. 255–256, 13n. Faulkner used the exotic word "caryatid" in connection with sovereignty to describe Elnora and Narcissa, attendants to Miss Jenny Sartoris DuPre, in the 1929 story "There Was a Queen." cswf, pp. 731, 738.

13. Blotner notes, "Set in Beverly Hills, its every page seemed imbued with the distaste and unhappiness he had felt. The terrain, the climate, the architecture, the people, their behavior, their dress—all displeased him." *Biography* (1984), p. 342.

14. Faulkner began working with Howard Hawks on the film titled *Today We Live* from the story "Turnabout" in April 1932. Paramount took an option on *Sanctuary* in June 1933 and the film opened as *The Story of Temple Drake* in May the following year.

15. The Hotel Vista del Mar may be based on the Hotel Miramar in Santa Monica where Faulkner stayed with Meta Carpenter the following year. See Blotner, *Biography* (1984), p. 369.

16. Poirier, *Renewal of Literature*, p. 29. I am indebted to Poirier's opening "Prologue: The Deed of Writing," the title of which has direct relation to my argument that writing for Faulkner always was a compulsively individual *deed.*

17. Meriwether, "An Introduction to *The Sound and the Fury*," *A Faulkner Miscellany*, p. 160.

18. Poirier, *Renewal of Literature*, p. 30.

19. On Faulkner's interest in Cubism, see the work of Panthea Broughton, Ilse Dusoir Lind, and G. Watson Branch.

20. This comment to Jean Stein, his new young lover, speaks to his having broken with her immediate predecessor, Joan Williams, whom he had encouraged early in his courtship of her to join him as a collaborator on *Requiem for a Nun*. See Chapter vi, "Old Moster."

21. Karl Zender points out, "The nature of the reporter's disenchantment with journalism suggests obvious parallels to Faulkner's attitude toward writing for the movies—both to his sense that 'a moving picture is by its nature a collaboration and any collaboration is compromise' and to his more general sense of the threat posed to serious literature by the popular media." *The Crossing of the Ways*, p. 52.

22. Michael Zeitlin notes critical opinion that identifies "the central irritating feature of *Pylon*" as "Faulkner's apparently imitative, stylized, and unaccountable return to the twin pylons of modernism, Eliot and Joyce." He finds, however, that "Faulkner absorbs and transfigures Joyce not only for parodic purposes but also to solve a range of narrative problems uniquely relevant to Faulkner's predicament as both an artist and a historical subject in the year 1934. For Faulkner writing *Pylon*, Joyce was a means of structuring an apocryphal geography, of 'contemplating sheer language calmly,' of widening the scope of his representational possibilities, and, accordingly, of probing into some of the dominant structures of contemporary history itself." "*Pylon*, Joyce and Faulkner's Imagination," pp. 186, 188.

23. Sensibar enumerates several of these with respect to creativity and gender in her "Faulkner's Fictional Photographs: Playing with Difference."

24. The word "shadow" and synonyms "shade," "shades," "shadowy" occur fifty-five times in *Absalom, Absalom!*. See Polk and Hart, "*Absalom, Absalom!*": *A Concordance to the Novel.*

25. Given the pervasive photographic dimension of *Absalom, Absalom!*, including Quentin's immediate association of Rosa's story with photography, Faulkner may have adapted the surname Coldfield from his friend, the Oxford photographer J. R. Cofield.

26. Hans Skei notes that Morton Goldman sold "Wash" to *Harper's* on November 2, 1933. Two earlier, related stories are "The Big Shot" and "Evangeline," which Skei dates from Faulkner's Short Story Sending Schedule as written in 1930 and 1931, respectively. *William Faulkner: The Short Story Career*, pp. 79, 36–37.

27. There is some manuscript evidence that Faulkner did not entirely abandon *Absalom, Absalom!* during the composition of *Pylon*. Polk points out, "The fact that certain pages of the manuscript of *Absalom, Absalom!* are written in the same green ink that he used to write the entire *Pylon* manuscript suggests that even though he put his problems with *Absalom* aside long enough to write *Pylon*, he didn't completely abandon the former." *Children of the Dark House*, pp. viii. Pages and parts of pages in green ink are intermittent in *Absalom, Absalom!* Chapter 2 (AA!, 33, 34–36) and Chapter 8 (AA!, 257–263, 265–276, 277–278, 278–279). I am grateful to Karen Pavelka at the Harry Ransom Humanities Research Center for identifying the green ink sheets for me and sharing with me her work on them.

28. Blotner (1984), p. 371.

29. Some contradictions are editorially repaired in the 1986 "Corrected Edition" of *Absalom, Absalom!*. See Polk, "Editor's Note," p. 311.

30. Galley 59A; AA!, 148.4. The galleys of *Absalom, Absalom!*, dated August 17 and August 21, 1936, are in the William Faulkner Collection at the Harry Ransom Humanities Research Center. Citations here are by galley and by page and line of the 1986 Corrected Edition.

31. Galley 65; AA!, 161.4.

32. Galley 79A; AA!, 194.21. Brackets indicate a cancellation.

33. Galley 68A; AA!, 168.13.

34. Galley 68A; AA!, 168.5. Elinor Glyn (1861–1943) was an English novelist whose public popularity rested upon slightly scandalous romances such as *The Vicissitudes of Evangeline* (1905) and *Three Weeks* (1907).

35. Galleys 91–91A.

36. Blotner (1984), pp. 358–359, 371–372.

37. Galley 21; AA!, p. 54.

38. Meriwether and Millgate, *Lion*, p. 253.

39. The imagery of this section is rooted in Shakespearean drama, which it strongly reflects. Note especially King Lear's "wheel of fire" (*Lear*, IV, vii, 48) and Kent's "O, let him pass! He hates him / That would upon the rack of this tough world / Stretch him out longer" (*Lear*, V, iii, 319–321).

40. Poem 125 was first published in 1891 in *Poems of Emily Dickinson*, Second Series, edited by T. W. Higginson and Mabel Loomis Todd and republished in 1924 in *Complete Poems*. The entire poem reads:

For each ecstatic instant
We must an anguish pay

In keen and quivering ratio
To the ecstasy.

For each beloved hour
Sharp pittances of years—
Bitter contested farthings—
And Coffers heaped with Tears!
—T. H. Johnson, ed., *Complete Poems*, p. 58.

I am indebted to Andrea Bradley for pointing out this connection.

41. Edwin T. Arnold provides a somewhat different, and somewhat fuller, gloss to this passage in *Mosquitoes Annotated*, pp. 45–46.

42. Eliot, "The Love Song of J. Alfred Prufrock," *T. S. Eliot: The Collected Poems and Plays, 1909–1950*, p. 4.

43. Blotner, *A Biography* (1984), pp. 141, 182.

44. Thoreau, *Walden*, pp. 134–135.

45. Thoreau, *Walden*, p. 1.

46. Thoreau, *Walden*, p. 219.

47. Faulkner's reading is a complicated issue and his own library, while important, is not always a reliable guide. He was encouraged to read by his family from an early age, and living in a university town he had access to the university as well as family libraries. Even favorite books are missing from the library at Rowan Oak. There is no copy of *Moby-Dick* there, for example, although Phil Stone purchased the book in 1922 and Faulkner could well have read Stone's copy as he did many of his other books. The only copy of *The Scarlet Letter*, which he knew well at least as early as *As I Lay Dying*, is in Malcolm Cowley's *The Portable Hawthorne* (1948). See Blotner, *William Faulkner's Library: A Catalogue* and his "Introduction," pp. 3–12.

48. Thoreau, *Walden*, p. 48.

49. Thoreau, *Walden*, p. 29. *Walden* itself is highly allusive, as shown by the quotation in this passage from Richard Lovelace, "To Althea from Prison": "If I have freedom in my love / And in my soul am free . . . ."

50. Thoreau, *Walden*, p. 48.

51. Thoreau, *Walden*, p. 372.

52. Thoreau, *Walden*, p. 233.

53. Thoreau, *Walden*, p. 3.

54. Thoreau, *Walden*, p. 11.

55. Thoreau, *Walden*, p. 3. There is a scattering of other echoes of *Walden* in *The Sound and the Fury*. In "Sounds" Thoreau tells the story of a boy who lives too far out in the Massachusetts countryside to hear factory whistles; he himself hears the Sunday sound of bells (*Walden*, 115, 123). Quentin flees the sound of bells and factory whistles for the country. In "Solitude" Thoreau imagined the solitary existence of a student like Quentin "in one of the crowded hives of Cambridge College" (*Walden*, 135), and anticipated Quentin's sense of loving Caddy in hell in "Sounds" where he described owls' hooting as "the mutual consolations of suicide lovers remembering the pangs and delights of supernal love in the infernal groves" (*Walden*, 138).

56. Melville, "Hawthorne and His Mosses," p. 249. In the same essay, Melville also proposed, "Would that all excellent books were foundlings, without father or mother, that so it might be, we could glorify them, without including their ostensible authors," all of whose names are "fictitious ones" (239). In this he anticipated Faulkner's declaration to Malcolm Cowley when he was protesting the proposed *Life* magazine story in 1949 that he would like to have left his books unsigned. Cowley, *The Faulkner-Cowley File*, p. 126.

57. Hawthorne, *The Scarlet Letter*, pp. 3–4.

58. Whitman, *Complete Poetry and Selected Prose*, p. 27.

59. Whitman, "So Long," *Complete Poetry and Selected Prose*, p. 349.

60. Meta Carpenter Wilde remembered that she met Faulkner in December 1935 when he was working with Hawks on *Road to Glory*. Broughton, "An Interview with Meta Carpenter Wilde," pp. 791–792. In her *A Loving Gentleman* she is clear on the fact that they did not immediately become lovers. Dates and events in the following discussion are based on *A Loving Gentleman*, the 1981 Broughton chronology, Blotner's revised *Biography* (1984), and letters in the Meta Carpenter Wilde Collection at the Harry Ransom Humanities Research Center.

61. Wilde and Borsten, *A Loving Gentleman*, pp. 171–175; Wasson, *Count No 'Count*, pp. 145–149.

62. See WF–MC AL (February 7, 1937), Meta Carpenter Wilde Collection, HRHRC. The cartoon was published in an article by Sally Davis, "The Secret Hollywood Romance of William Faulkner" (132–133) and is reproduced in Robert Dale Parker, "Sex and Gender, Feminine and Masculine: Faulkner and the Polymorphous Exchange of Cultural Binaries" (87).

63. Blotner, *Biography* (1984), p. 385; McHaney, *"The Wild Palms": Holograph Manuscript*, p. vii.

64. Blotner, *Biography* (1984), p. 738, 3n.

65. Blotner, *Biography* (1984), pp. 386–389; Wilde and Borsten, *A Loving Gentleman*, p. 230. Although Wilde's memory of this meeting, on which Blotner's account is based, is very clear, Faulkner did not write those words into his novel until a year later.

66. Gray, *Life*, p. 248.

67. Wilde and Borsten, *A Loving Gentleman*, p. 52; Blotner, *Biography* (1984), p. 369.

68. Gray summarizes critical opinion when he writes that "the trauma of breakup with Meta seems to have carried him back to an earlier erotic trauma, his frustrated longing for another woman who had married someone else. *Life*, p. 241.

69. Bonner, *William Faulkner: The William B. Wisdom Collection*, p. 4. See *Jerusalem*, p. 5. Collins lists several of these similarities in his "Biographical Background for Faulkner's *Helen*," pp. 86–87.

70. Melville, *Moby-Dick*, p. 164.

71. Wilde and Borsten, *A Loving Gentleman*, p. 173. See also Gray, *Life*, pp. 240–241.

72. Wilde and Borsten, *A Loving Gentleman*, p. 76.

73. Rosa at this stage, like Miranda, is an innocent, overprotected by her father, and as Prospero tells Miranda when she discovers the "brave new world" of Neapolitan aristocrats, " 'Tis new to thee." Shakespeare, *The Tempest*, V, i, 185–187.

74. Shakespeare, *Tempest*, III, ii, 145.

75. Melville, *Moby-Dick*, p. 164.

76. Shakespeare, *Hamlet*, III, iv, 24. McHaney speculates additionally that Faulkner drew the name Wilbourne from the speech in which Hamlet considers and rejects suicide, which includes the lines, "The undiscovered country from whose *bourne* / No traveller returns, puzzles the *will*" (*Hamlet*, III, 1, 79–80; italics added). *Faulkner's "The Wild Palms,"* pp. xviii, 124.

77. See McHaney, *Faulkner's "The Wild Palms,"* p. 26, 1n.

78. Broughton, "An Interview with Meta Carpenter Wilde," p. 777. He visited them in January and accidentally left the manuscript of *Absalom, Absalom!* behind when he left. In October, he gave the first copy of the published novel to Meta.

79. The reunion may also have prompted Faulkner's *If I Forget Thee, Jerusalem* parody of Hemingway, whom Anderson also believed had betrayed him. As Blotner notes, Anderson remembered that Faulkner asked, "Sherwood, what the hell is the matter with you? Do you think I am also a Hemy?" *Biography* (1984), p. 387.

80. Melville, *Moby-Dick*, p. 123. I am indebted to Alicia Mosier for pointing out this similarity.

81. Dr. Pigford's widow, Helen Pigford, remembered that Faulkner and Pigford saw each other frequently in New Orleans and on at least one occasion visited Charity Hospital, where Faulkner saw the overcrowded conditions and talked with the nurses and nuns. Helen Pigford to the author.

82. See especially McHaney, *William Faulkner's "The Wild Palms,"* pp. 3–24.

83. A copy of the 1933 edition of *Miss Lonelyhearts* is dated at Rowan Oak July 1946, too late to have influenced *If I Forget Thee, Jerusalem*. Like other source books, of course, it was widely available. Faulkner could very well have read it in the 1930s in California. Blotner, *William Faulkner's Library*, p. 56.

84. The existence of the maps indicates only that Faulkner knew the terrain well. Gabriele Gutting has shown that the maps are drafts locating hunting camps where Faulkner and his fellow hunters stayed on their November trips to the Delta. "Mysteries of the Map-Maker: Faulkner, *If I Forget Thee, Jerusalem*, and the Secret of a Map," pp. 85–89.

85. Wilde and Borsten, *A Loving Gentleman*, p. 140; Gray, *Life*, p. 240. Although Meta identifies this behavior with Faulkner's work on *If I Forget Thee, Jerusalem*, the chronology of their relationship shows that he worked on only the six-page holograph manuscript of "The Wild Palms" short story while they were lovers in 1936–1937. The novel was written after her marriage in April 1937.

86. Wilde and Borsten, *A Loving Gentleman*, pp. 117, 330, 264. Two other letters, not quoted in her book, document masturbation by both partners. See WF–MC TL (June 25, 1936), WF–MC TL (July 2, 1936), Meta Carpenter Wilde Collection, HRHRC.

87. Grimwood, *Heart in Conflict*, pp. 91, 99.

88. Grimwood, *Heart in Conflict*, pp. 4, 6.

89. Faulkner portrayed Trueblood as a critic in a 1961 letter to Albert Erskin where he proposed a dust jacket blurb for *The Reivers* reading: "'An extremely important message. . . . eminently qualified to become the Western World's bible of free will and

private enterprise.' / Ernest V. Trueblood, / Literary & Dramatic Critic, / Oxford, (Miss.)
Eagle." SLWF, p. 455.

90. Melville, *Moby-Dick*, p. 164.

91. Melville, *Moby-Dick*, pp. 79, 571.

Chapter VI. Old Moster

1. Blotner, *Biography* (1984), p. 319.

2. *Absalom, Absalom!*, endpapers. The Suratt named there is the sewing machine agent
in *Flags in the Dust* and "Lizards in Jamshyd's Courtyard" whose name Faulkner
changed to Ratliff in *The Hamlet*. The other plantation house on the map is obliquely
associated with the rise of the Snopeses, as well. Sutpen's Hundred was "later bought
and restored by Major Cassius DeSpain" who became the Major DeSpain whose barn
Ab Snopes burns in "Barn Burning" (1938) and Eula's lover whose bank Flem acquires
in *The Town*, where he is named Manfred DeSpain.

3. Blotner, *Biography* (1984), p. 392.

4. Quoted in Bezzerides, *William Faulkner: A Life on Paper*, p. 71. Louis J. Budd notes
that Faulkner paid taxes "on more real estate within the city limits of Oxford than anybody else." "Playing Hide and Seek with William Faulkner: The Publicly Private Artist," p. 52.

5. Blotner, *Biography* (1984), p. 408.

6. Blotner, *Biography* (1984), p. 408.

7. Rubin, *The Faraway Country*, p. 18.

8. Blotner, *Biography* (1974), p. 151.

9. See John Faulkner, *My Brother Bill*, pp. 128–129; and Blotner, *Biography* (1984),
p. 406.

10. Honnighausen characterizes football at the university as "a sphere of cultural play."
Faulkner: Masks and Metaphors, p. 241. Poems such as Faulkner's translations of Ver-
laine and the verse play he wrote while there are analogous forms of play and playing.

11. Minter makes the important point about Faulkner's relationship to another woman,
Helen Baird, "that there was a doubleness in his emotional entanglements; that he
deliberately cultivated emotions with the intention of transmuting them; and that
he found her more compelling because he knew her to be unattainable." *Life and
Work*, p. 64.

12. In a letter to Phil Mullen about Robert Coughlan's 1953 *Life* articles, Faulkner
wrote, "There seems to be in this the same spirit which permits strangers to drive into
my yard and pick up books or pipes I left in the chair where I had been sitting, as sou-
venirs" (SLWF, 354). Joan Williams approached him in nearly the same way in 1949
when she and friends came to Rowan Oak unannounced and found him at work in
his yard.

13. Cowley, *The Portable Faulkner*, p. viii.

14. See Polk, *Children of the Dark House*, p. 253. Polk attributes the insight to James
B. Meriwether.

15. I have argued elsewhere that "the poetry given [Ike's] story obscures no deprav-

ity. Rather, it elevates Ike's inchoate virtues of gentleness, love, and devotion to a standard against which all other lovers are implicitly judged." Watson, *The Snopes Dilemma*, p. 47.

16. See Honnighausen, *Faulkner: Masks and Metaphors*, pp. 229–230.

17. Polk, *Children of the Dark House*, p. 157.

18. Polk, *Children of the Dark House*, p. 152.

19. Brodsky and Hamblin, *A Comprehensive Guide to the Brodsky Collection*, Vol. 5, pp. 365, 366. The wills of 1930, 1951, and 1954 were prepared by Phil Stone and are also in the Brodsky Collection.

20. Minter, *Life and Work*, p. 187.

21. Grimwood ties the "paradigm of depletion" in the genealogical structure of *Go Down, Moses* to the diminution of Faulkner's family and "his experience of personal reduction." He veers away from that argument, however, in finding that the major failure the book embodies is the artistic one of Faulkner's "final inability to penetrate the Negro stereotypes he had set out at first to destroy." *Heart in Conflict*, p. 275.

22. See Watson, *William Faulkner, Letters and Fictions*, pp. 129–132; Matthews, *The Play of Faulkner's Language*, p. 260.

23. Polk comes to a similar conclusion from a slightly different angle. Arguing that there is no proof in the novel that Bon is black, Polk concludes, "Race is, in *Absalom* and in Faulkner generally, a mask for very serious matters of sexuality and gender." *Children of the Dark House*, 139.

24. Eric Sundquist takes the opposite approach of analyzing Southern race culture and reading the novels as Faulkner's condemnation of it. With respect to *Light in August* and *Absalom, Absalom!*, Sundquist argues that Faulkner "turned from the tragedy of Jim Crow to the tragedy that made him possible—indeed, it seems, inevitable—and he did so by turning, as Stowe had, to the sins of the fathers that led necessarily to the violence of the brothers." The cultural realities Sundquist identifies and examines—that miscegenation "made a mockery of white marriage," for example, and that the slave son of a white father "had, therefore, no father at all"—are not issues that Faulkner dramatizes in either book. See *The House Divided*, pp. 100, 110, 125.

25. Faulkner repeatedly declared his love to Meta Carpenter Wilde in letters published in *A Loving Gentleman* that he began writing her in 1936. He wrote the same to Joan Williams, sometimes in the same language, telling her almost immediately in their correspondence that he wanted to write her love letters. Williamson, *William Faulkner and Southern History*, p. 279. He first mentioned Jean Stein in a March 1954 letter to Saxe Commins, where he wrote, "She doesn't want anything of me—only to love me, be in love." Brodsky and Hamblin, *A Comprehensive Guide to the Brodsky Collection*, Vol. 2, p. 138.

26. Zender treats the cultural differences between parent-child and sibling incest in Faulkner's work in his "Faulkner and the Politics of Incest."

27. Grimwood describes Faulkner's revisions of the stories in *Go Down, Moses* as attempts "to salvage work that had been cheaply conceived and crassly executed." *Heart in Conflict*, p. 230.

28. See Williamson, *William Faulkner and Southern History*, pp. 64–71. Williamson argues, "The kinship between fact and fiction is not coincidental. Through Emeline and

her children, Faulkner was personally intimate with a real story, a historical happening, fully as powerful as any that he ever conceived in his imagination" (64). He concludes that because of her close relationship to her master and lover, "Emeline in the end was insistent in an extraordinary degree that she was a married woman. . . . Emeline, of course, could not describe herself as the wife of Colonel William C. Falkner, but she did establish firmly the fact—indeed had it written in stone—that she was 'Mrs. Falkner.' She is, in truth, the only Mrs. Falkner in the cemetery where *his* marble self rises above all" (70). Williamson also documents Faulkner's maternal grandfather Charlie Butler's liaison with an octoroon woman at the time he deserted his wife Leila, Maud Falkner's mother (123).

29. Williamson, *William Faulkner and Southern History*, pp. 67, 68–69.

30. Williamson cites family testimony that the Old Colonel not only paid Fannie's bills but visited her at Rust College, often bringing her flowers. *William Faulkner and Southern History*, p. 67.

31. Gray calls Roth Edmonds "perhaps the closest there is to an autobiographical character in 'The Fire and the Hearth,' if only because his relationship with Molly Beauchamp replicates that of Faulkner with Caroline Barr." *Life*, p. 279.

32. Snell, *Phil Stone of Oxford*, pp. 3, 13–14. Snell also suggests that one of Phil Stone's poker hands became the hand dealt Uncle Buddy McCaslin by Turl in "Was," the opening chapter of *Go Down, Moses*.

33. Brodsky and Hamblin, *A Comprehensive Guide to the Brodsky Collection*, Vol. 2, p. 136.

34. Minter relates the scene between Ike and Edmonds to the confrontation between the Corporal and the Old Marshall in *A Fable*, both characterized by "abstraction and didacticism." *Life and Work*, p. 228. Gray finds that *Go Down, Moses* "marks a significant moment in the development of Faulknerian language. . . . towards the declamatory." *Life*, p. 275.

35. Sundquist, *Faulkner: The House Divided*, p. 133.

36. Bleikasten has assessed Faulkner's debt to *The Scarlet Letter* in his *Faulkner's "As I Lay Dying,"* pp. 18–19. See also Douglas and Daniel, "Faulkner and the Puritanism of the South."

37. Hawthorne, "The Custom House," p. 10.

38. Hawthorne, "The Custom House," p. 32; cf. *The Scarlet Letter*, pp. 259–260.

39. In this there is a further connection of *Go Down, Moses* to *Moby-Dick*. Sundquist says, "Ike discovers, as Ishmael asserts, that the secret of his 'paternity' lies in the grave of an unwedded mother—not his own mother, of course, but the slave mother who carries the white McCaslin blood into the black Beauchamp family." *Faulkner: The House Divided*, pp. 133–134.

40. Hawthorne, *The Scarlet Letter*, p. 264.

41. Hawthorne, "The Custom House," p. 4.

42. Hawthorne, *The Scarlet Letter*, pp. 256–257.

43. Hawthorne, "The Custom House," p. 36.

44. WF–JW TLs, "Oxford, Wednesday" (August 31, 1949) FCVA. Quoted in Blotner, *Biography* (1984), p. 507.

45. Joan Williams, "Twenty Will Not Come Again," p. 63.

46. He wrote Cowley from Oxford in December 1946, "It's a dull life here. I need some new people, above all probably a new young woman" (SLWF, 245).

47. Gertrude Stegbauer was Phil Stone's stenographer in Charleston, Mississippi. Faulkner made her a book of poems and she was the model for Jenny Steinbauer in *Mosquitoes*. Blotner, *Biography* (1984), p. 141. See also Snell, *Phil Stone of Oxford*, p. 124.

48. Blotner, *Biography* (1984), p. 507.

49. WF–JW TLs (January 7, 1950) FCVA. See Williamson, *William Faulkner and Southern History*, p. 279, and Blotner, *Biography* (1984), p. 512.

50. WF–JW TLs (July 13, 1950) FCVA. See Joan Williams, "Twenty Will Not Come Again," p. 63.

51. WF–JW ALs (February 11, 1950) FCVA. Quoted in Blotner, *Biography* (1974), p. 1309. On the composition of *Requiem for a Nun*, see Noel Polk, *Faulkner's Requiem for a Nun: A Critical Study*, pp. 337–345.

52. WF–JW TLs (March 22, 1950) FCVA.

53. Quoted in Blotner, *Biography* (1974), p. 1313.

54. WF–JW TL (January 7, 1950) FCVA. Quoted in Blotner, *Biography* (1984), p. 512.

55. There were literary models, as well, notably in Shakespeare and Hemingway. For a discussion of Temple's letters and their sources, see Watson, *William Faulkner, Letters and Fictions*, pp. 140–154.

56. WF–JW TL "Monday" (February 4, 1952) FCVA.

57. WF–JW TL (August 20, 1952) FCVA. "A Virginal" is from *Ripostes* (1912) in *Personae: Collected Shorter Poems of Ezra Pound*, p. 71.

58. WF–JW TL "Wednesday" (April 29, 1953) FCVA. Meta reports that he said, "I weigh 129 pounds and I want to put it all on you and as much in you as I can can can can must must will will shall." Quoted in Wilde and Borsten, *A Loving Gentleman*, p. 264. Cf. the somewhat different phrasing in WF–MC TL (July 9, 1936) HRHRC. Blotner deleted the erotic passage in the letter to Joan (SLWF, 348).

59. WF–JW TL "Friday evening" (August 7, 1952) FCVA. Quoted in Blotner, *Biography* (1984), p. 559.

60. Wilde and Borsten, *A Loving Gentleman*, p. 78.

61. Joan Williams, "Twenty Will Not Come Again," p. 63.

62. WF–JW TLs (May 9, 1950) FCVA.

63. WF–JW ALs "St Moritz / Saturday night" (December 19, 1953) FCVA.

64. WF–JW TLs "Monday 11th" (January 1954) FCVA. He told Commins, as he had Joan, "A queer thing has happened to me, almost a repetition; this one is even named Jean," and went on to tell Commins that Jean had "none of the emotional conventional confusion which poor Joan had." Brodsky and Hamblin, *A Comprehensive Guide to the Brodsky Collection*, Vol. 2, p. 138.

65. WF–JW TL "Thursday" (January 8, 1953) FCVA. Quoted in Blotner, *Biography* (1974), p. 1445.

66. WF–JW ALs (March 2, 1950) FCVA. Quoted in Blotner, SLWF, p. 300.

67. WF–JW TL (May 19, 1950) FCVA. Quoted in Blotner, SLWF, p. 304.

68. WF–MC TLs (March 6, 1950) HRHRC; WF–JW TLs (July 13, 1950) FCVA.

69. WF–JW TLs (January 21, 1951) FCVA; WF–MC ALs (January 29, 1951) HRHRC.

70. WF–JW ALs (March 4, 1951) FCVA.

71. Brodsky and Hamblin, *A Comprehensive Guide to the Brodsky Collection*, Vol. 2, pp. 66–67.

72. WF–MC TL (October 19, 1951) HRHRC; WF–JW ALs (October 21, 1951) FCVA.

73. WF–MC TL (January 15, 1952) HRHRC; WF–JW TL Tuesday (January 15, 1952) FCVA.

74. WF–JW ALs "Friday" (December 15, 1950) FCVA; WF–JW TL (May 7, 1952) FCVA.

75. WF–JW TL (July 11, 1952) FCVA.

76. WF–JW TLs (June 12, 1960) FCVA.

77. Faulkner mentions reading *The Spanish Farm* in a letter to Sherwood Anderson written in New Orleans early in 1925. WF–SA TL n.d. Carvel Collins Collection, HRHRC. He described walking tours of the battlefields in letters from France in September 1925 (SLWF, 25) and visited French war sites with Else Jonsson in 1951. Blotner, *Biography* (1984), p. 541.

78. Mahon's wound is repeated in the film script *Today We Live* (1932–1933) in Claude's being blinded at the Front. *Today We Live*, pp. 220ff. As late as 1945 Malcolm Cowley believed Faulkner had been wounded in combat, and Faulkner was at some pains to keep that invention out of the preface to *The Portable Faulkner*. See Watson, *William Faulkner, Letters and Fictions*, pp. 5–8.

79. Polk finds in the old general's small size and delicate features another Faulknerian self-portrait. *Children of the Dark House*, p. 271.

80. Polk comments on the difference between photographs taken in the 1950s and that taken to publicize *Sanctuary* in the early 1930s as evidence of Faulkner's enjoying his post-Nobel Prize celebrity. *Children of the Dark House*, pp. 244–247.

81. Herman Melville, *Moby-Dick*, p. 450.

82. Budd, "Playing Hide and Seek with William Faulkner: The Publicly Private Artist," p. 52.

83. James, *The Bostonians*, p. 34.

84. See Budd, "Playing Hide and Seek with William Faulkner: The Publicly Private Artist," pp. 37–39.

Works Cited

Adams, Richard. "The Apprenticeship of William Faulkner." *Tulane Studies in English* 12 (1962), 113–156.

Anderson, Sherwood. *Sherwood Anderson's Memoirs: A Critical Edition*, ed. Ray Lewis White. Chapel Hill: University of North Carolina Press, 1969.

———. *Winesburg, Ohio.* New York: Viking, 1960.

Arnold, Edwin T. *Mosquitoes Annotated.* New York: Garland, 1989.

Bachelard, Gaston. *The Poetics of Space*, trans. Maria Jolas. Boston: Beacon Press, 1964.

Barthes, Roland. *Camera Lucida: Reflections on Photography*, trans. Richard Howard. New York: Hill and Wang, 1981.

Berger, John. *About Looking.* New York: Vintage, 1980.

Bezzerides, A. I. *William Faulkner: A Life on Paper.* Jackson: University Press of Mississippi, 1980.

Bleikasten, Andre. "Fathers in Faulkner." In *The Fictional Father: Lacanian Readings of the Text*, ed. Robert Conn Davis, 115–146. Amherst: University of Massachusetts Press, 1981.

———. *Faulkner's "As I Lay Dying."* Bloomington: University of Indiana Press, 1973.

———. *The Most Splendid Failure: Faulkner's "The Sound and the Fury."* Bloomington: Indiana University Press, 1967.

———. "A Private Man's Public Voice." In *Faulkner After the Nobel Prize*, ed. Michel Gresset and K. Ohashi, 45–60. Tokyo: Yamaguchi, 1987.

———. "Reading Faulkner." In *New Directions in Faulkner Studies*, ed. Doreen Fowler and Ann J. Abadie, 1–17. Jackson: University Press of Mississippi, 1984.

Blotner, Joseph L. *Faulkner: A Biography.* 2 vols. New York: Random House, 1974.

———. *Faulkner: A Biography.* One-Volume Edition. New York: Random House, 1984.

———. "William Faulkner's Essay on the Composition of *Sartoris*," *Yale University Library Gazette* 47 (January 1973), 121–124.

———. *William Faulkner's Library: A Catalogue.* Charlottesville: University of Virginia Press, 1964.

———, ed. *Selected Letters of William Faulkner.* New York: Random House, 1977.

Bonner, Thomas. *William Faulkner: The William B. Wisdom Collection*. New Orleans: Tulane University Libraries, 1980.

Branch, G. Watson. "Darl Bundren's 'Cubistic' Vision." *Texas Studies in Language and Literature* (Spring 1977), 42–59.

Brodsky, Louis Daniel. *William Faulkner, Life Glimpses*. Austin: University of Texas Press, 1990.

Brodsky, Louis Daniel, and Robert W. Hamblin, eds. *A Comprehensive Guide to the Brodsky Collection*. Vol. 1, *The Bio-bibliography*. Jackson: University Press of Mississippi, 1982.

———, eds. *A Comprehensive Guide to the Brodsky Collection*. Vol. 2, *The Letters*. Jackson: University Press of Mississippi, 1984.

———, eds. *A Comprehensive Guide to the Brodsky Collection*. Vol. 5, *Manuscripts and Documents*. Jackson: University Press of Mississippi, 1988.

Brooks, Cleanth. *Toward Yoknapatawpha and Beyond*. New Haven: Yale University Press, 1978.

Broughton, Panthea Reed. "The Cubist Novel: Toward Defining the Genre." In *A Cosmos of My Own*, ed. Doreen Fowler and Ann J. Abadie, 36–58. Jackson: University Press of Mississippi, 1981.

———. "Faulkner's Cubist Novels." In *A Cosmos of My Own*, ed. Doreen Fowler and Ann J. Abadie, 59–94. Jackson: University Press of Mississippi, 1981.

———. "An Interview with Meta Carpenter Wilde." *Southern Review* 18 (October 1982), 776–801.

Bruccoli, Matthew J. *Some Sort of Epic Grandeur: The Life of F. Scott Fitzgerald*. New York: Harcourt Brace Jovanovich, 1981.

Budd, Louis J. "Playing Hide and Seek with William Faulkner: The Publicly Private Artist." In *Faulkner and Popular Culture*, ed. Doreen Fowler and Ann J. Abadie, 34–58. Jackson: University Press of Mississippi, 1990.

Cofield, J. R. "Many Faces, Many Moods." In *William Faulkner of Oxford*, ed. James W. Webb and A. Wigfall Green, 107–112. Baton Rouge: Louisiana State University Press, 1965.

Cohen, Philip, and Doreen Fowler. "Faulkner's Introduction to *The Sound and the Fury*." *American Literature* 62 (June 1990), 262–284.

Coindreau, Maurice Edgar. "Preface to *The Sound and the Fury*." In *The Time of William Faulkner*, ed. Maurice Coindreau, 41–50. Columbia: University of South Carolina Press, 1971.

Collins, Carvel. "'Ad Astra' through New Haven: Some Biographical Sources of Faulkner's War Fiction." In *Faulkner and the Short Story*, ed. Evans Harrington and Ann J. Abadie, 108–127. Jackson: University Press of Mississippi, 1992.

———. "Biographical Background for Faulkner's *Helen*." In *Helen: A Courtship and Mississippi Poems*, ed. Carvel Collins and Joseph L. Blotner, 9–105. Oxford, Miss., and New Orleans: Yoknapatawpha Press and Tulane University Press, 1981.

———. "A Note on *Sanctuary*." *Harvard Advocate* (November 1951), p. 16.

———, ed. *William Faulkner: Early Prose and Poetry*. Boston: Little, Brown, 1962.

Cowley, Malcolm, ed. *The Faulkner-Cowley File: Letters and Memories, 1944–1962*. New York: Viking, 1966.

———, ed. *The Portable Faulkner*. New York: Viking, 1946.

Dahl, James, "A Faulkner Reminiscence: Conversations with Mrs. Maud Falkner." *Journal of Modern Literature* 3 (April 1974), 1026–1030.

Davis, Sally. "The Secret Hollywood Romance of William Faulkner." *Los Angeles* 21, no. 11 (November 1976), 131–134, 206–207.

Dimock, Wai-chee. *Empire for Liberty: Melville and the Poetics of Individualism.* Princeton: Princeton University Press, 1989.

Douglas, Harold J., and Robert Daniel. "Faulkner and the Puritanism of the South." *Tennessee Studies in Literature* 2 (1957), 1–13.

Eliot, Thomas Stearns. "Tradition and the Individual Talent." In *Selected Essays of T. S. Eliot*, 3–11. New York: Harcourt, Brace & World, 1964.

———. *T. S. Eliot: The Complete Poems and Plays, 1909–1950.* New York: Harcourt, Brace & World, 1971.

Falkner, Murry C. *The Falkners of Mississippi.* Baton Rouge: Louisiana State University Press, 1967.

Faulkner, John. *My Brother Bill: An Affectionate Reminiscence.* New York: Trident Press, 1963.

Faulkner, William. *Absalom, Absalom!.* New York: Random House, 1936. Corrected Edition, New York: Vintage, 1986.

———. "Appendix: Compson." In *The Portable Faulkner*, ed. Malcolm Cowley, 704–721. Rev. ed. New York: Viking, 1967.

———. *As I Lay Dying.* New York: Random House, 1930. Corrected Edition, New York: Vintage, 1985.

———. *Collected Stories of William Faulkner.* New York: Random House, 1950.

———. *Elmer*, ed. Diane L. Cox. *Mississippi Quarterly* 36 (Summer 1983): 343–448.

———. *A Fable.* New York: Random House, 1954.

———. *Flags in the Dust*, ed. Douglas Day. New York: Random House, 1973.

———. "Foreword to *The Faulkner Reader*." In *Essays, Speeches and Public Letters by William Faulkner*, ed. James B. Meriwether, 179–182. New York: Random House, 1965.

———. *Go Down, Moses.* New York: Random House, 1942. Corrected Edition, New York: Vintage, 1990.

———. *A Green Bough.* In *The Marble Faun and A Green Bough.* New York: Random House, 1960.

———. *The Hamlet.* New York: Random House, 1940. Corrected Edition, New York: Vintage, 1991.

———. *Helen: A Courtship.* In *Helen: A Courtship and Mississippi Poems by William Faulkner*, ed. Carvel Collins and Joseph L. Blotner. Oxford, Miss., and New Orleans: Yoknapatawpha Press and Tulane University Press, 1981.

———. *If I Forget Thee, Jerusalem* [*The Wild Palms*]. New York: Random House, 1939. Corrected Edition, New York: Vintage, 1995.

———. *Intruder in the Dust.* New York: Random House, 1948. Corrected Edition, New York: Library of America, 1994.

———. *Knight's Gambit.* New York: Random House, 1949.

———. *Light in August.* New York: Random House, 1932. Corrected Edition, New York: Vintage, 1990.

———. *The Mansion.* New York: Random House, 1959.

———. *The Marionettes*, ed. Noel Polk. Charlottesville: Bibliographical Society of the University of Virginia and the University Press of Virginia, 1977.

———. *Mayday*, ed. Carvel Collins. Notre Dame: University of Notre Dame Press, 1978.

————. *Mississippi Poems*. In *Helen: A Courtship and Mississippi Poems by William Faulkner*, ed. Carvel Collins and Joseph L. Blotner. Oxford, Miss., and New Orleans: Yoknapatawpha Press and Tulane University Press, 1981.

————. *Mosquitoes*. New York: Liveright, 1927.

————. *New Orleans Sketches*, ed. Carvel Collins. New York: Random House, 1958.

————. *Pylon*. New York: Random House, 1935. Corrected Edition, New York: Vintage, 1987.

————. *The Reivers*. New York: Random House, 1962.

————. *Requiem for a Nun*. New York: Random House, 1951. Corrected Edition, New York: Library of America, 1994.

————. *Sanctuary*. New York: Cape and Smith, 1931. Corrected Edition, New York: Vintage, 1993.

————. *Sanctuary. The Original Text*, ed. Noel Polk. New York: Random House, 1981.

————. *Soldiers' Pay*. New York: Liveright, 1926.

————. *The Sound and the Fury*. New York: Cape and Smith, 1929. Corrected Edition, New York: Vintage, 1984.

————. *Today We Live*. In *Faulkner's MGM Film Scripts*, ed. Bruce Kawin, 128–256. Knoxville: University of Tennessee Press, 1982.

————. *The Town*. New York: Random House, 1957.

————. *Uncollected Stories of William Faulkner*, ed. Joseph L. Blotner. New York: Random House, 1979.

————. *The Unvanquished*. New York: Random House, 1938. Corrected Edition, New York: Vintage, 1991.

————. "Verse Old and Nascent: A Pilgrimage." In *William Faulkner: Early Prose and Poetry*, ed. Carvel Collins, 114–118. New York: Little, Brown, 1958.

————. *Vision in Spring*, ed. Judith L. Sensibar. Austin: University of Texas Press, 1984.

————. *The Wild Palms*. New York: Random House, 1939.

Fenton, Charles A., ed. *Selected Letters of Stephen Vincent Benet*. New Haven: Yale University Press, 1960.

Fitzgerald, F. Scott. "Absolution." In *All the Sad Young Men*, 109–132. New York: Scribner's, 1926.

————. *The Great Gatsby*. Scribner's, 1925.

Fowler, Doreen, and Philip Cohen, eds. "Faulkner's Introduction to *The Sound and the Fury*." *American Literature* 62 (June 1990), 262–283.

Franklin, Malcolm. *Bitterweeds: Life with William Faulkner at Rowan Oak*. Irving, Tex.: The Society for the Study of Traditional Culture, 1977.

Gray, Richard. *The Life of William Faulkner*. Oxford, U.K.: Blackwell, 1994.

Gresset, Michel. *Fascination: Faulkner's Fiction, 1919–1936*. Durham: Duke University Press, 1989.

————. *A Faulkner Chronology*. Jackson: University Press of Mississippi, 1985.

————. "Faulkner, Home and the Ocean." In *Faulkner and the Artist*, ed. Donald M. Kartiganer and Ann J. Abadie, 41–50. Jackson: University Press of Mississippi, 1996.

————. "Faulkner's Self-Portraits." *The Faulkner Journal* 2 (Fall 1986), 2–13.

————. "A Public Man's Private Voice: Faulkner's Letters to Else Jonsson." In *Faulkner After the Nobel Prize*, ed. Michel Gresset and K. Ohashi, 61–73. Tokyo: Yamaguchi, 1987.

Grimwood, Michael. *Heart in Conflict: William Faulkner's Struggles with Vocation*. Athens: University of Georgia Press, 1987.

Gutting, Gabriel. "Mysteries of the Map-Maker: Faulkner, *If I Forget Thee, Jerusalem*, and the Secret of a Map." *Faulkner Journal* 3 (Spring 1993), 85–89.

Gwynn, Frederick, and Joseph L. Blotner, eds. *Faulkner in the University: Class Conferences at the University of Virginia, 1957–1958*. Charlottesville: University Press of Virginia, 1958.

Harrington, Gary. *Faulkner's Fables of Creativity*. Athens: University of Georgia Press, 1990.

Hawthorne, Nathaniel. "The Custom House." In *The Scarlet Letter*, ed. William Charvat et al., 3–45. Columbus: Ohio State University Press, 1962.

———. *The Scarlet Letter*, ed. William Charvat et al. Columbus: Ohio State University Press, 1962.

Hemingway, Ernest. *By-Line Ernest Hemingway*, ed. William White. New York: Scribner's, 1967.

———. *The Sun Also Rises*. New York: Scribner's, 1926.

Honnighausen, Lothar. *Faulkner: Masks and Metaphors*. Jackson: University Press of Mississippi, 1997.

Howard, Peter, ed. *William Faulkner: The Carl Petersen Collection*. Catalogue 48. Berkeley, Calif.: Serendipity Books, 1991.

Howell, John M. "Hemingway and Fitzgerald in *The Sound and the Fury*." *Papers on Language and Literature* (1966), 234–242.

James, Henry. *The Bostonians*. In *Henry James: Novels 1881–1886*. New York: Library of America, 1985.

Johnson, Susan P. *Annotations to Faulkner's "Pylon"*. New York: Garland, 1989.

Johnson, Thomas H., ed. *The Complete Poems of Emily Dickinson*. Boston: Little, Brown, 1955.

Jones, Howard Mumford, and Walter B. Rideout, eds. *Letters of Sherwood Anderson*. Boston: Little, Brown, 1953.

Joyce, James. *Dubliners*. New York: Viking, 1958.

Kartiganer, Donald M. "Introduction." In *Faulkner and the Artist*, ed. Donald M. Kartiganer and Ann J. Abadie, ix–xxiv. Jackson: University Press of Mississippi, 1996.

Kawin, Bruce F. "Faulkner's Film Career: The Years with Hawks." In *Faulkner, Modernism and Film*, ed. Evans Harrington and Ann J. Abadie, 163–181. Jackson: University Press of Mississippi, 1979.

———. "The Montage Element in Faulkner's Fiction." In *Faulkner, Modernism and Film*, ed. Evans Harrington and Ann J. Abadie, 103–126. Jackson: University Press of Mississippi, 1979.

———, ed. *Faulkner's MGM Screenplays*. Knoxville: University of Tennessee Press, 1982.

Krause, David. "Reading Bon's Letters and Faulkner's *Absalom, Absalom!*." *PMLA* 99 (March 1984), 225–241.

———. "Reading Shreve's Letters and Faulkner's *Absalom, Absalom!*." *Studies in American Fiction* 2 (Autumn 1983), 153–169.

Lind, Ilse Dusoir. "The Effect of Painting on Faulkner's Poetic Form." In *Faulkner, Modernism and Film*, ed. Evans Harrington and Ann J. Abadie, 127–148. Jackson: University Press of Mississippi, 1979.

Martin, Jay. "'The Whole Burden of Man's History and His Impossible Heart's Desire'" *American Literature* 53 (January 1982), 123–164.

Matthews, John T. "The Elliptical Nature of *Sanctuary*." *Novel* 17 (1984), 246–265.

———. "Faulkner's Narrative Frames." In *Faulkner and the Craft of Fiction*, ed. Doreen
      Fowler and Ann J. Abadie, 71–91. Jackson: University Press of Mississippi, 1989.
———. *The Play of Faulkner's Language*. Ithaca: Cornell University Press, 1982.
———. "The Rhetoric of Containment in Faulkner." In *Faulkner's Discourse*, ed. Lothar
      Honnighausen, 55–67. Tubingen: Max Niemeyer Verlag, 1989.
McHaney, Thomas L. "The Elmer Papers: Faulkner's Comic Portraits of the Artist."
      Mississippi Quarterly 26 (Summer 1973), 281–311.
———. *"The Wild Palms": Holograph Manuscript and Miscellaneous Rejected Holo-
      graph Pages*. William Faulkner Manuscripts, 14. Vol. 1. New York: Garland,
      1986.
———. *William Faulkner's "The Wild Palms."* Jackson: University Press of Missis-
      sippi, 1975.
Melville, Herman. "Hawthorne and His Mosses." In *The Piazza Tales and Other Prose
      Pieces, 1839–1860. The Writings of Herman Melville*, Vol. 9, ed. Harrison Hay-
      ford et al., 239–253. Evanston: Northwestern University Press, 1987.
———. *Moby-Dick. The Writings of Herman Melville*, Vol. 6, ed. Harrison Hayford
      et al. Evanston: Northwestern University Press, 1988.
Meriwether, James B., ed. *Essays, Speeches and Public Letters by William Faulkner*.
      New York: Random House, 1965.
———, ed. "Faulkner's Short Story Sending Schedule." In *The Literary Career of
      William Faulkner*, ed. James B. Meriwether, 167–180. Columbia: University of
      South Carolina Press, 1971.
———, ed. "An Introduction to *The Sound and the Fury*." *Southern Review* 8 (1972),
      705–710.
———, ed. "An Introduction to *The Sound and the Fury*." In *A Faulkner Miscellany*,
      ed. James B. Meriwether, 156–161. Jackson: University Press of Mississippi,
      1973.
Meriwether, James B., and Michael Millgate, eds. *Lion in the Garden: Interviews with
      William Faulkner, 1926–1962*. New York: Random House, 1968.
Millgate, Michael. *The Achievement of William Faulkner*. New York: Random House,
      1968.
Minter, David. "Faulkner, Childhood and the Making of *The Sound and the Fury*."
      American Literature 51 (November 1979), 376–393.
———. *William Faulkner: His Life and Work*. Baltimore: Johns Hopkins University
      Press, 1980.
Moser, Thomas. "Faulkner's Muse: Speculations on the Genesis of *The Sound and
      the Fury*." In *Critical Reconstructions: The Relationship of Fiction to Life*, ed.
      Robert M. Polhemus and Roger Henkle, 187–212. Stanford: Stanford University
      Press, 1994.
Parker, Robert Dale. "Sex and Gender, Feminine and Masculine: Faulkner and the Poly-
      morphous Exchange of Cultural Binaries." In *Faulkner and Gender*, ed. Donald
      M. Kartiganer and Ann J. Abadie, 73–96. Jackson: University Press of Missis-
      sippi, 1996.
Poirier, Richard. *The Performing Self*. New York: Oxford University Press, 1971.
———. *The Renewal of Literature: Emersonian Reflections*. New York: Random House,
      1987.
Polk, Noel. Afterword to *"Sanctuary": The Original Text*, 293–306. New York: Ran-
      dom House, 1981.

————. *Children of the Dark House*. Jackson: University Press of Mississippi, 1996.

————. "'The Dungeon Was Mother Herself': William Faulkner, 1927–1931." In *New Directions in Faulkner Studies*, ed. Doreen Fowler and Ann J. Abadie, 61–93. Jackson: University Press of Mississippi, 1984.

————. *Faulkner's "Requiem for a Nun": A Critical Study*. Bloomington: Indiana University Press, 1981.

————. "'Hong Li' and *Royal Street*: The New Orleans Sketches in Manuscript." In *A Faulkner Miscellany*, ed. James B. Meriwether, 143–144. Jackson: University Press of Mississippi, 1974.

————. Introduction to *The Marionettes*, ed. Noel Polk, ix–xxii. Charlottesville: Bibliographical Society of the University of Virginia and the University Press of Virginia, 1977.

————. "The Space Between *Sanctuary*." In *Intertextuality in Faulkner*, ed. Michel Gresset and Noel Polk, 16–35. Jackson: University Press of Mississippi, 1985.

————, ed. *Sanctuary: The Holograph Manuscript and Miscellaneous Pages*. William Faulkner Manuscripts 8. New York: Garland, 1987.

Polk, Noel, and John D. Hart, eds. *"Absalom, Absalom!": A Concordance to the Novel*. West Point, NY: Faulkner Concordance Advisory Board. Ann Arbor: UMI Research Press, 1989.

Pound, Ezra. *Personae: Collected Shorter Poems of Ezra Pound*. New York: New Directions, 1971.

Putzel, Max. "Faulkner's Trial Preface to *Sartoris*." *Papers of the Bibliographical Society of America* 64 (1980), 361–378.

————. *Genius of Place: William Faulkner's Triumphant Beginnings*. Baton Rouge: Louisiana State University Press, 1985.

————. "Text of the Yale Preface [to *Sartoris*]." In Max Putzel, *Genius of Place: William Faulkner's Triumphant Beginnings*, 295–298. Baton Rouge: Louisiana State University Press, 1985.

Reed, Joseph. *Faulkner's Narrative*. New Haven: Yale University Press, 1973.

Rollyson, Carl E. "'Counterpull': Estelle and William Faulkner." *South Atlantic Quarterly* 85 (1985), 215–227.

Rubin, Louis D., Jr. *The Faraway Country: Writers of the Modern South*. Seattle: University of Washington Press, 1963.

Sensibar, Judith L. "'Drowsing Maidenhead Symbol's Self': Faulkner and the Fictions of Love." In *Faulkner and the Craft of Fiction*, ed. Doreen Fowler and Ann J. Abadie, 124–147. Jackson: University Press of Mississippi, 1989.

————. "Faulkner's Fictional Photographs: Playing with Difference." In *Out of Bounds*, ed. Laura Claridge and Elizabeth Langland, 290–315. Amherst: University of Massachusetts Press, 1990.

————. *Faulkner's Poetry: A Bibliographical Guide to Texts and Criticism*. Ann Arbor: UMI Research Press, 1988.

————. *The Origins of Faulkner's Art*. Austin: University of Texas Press, 1984.

Shakespeare, William. *Hamlet*. In *Shakespeare: Four Tragedies*, ed. David Bevington et al. New York: Bantam, 1988.

————. *King Lear*. In *Shakespeare: Four Tragedies*, ed. David Bevington et al. New York: Bantam, 1988.

————. *Macbeth*. In *Shakespeare: Four Tragedies*, ed. David Bevington et al. New York: Bantam, 1988.

————. *The Tempest*. In *Shakespeare: The Tempest*, ed. David Bevington et al. New York: Bantam, 1988.

Shloss, Carol. *In Visible Light: Photography and the American Writer: 1840–1940*. New York: Oxford University Press, 1987.

Skei, Hans. *William Faulkner: The Short Story Career*. Oslo: Universitetsforlaget, 1981.

Snell, Susan. *Phil Stone of Oxford*. Athens: University of Georgia Press, 1991.

Sontag, Susan. *On Photography*. New York: Anchor, 1977.

Spratling, William. "Chronicle of a Friendship." In William Spratling and William Faulkner, *Sherwood Anderson and Other Famous Creoles*, 11–16. 1926. Reprint, Austin: University of Texas Press, 1966.

Spratling, William, and William Faulkner. *Sherwood Anderson and Other Famous Creoles*. 1926. Reprint, Austin: University of Texas Press, 1966.

Sundquist, Eric J. *Faulkner: The House Divided*. Baltimore: Johns Hopkins University Press, 1983.

Thoreau, Henry David. *Walden*, ed. J. Lyndon Shanley. Princeton: Princeton University Press, 1991.

Wasson, Ben. *Count No 'Count: Flashback to Faulkner*. Jackson: University Press of Mississippi, 1983.

Watson, James G. "Carvel Collins's Faulkner: A Newly Opened Archive." *Library Chronicle of the University of Texas* 20 (1990), 17–35. Repr. *Mississippi Quarterly* 44 (Summer 1991), 257–272.

————. "Faulkner in New Orleans: The 1925 Letters." In *Faulkner, His Contemporaries, and His Posterity*, ed. Waldemar Zacharasievicz, 196–206. Tubingen: Francke Verlag, 1993.

————. "Faulkner's 'What Is the Matter with Marriage.'" *Faulkner Journal* 5 (Spring 1990), 69–72.

————. "Literary Self-Criticism: Faulkner on Fiction in Fiction." *Southern Quarterly* 20 (Fall 1981), 46–63.

————. "'My Father's Unfailing Kindness': William Faulkner and the Idea of Home." *American Literature* 64 (December 1992), 749–761.

————. *The Snopes Dilemma: Faulkner's Trilogy*. Coral Gables: University of Miami Press, 1970.

————. "Two Letters about William Faulkner, 1918." *Faulkner Journal* 8 (Fall 1992), 15–19.

————. *William Faulkner, Letters and Fictions*. Austin: University of Texas Press, 1987.

————, ed. *Thinking of Home: William Faulkner's Letters to His Mother and Father, 1918–1925*. New York: W. W. Norton, 1992.

West, Nathaniel. *Miss Lonelyhearts and The Day of the Locust*. New York: New Directions, 1962.

White, William, ed. *By-Line Ernest Hemingway*. New York: Scribner's, 1967.

Whitman, Walt. *Complete Poetry and Selected Prose of Walt Whitman*, ed. James E. Miller. New York: Riverside, 1959.

Wilde, Meta Carpenter, and Orin Borsten. *A Loving Gentleman: The Love Story of William Faulkner and Meta Carpenter*. New York: Simon and Schuster, 1976.

Williams, Joan. "Twenty Will Not Come Again." *Atlantic Monthly* 245 (May 1980), 58–65.

Williamson, Joel. *William Faulkner and Southern History.* New York: Oxford University Press, 1993.

Wittenberg, Judith. *Faulkner: The Transfiguration of Biography.* Lincoln: University of Nebraska Press, 1979.

Zeitlin, Michael. "*Pylon,* Joyce and Faulkner's Imagination." In *Faulkner and the Artist,* ed. Donald M. Kartiganer and Ann J. Abadie, 181–207. Jackson: University Press of Mississippi, 1996.

Zender, Karl. *The Crossing of the Ways: William Faulkner, the South and the Modern World.* New Brunswick: Rutgers University Press, 1989.

———. "Faulkner and the Politics of Incest." *American Literature* 70 (December 1998), 739–765.

Index